Teaching Together

School/University Collaboration to Improve Social Studies Education

EDITED BY
Mary Christenson • Marilyn Johnston • Jim Norris

NCSS

**Bulletin
98**

National Council for the Social Studies
8555 Sixteenth Street
Suite 500
Silver Spring, Maryland 20910

(ADDRESS AS OF JULY 2001)

Editorial staff on this publication: Terri Ackerman, Steven Lapham, David Morse, Michael Simpson.
Design by Gene Cowan.

TODAY'S SOCIAL STUDIES
Creating Effective Citizens

LIBRARY OF CONGRESS CATALOG CARD NUMBER: 2001089188
ISBN 0-87986-088-X

Table of Contents

Introduction

Elementary

Middle School

High School

Teaching Together: School/University Collaboration to Improve Social Studies Education

MARY CHRISTENSON
MARILYN JOHNSTON
JIM NORRIS

ACKNOWLEDGMENT

The genesis of this book lies in the efforts of Merry Merryfield. As chair of the College and University Faculty Assembly (CUFA) Board of National Council for the Social Studies (NCSS), Merry wrote the proposal for this book to demonstrate the connections between CUFA and NCSS, or between professors and classroom teachers. Merry has a long history of working closely with classroom teachers in her Professional Development School Network for Social Studies and Global Education at The Ohio State University. This book was motivated by her dedication to the principle that we (professors and teachers) work best when we share our expertise, experience, and enthusiasm for social studies education.

Introduction

Teaching Together: School/University Collaboration to Improve Social Studies Education is about innovative social studies curriculum developed through collaboration between classroom teachers and university professors. By working collaboratively, we challenge the traditional isolation of schools and universities. Working together, we share our expertise and create innovative ways to improve social studies teaching and learning.

This book provides preservice, beginning, and experienced teachers with provocative ideas as well as a realistic look at the challenges of school/university collaboration. Many examples of innovative social studies practices situated in collaborative relations are presented. In addition, this book provides rich, contextualized teaching practices that can be adapted to individual classrooms and various grade levels. We hope this book will enrich teaching at all levels and encourage educators from elementary through university levels to work collaboratively with colleagues to improve social studies education.

About This Book

The sixteen chapters in this book are divided into three grade-level sections—elementary, middle, and high school—with diverse projects described within each section. There are projects in different kinds of schools; some chapters focus on social studies exclusively while others are highly integrated with other fields of study; some collaborations are between a single teacher-professor pair while others are much larger; some are connected to national and international projects or partners; some projects are just beginning while others have been going on for years.

The ideas in this book, regardless of the level in which they were developed, are easily adaptable. A good teaching strategy used in an elementary classroom can be adapted to a secondary classroom. Good ideas can work at any level—elementary, middle, secondary, or university. For example, in chapter 15 we present the collaboration of a university, a high school, and a local historical society. In this project, high school students collected oral histories that were placed in the society's archives; preservice teachers from the university helped facilitate the oral history collections. Even primary students, however, can collect oral histories from family and community members. They can contribute to the construction of histories meaningful to their social context by collecting these oral histories. The strategies and organization of the high school project might give elementary and middle level teachers helpful ideas for oral history projects.

Likewise, chapter 4 describes an elementary school in which the study of different cultures involved a wide partnership. Parents of students were drawn into the learning process. A ripple effect occurred when they learned about the cultures of their international neighborhood. This project could easily serve as a model for work in a high school or university classroom.

School/University Collaboration

Is collaboration a viable means for improving social studies education? Is it worth the time and effort required? Can collaboration facilitate increased student learning and professional development? This book may help answer these questions.

Traditionally, schools and universities have not worked well together, nor used their different expertise to solve the complex challenges facing social studies education. Nevertheless, the enthusiasm of these collaborative participants shines through these articles. Their enthusiasm often stems from the successes of their students, but also from what they themselves have learned. This enthusiasm is biased, of course, because we do not have chapters on collaborative projects that failed. Even so, the benefits of collaboration are clear.

In the literature on collaboration, differences in perspective pose a major challenge to collaborative partnerships.[1] Social studies, however, has always needed to accommodate and use different perspectives as part of its day-to-day practice. Social scientists from varied disciplines bring different methodologies and orientations to social studies; these are not easily unified into an integrated whole. In addition, diverse goals and social studies programs (multicultural education, moral education, social education, and civics education, to name but a few) tug at teachers' allegiances and must be accommodated within limited instructional time and in line with standards. As social studies educators, we are used to managing different perspectives and working across disciplinary boundaries. It seems logical that we would also seek the different perspectives and expertise of our school or university colleagues.

So why have social studies teachers and professors not consistently worked together? The authors of this book, while lauding the value of collaboration, also point to its difficulties. Some of the difficulties stem from the inherent tensions that are demanding on teachers and professors alike, such as those accompanied by authentic teaching and issue-oriented social studies and the need to prepare students for mandated tests. There is also the struggle to balance the desire for rich social studies curricula while managing the time that it takes to collaborate. There is a tension between managing the needs and interests of students and teachers with the institutional constraints of bureaucracies and political influences on schools. There are many others, such as the struggle to balance content and process, substance and skills, student interests and mandated curricula, and the differing norms of schools and universities.

Although these tensions sometimes pull the authors in many directions, it is apparent that collaboration results in a richer experience for participants and students alike—two heads are truly better than one. Nevertheless, it takes more time to collaborate than to work alone. It particularly takes more time if there are differences in orientations, perspectives, or goals that must be negotiated.

School/University Stereotypes

The differences between schools and universities are reflected in many of the stereotypes that teachers and professors hold about each other. For example, it is a common stereotype that university professors live in ivory towers and can only spout theories; and conversely, that teachers are wedded to practice and see theories as irrelevant. Such stereotypes reflect prejudices and simplifications that we have tried to overcome in this book. In these chapters, what becomes clear is that the complementary expertise of teachers and professors is much more complicated and interesting than the stereotypes would suggest.

The saying "There's nothing as practical as a good theory" frames our perspective as editors of this book. Whether we talk out loud about our theories or not, we cannot escape having them. We are inescapably embedded in teaching practices that reflect our theories. We try to teach in ways that reflect our beliefs about best practices. We make minute-by-minute decisions as well as set long-term goals that are informed by our theories. Whether we teach in schools or universities, our practices and theories are embedded in what we do, and neither theory nor practice is the sole domain of teachers or professors. Our teaching realities are much more complicated than the stereotypes allow. We think this book works against simple stereotypes.

Nevertheless, there are important institutional differences between schools and universities that are at play in these collaborative projects. The differences are real, and they often make school/university collaboration challenging. One difference has to do with the institutional structures themselves. Universities and schools operate differently and have distinct rewards structures. Teachers are under pressure to produce results on test scores, appease parents, and deal with all kinds of situations that children bring with them to school. Teachers value collegial relationships in order to maintain environments that are positive for both teachers and students. The norm in schools is often to avoid debate because it interferes with the collegiality needed to buffet outside demands and pressures.

Universities, by contrast, are more individualistic and entrepreneurial. The demands for research and service are different from the pressures faced by teachers. Professors are expected to create their own research agendas and debate their differences heartily. Such cultural differences between schools and universities sometimes make collaboration challenging.

In this book, fifty-one teachers and professors struggle creatively with their different agendas. Different demands make communication and goal setting difficult. For example, research and writing are a required part of what professors must do. Is it fair to ask teachers to participate in these time-consuming efforts if there are no structural rewards for them and if these efforts sometimes expose teachers to criticism? Teachers are co-authors of all of these chapters. Is this an imposition of university norms? Professors get tenure and promotion for publishing chapters in books; teachers usually get little time or recognition for these kinds of professional endeavors.

The Value of Collaboration

So what is the value of collaboration? One positive aspect of collaboration evident in these chapters is the value of learning from each other. Because teachers and professors do different things, they have different expertise. There is value in sharing what we know and in learning from our differences. Learning from and about each other makes us more tolerant of our differences, and also opens doors to new ideas and teaching practices. Teachers begin to understand the pressures that professors are under; professors, many of whom were public school teachers at one time, are helped to remember the pressures and pleasures of teaching children everyday. Teachers learn ways to be more articulate about their theories; professors learn more about the specific application of theories in particular contexts. Collaboration has the potential to create dynamic communities of practice[2] as we share, debate, collaborate, and build better contexts for our students.

What Readers Will Find in This Book

There are similarities and differences across the collaborations described in chapters of this book. One difference is the way they started. Some began with a funded project. Typically, the university participant received a grant and defined the project. Teachers were invited to join and had little initial ownership. With shared decision making, however, the project became more collaborative over time. In contrast, other projects began with teachers who were looking for professors to help them with a project where a particular expertise was needed. Other teachers were looking for student teachers to bring additional human resources into the classroom; or conversely, social studies methods teachers were looking for classrooms where student teachers could have meaningful teaching experiences.

Accountability is a common theme across these chapters. In these times, teachers and professors alike are immersed in demands for accountability and "higher" standards. Unfortunately, these are too often defined in terms of narrow guidelines and high-stakes testing. This theme is present, but not critiqued, in these chapters. Our focus is on what is happening in classrooms and not on how we are dealing with the

Chart 1: **Overview of Bulletin Chapters and their Common Elements**

Chapter Number, First Author	Pre-service Teachers	Rural Schools	Suburban Schools	Urban Schools	Grade Level	Social Studies Content	Inter-disciplinary	Multi- or Cross-cultural
1: Alleman				✓	Elem.	cultural universals		
2: Barton				✓	Elem.	history	✓	
3: Beisser	✓		✓	✓	Elem.	service-learning	✓	✓
4: Cozza	✓				Elem.	multicultural/ global educ.	✓	✓
5: McCall				✓	Elem.	history		✓
6: Alibrandi				✓	Middle	geography history service-learning		
7: Carlson				✓	Middle	geography global studies service-learning		✓
8: Harwood	✓			✓	Middle	civics service-learning	✓	
9: Kunkel	✓			✓	Middle	civic action service-learning	✓	
10: Milson	✓			✓	Middle	social issues/ values		
11: Gerwin				✓	High Sch.	social history literature	✓	
12: Merryfield				✓	High Sch.	global studies		
13: Mallory				✓	High Sch.	economics		
14: Oldendorf	✓	✓			High Sch.	history	✓	✓
15: Wilen	✓			✓	High Sch.	history service-learning		
16: Prior					High Sch. Industry	work place experience		

political context. This silence should not be taken as compliance. These projects are explicitly about doing rich, integrated, and meaningful social studies that press against expectations to teach in more segmented, teach-to-the-test approaches.

Another commonality is the constructivist learning orientation of many of the chapters. Authors in this book are searching for ways to make social studies learning active, participatory, and socially constructed. Democracy and negotiation are common themes. Students working in their communities and dealing with real-life issues and complexities are central to many of these projects. Active citizenship and critical decision making also pervade the activities described in this book.

Throughout this book, within chapters, there are times when only one author of several is writing from his or her perspective. In some cases where this has occurred, we have placed the author's initials within parentheses for clarification. For example, "(J.S.)" would indicate that a section was written by "John Smith" individually, not by all of the co-authors together.

In addition, there are many chapters that contain sections (with titles like "Remarks for Fellow Teachers") that are written by just one of the co-authors of that chapter (in this case, the classroom teacher). We hope it will be helpful for classroom teachers to read remarks addressed especially to them, written by another classroom teacher. Likewise, college professors often have comments that would be especially useful for other professors. In sum, each side of the collaboration has special advice about how to construct a school/university project while meeting the demands of its respective professional environment. The editing convention of using an author's initials at the beginning of a section is designed to help readers keep track of who (among the various co-authors) is speaking.

Reading This Book

There are many ways to read this book. Of course, we invite readers to travel from cover to cover, but selective reading of chapters with shared topics or other common elements is another strategy. For example, several chapters have a service-learning focus; others include multicultural education or community-based projects. The chart on the facing page reveals some of the common elements within chapters. The introduction to each chapter also provides a snapshot of the chapter.

NOTES
1. Susan M. Brookhart and William E. Loadman, "School-University Collaboration: Different Workplace Cultures," *Contemporary Education* 61 (1990): 125-128; Lawrence Cuban, "Managing Dilemmas While Building Professional Communities," *Educational Researcher* 21 (1992): 4-11; Sharon Feiman-Nemser and Robert Floden, "The Culture of Teaching," in *Handbook of Research on Teaching*, ed. Merlin C. Wittrock (New York: Macmillan, 1986): 505-526; Marilyn Johnston and PDS Colleagues, *Contradictions in Collaboration* (New York: Teachers College Press, 1997); Seymour Sarason, *The Culture of the School and the Problem of Change* (Boston, Mass.: Allyn and Bacon, 1982).
2. Etienne Wenger, *Communities of Practice: Learning, Meaning, and Identity* (Cambridge, England: Cambridge University Press, 1999).

Elementary

Teaching Primary-Grade Students about Cultural Universals

One

JANET ALLEMAN
JERE BROPHY
BARBARA L. KNIGHTON
GINA M. HENIG

The Scene

"Why are the kids doing all the work and the teachers just standing around?" Normally, a question like that from a parent would raise our blood pressure and cause us to launch a defense immediately. Instead, we just smiled and laughed along with the parent because we knew that our first and second grade students were demonstrating, in a very authentic setting, how much they had already learned. At the end of our Family Unit collaboration with Dr. Janet Alleman and Dr. Jere Brophy from Michigan State University (MSU), we (B.K. and G.H.) scheduled a special night for students to bring their families to school, share their portfolios, displays, and timelines, and explain what they had learned. Depth of understanding (not just memory of simple facts) was apparent as children carried out sustained conversations with family members. The parent's quote was one of the many compliments that we received from parents, grandparents, and other family members after they realized how much their children had learned.

More than 90 percent of our families were excited enough about our unit that they rearranged their lives to come to school for the Family Night Celebration. We suddenly realized that our university collaboration had elevated our social studies program to places we never expected it to go. Our project demonstrated that social studies, even in the early grades, really can focus on networks of powerful ideas for advancing students' social understanding and civic efficacy, and still allow for students to develop language skills, participate in groups, and contribute ideas to their classmates, families, and community. Students blossom as they realize that their ideas matter.

We found that kids talk about social studies even during lunch, recess, and at home. We assigned several different out-of-school learning opportunities during the units, which were a true collaboration between university ideals and knowledge and classroom practicality and reality. Students averaged 80 to 85 percent completion of the home assignments, and parents often commented that they have had interesting conversations at home—with children occasionally influencing parental decisions and actions.

The bottom line is that our collaboration is resulting in an enriched social studies program—and a show of enthusiasm.

Our Conceptualization of Improving Social Studies

Critics of social studies have long characterized the content taught in the early grades as trite, redundant, and unlikely to help students achieve significant social education goals. They often blame the problem on the expanding-communities framework commonly used to organize the curriculum.[1] Within this framework, students begin by studying the familiar in the here and now and only gradually move backward in time and outward in space.

Our analyses of instructional materials suggest that the content problems in early elementary social studies are not so much due to the expanding-communities framework or the choice of topics addressed but to the way these topics have been taught. Many of the topics—families, communities, food, shelter, clothing, government, transportation, and communication, among others—provide a sound basis for developing fundamental understandings about the human condition. They tend to be cultural universals—basic human needs and social experiences found in all societies, past and present. We posit that if these topics are taught with an appropriate focus on powerful ideas, students will develop a basic set of connected understandings about how the social system works, how and why it came to be the way it is, how and why it varies across locations and cultures, and what all of this might mean for personal, social, and civic decision making.

Working from these assumptions, we (J.A. and J.B.) have been developing instructional units designed to teach cultural universals for understanding, appreciation, and life application. Each unit is structured around networks of powerful ideas and informed by the disciplines of history, geography, and the social sciences. Unit content, however, is selected and organized primarily to promote general preparation for life in our society, not as an induction into these disciplines, and instruction and assessment are designed accordingly. Our units develop big ideas in-depth, in contrast to the broad but shallow coverage found in most early elementary texts. Discourse is designed to develop thoughtfulness as described by Newmann,[2] and authentic activities are planned to promote application of learning to life outside of school. Another significant element is teaching for conceptual change. In this regard, we have adapted the theory developed by Kathleen Roth,[3] which places at least as much emphasis on connecting with students' valid prior knowledge as it does on identifying and addressing their misconceptions. Our units also reflect our concern for achieving an optimal balance between transmission of knowledge and social constructivist pedagogy, given that the students are young learners with limited prior knowledge of or structured experiences with most of the topics addressed.

Our unit on shelter exemplifies the application of these principles for selecting and developing content. First, incorporating contemporary and familiar examples, the unit helps students understand how and why this cultural universal functions as it does in the contemporary United States. The unit begins with the forms of shelter commonly found in the students' own neighborhoods. Instruction helps students to articulate the tacit knowledge that they already possess, to expand on it, and to embed it within a knowledge network structured around powerful ideas.

Second, the unit includes a historical dimension illustrating how human responses to shelter needs have evolved over time by means of inventions and other cultural advances. For example, shelters evolved from caves and simple huts to sturdier and more permanent homes such as log cabins, to modern, weatherproofed homes that feature running water, heat, light, and insulation. Technological advances have enabled us to meet our needs and wants for shelter and related services more effectively, yet with less investment of personal time and effort than in the past.

The unit also includes a geographical-cultural dimension that exposes students to current variations in forms of shelter in different places and cultures, variations that result from differences in geography, climate, and the availability of construction materials, as well as differences in cultures and customs. Along with the historical dimension, this geographical-cultural dimension of the unit extends students' concepts about shelters. Students place themselves and their familiar social environment into perspective as part of the larger human condition that evolves through time and varies across cultures.

The unit also emphasizes applications to students' current and future lives. This is accomplished through critical thinking and decision-making activities designed to raise students' consciousness about the fact that they will be making shelter-related choices, both as individuals and as citizens. The emphasis is not on inculcating preferences for particular choices but instead on building knowledge about the trade-offs associated with the major choice options. Thus, the unit includes discussions of the trade-offs offered by different housing types and locations (urban, suburban, and rural) and of the problem of homelessness (including what even young children and their families can do to help others when a crisis strikes due to a flood, fire, loss of job, poverty, and so forth).

Our data on the teaching of particular topics suggest which aspects of the topic of shelter are worth developing and which are not. For example, concerning home mortgages, we have found that students are able to understand the motives of the parties involved (banks are businesses and make money by requiring families to pay interest; families agree to do this because it allows them to move into a house now, without having to wait until they accumulate the full price). Also, instruction on these aspects of mortgage loans helps students develop a sense of efficacy for future action ("When I grow up, I will be able to borrow part of the money to buy a house if I want to."). Worthwhile social education goals are promoted by teaching these aspects of mortgage loans, but we do not think that attempts to teach the abstract economics concepts or financial details involved (escrow, equity, interest rates, and so forth) would be appropriate for the primary grades.

Students' comments and questions in class sometimes indicate that we should broaden our approach to a topic or develop it further than we had intended. For example, our plans for teaching about Native American tipis included emphasizing their portability as a key feature. However, we found that students had never heard of nomadic societies and thus had difficulty accepting the notion that some people moved periodically without possessing a more permanent home base. Comments and questions about other forms of housing indicated that students frequently understood that different forms of shelter exist, but not why they exist. For example, second graders typically know or easily learn that stilt houses are situated high on poles to keep them dry from water below them, but they do not understand (or even appear to wonder) why people live in marshes or flood plains in the first place. These findings led us to elaborate our unit plans to say more about functions and cause-effect relationships (for example, by explaining that portable shelters allowed Native Americans to follow buffalo herds).

Our classroom data allow us to assess the value of children's literature sources, both as vehicles for teaching content and as ways to connect to students' interests and emotions. Sometimes a book that initially looks promising proves ineffective in classroom tryouts. For example, *A House Is a House For Me*[4] seemed ideal for introducing a unit on shelter, but when we observed the students' reactions to the story, we realized that the book's fancifulness in its use of the word house was communicating misconceptions and thus was not supportive of our instructional goals. For example,

"A box is a house for a tea bag.
A teapot is a house for some tea.
If you pour me a cup and I drink it all up,
Then the teahouse will turn into me."

Other ideas about developing content that have emerged from our classroom observations concern the use of games, pantomime, props, or drama. Sometimes these ideas evolved as a result of preplanning with classroom teachers, and at other times, they added ideas on their own. These varied approaches have broadened the scope and appeal of the lessons.

Our units feature home assignments that engage students in sustained conversations with their parents about what they are learning in the classroom and how it applies to their everyday lives. Interviews with some of the parents have increased our awareness of affective outcomes that accompany students' involvement in the units. In particular, parents' comments have led us to increase our emphasis on self-efficacy.

We plan to analyze the data from our educational studies much more closely and systematically. Then, we plan to begin intensive studies of polished versions of some of our units, revised in light of what we learn.

Process of Collaboration and Some Tangible Outcomes

Our current collaboration began about three years ago and is expected to continue indefinitely. Having developed some of our units, we (the professors) sought to collaborate with an early elementary teacher who would agree to focus on powerful ideas in the social studies. We would create units focusing on cultural universals and study their classroom enactments.

Our initial attempts at collaboration with other teachers did not yield the high-quality implementations that we hoped to study (in one case, the teacher proved to be an ineffective classroom manager; in another, the teacher failed to maintain a significant focus on big ideas; and in a third, one of us (J.A.) served as the teacher and developed the big ideas adequately but felt frustrated by limited familiarity and contact with students and having to work within a physical setting and classroom climate that were ill-suited to our goals). Seeking a teacher who could reliably produce high-quality implementations of our units, we contacted local administrators with whom we shared common values associated with classroom management and learner expectations. We were seeking a teacher who valued social studies, appreciated an approach that was more powerful than lessons based on a textbook, understood the importance of developing big ideas in-depth, believed that students were capable of learning and could respond positively to challenging social studies curricula, and was willing to step outside the typical early elementary social studies program and try something new.

After Barbara was nominated by her principal, several conversations and classroom visits ensued in an effort to ensure that we had a "good working match" that would lead to high-quality implementations of our instructional units. We (the professors) agreed to provide unit plans that we developed and all of the accompanying instructional materials. Barbara agreed to critique early drafts of our units and engage in conversations regarding proposed changes. She also agreed to implement the units as finally designed and to allow us to collect data by interviewing students before and after the unit, audiotaping all lessons, observing and taking field notes, and interviewing the teacher and selected parents.

The collaboration has broadened over time, partly due to the school's method of organizing classes. Initially, Barbara taught a self-contained second grade, and then the school went on to a looping arrangement where first and second grade teachers stayed with the same class for two years, teaching first grade one year and second grade the next. Because this looping arrangement and professional collaboration were successful, Gina Henig (Barbara's colleague and eventual co-teacher) began to sit in on our collaborative work sessions and offer suggestions. Soon these two teachers decided to shift from self-contained classrooms to a team-teaching arrangement, wherein they taught about forty-five minutes in a double-sized classroom. One of the teachers focused on the first graders, and one focused on the second graders (depending on the year), but they used many common units and activities. Thus, Gina has become a more integral part of the collaboration, even though Barbara remains the primary pilot-test teacher for the social studies units. Currently, they work together in a multiage, ethnically diverse classroom in a working-class suburb where they share responsibility for all forty-five students. Children range from six to eight years of age. Special education children are mainstreamed into this classroom learning community.

The collaboration has expanded in other ways as well. For example, Barbara and Gina have begun sharing the results of our social studies work at professional meetings, at the district, state, and national levels. Through the extended dialogue surrounding our planning for these presentations, research questions that go beyond the requirements of our specific curriculum units have emerged. Toward this end, we are in the preliminary stage of finding released classroom time for Barbara so that she can engage in sustained conversations with us about early elementary social studies. In-depth analysis of the classroom data that we have collected so far would serve as the focus for this initiative.

Our tangible outcomes thus far have included detailed plans for seven units on cultural universals. For each unit, the associated data collection activities have produced a rich bank of information that we expect to analyze exhaustively over the next couple of years. Besides analyzing these data for relatively conventional unit assessment purposes (i.e., analyzing the transcripts and field notes to determine the degree to which the unit plans were implemented as intended, and analyzing the pre- and post-unit student interview data and the student work samples to assess the effectiveness of the unit in accomplishing student learning goals), we want to undertake a more comprehensive analysis of these unit implementations in collaboration with Barbara, who will provide the teacher's point of view.

Teachers Talk to Teachers (B.K. and G.H.)

One of the unusual things about our collaboration is that neither of us felt at first that social studies was a strength in our teaching. We had minimal preparation in this area before we began teaching. Before the collaboration, we followed district directives, but never emphasized or elaborated on social studies. To be successful with the new units, we needed to be open-minded and willing to try some ideas that might move us out of our "comfort zone." At first, the information that we received seemed cumbersome and unapproachable. The collaboration seemed one-sided; we were just receiving lessons and suggestions. Then we focused on bringing our strengths as classroom teachers and our experience working with children into the equation. We also found that the more we worked together, the more we built up our confidence. Also, we began to see how valuable our contributions were to the project. We could see our suggestions and ideas being valued and used often. It is important to believe and understand the value that both groups bring to the table. Learning this helped to build our confidence and opened the doors for new opportunities.

One of the first opportunities for us to share what we had learned during our collaboration was at the Michigan Council for the Social Studies convention during the spring of 1999. Together with Jan, we presented at two sessions. Before working with MSU professors, we never would have considered participating in a social studies convention. The idea seemed intimidating at first, but as we worked together, the task seemed more reasonable. From there, we went to the National Council for the Social Studies (NCSS) annual conference in the fall.

Another opportunity to come from the collaboration is this book chapter, which has given us the chance to take a close look at how we work together and acknowledge the best of what we do. We have also become more active within our district in social studies. We have taken the things that we have learned and put them to use working with benchmarks and curriculum.

Recently, we were asked to share a unit that we created using the same techniques that we developed in our collaborations with Jan and Jere. Using similar pedagogical ideas, we created and designed science and character education lessons and units. We did not realize going into the partnership that our work in social studies might eventually help us teach in other areas, too.

To others considering university collaboration, here are some recommendations for teachers. One crucial idea is to have and keep an open mind. Try not to make snap judgments. Give yourself some time and be willing to try some new things before you give up. Also, move away from the "it won't work" way of thinking. It can be easy to dismiss a new idea by listing all of the reasons why "it won't work." Instead, be willing to try things or thoughtfully discuss specific reasons for changing and adjusting the plans.

Try not to be overwhelmed when you first begin collaborating with someone from the university. Sometimes it might seem that you come from different worlds and speak different languages. Be patient and break tasks into pieces. Also, don't be afraid to ask for more information if you need it. This is the place where it is important to have a comfortable relationship with your fellow collaborators. You need to be honest about your comfort level. Don't agree to do more than you will be able to handle.

Time seems to be an eternal issue in education. Collaborating is no different from anything else. If you want to do it right, you have to be willing to put in the time. We've made it a habit at the end of each meeting always to schedule our next one. We try to meet regularly and make sure to schedule plenty of time to prepare for deadlines.

Communication is another important area. We have made sure to keep parents of our students informed and updated about our collaboration with the university. We share information in newsletters, home assignments, parent orientation and classes, and informal discussions. Some parents can be suspicious if they don't understand what you are doing. By being proactive and explaining your collaboration ahead of time, you can prevent problems. Also, be sure to share information with your administrators both at the building level and districtwide.

Finally, as you work and put more time into your collaboration, know that the benefits will be coming. You will find that collaborating will cause you to stretch and grow as an educator. It will also broaden your experiences and open new doors of opportunity. Also, even if it does not make your job easier, it will make it interesting and different.

Professors Talk to Professors (J.A. and J.B.)

The collaboration has already produced a wealth of useful information and insight. It has expanded beyond our initial plans because Barbara models good practice on dimensions that go beyond our original research questions. The collaboration has provided valuable assessment data on our units, validating our basic approach to constructing powerful teaching about cultural universals, but also suggesting many ways in which the units could be improved (we revised the unit plans in response to what we learned from each implementation). Because our collaboration has been useful for all parties, we have every reason to believe that all parties involved will continue indefinitely.

An unintended outcome of this collaboration has been the benefits reaped by one of us, Janet, who teaches undergraduate and graduate social studies classes. A wealth of actual classroom scenarios and techniques have been laced into her college classroom sessions. The professor's credibility is enhanced because she experiences what life is really like today in an elementary classroom. The many insights that this collaboration has produced about good teaching (both in general and in social studies specifically) in the early grades provide great commentary for the professor charged with teaching methods courses on the college campus.

Some of these insights were initially serendipitous, based on something Barbara said or did by way of elaborating on our plans, or on questions or comments made by the students in the classroom, or by parents describing activities carried out at home. Some serendipitous insights concerned events that occurred periodically (i.e., efficacy-building opportunities, citizenship considerations, cues for home assignments, direction giving, and so forth). We have begun to investigate these insights systematically.

Over and above information about the effectiveness of our units, the collaboration has produced (1) useful principles regarding issues such as methods of helping students see connections across units and between their school learning and their lives outside of school, (2) methods of developing students' perceptions of self-efficacy with respect to their potential for decision making about the cultural universals under study in their lives today and in the future, (3) the trade-offs offered by various forms of children's literature as instructional materials and principles for using these materials effectively, (4) methods of integrating social studies teaching with teaching in other subjects, and (5) methods of involving parents in curriculum-related discourse and activities at home in ways that parents and students find enjoyable and productive.

Through our experience, including a couple of false starts in our preliminary teacher-professor collaboration efforts, we have come to understand and appreciate classrooms more deeply. We experience firsthand the challenges that arise in trying to find the right mix that will be useful for all professionals involved and at the same time address the intended research questions.

Guiding Principles for Teacher-Professor Collaboration

FROM THE TEACHERS (B.K. AND G.H.)

We offer the following guidelines for other teachers to consider before entering into a partnership.

▶ If you are approached by a local university member and asked to collaborate, be sure to take time to consider your participation carefully.
▶ Don't be afraid to ask questions.
▶ Be sure that you understand your role and required participation.
▶ Spend some time talking with the collaborator to be certain that your philosophies about education match or at least are not in conflict.
▶ Avoid situations where you are expected to do something that you don't agree with.
▶ Try to talk with fellow teachers who might know the university collaborator.
▶ Be sure that you know what the timeline will look like.
▶ Don't decide to take on more than you can handle.

▶ Discuss the proposal with your administrator to be sure that you have the support of your district, especially if curriculum changes are involved.

FROM THE PROFESSORS (J.A. AND J.B.)
We offer the following guidelines for other professors.

▶ Observe potential field sites in advance. Is what you see compatible with what you want to do?
▶ Get good information from people in a position to provide it. For example, make sure that a hands-on approach is producing learning that can be assessed later. (We've seen lots of glitz that did not develop powerful ideas.)
▶ Make sure the teacher shares similar beliefs and orientations toward classroom management.
▶ Be clear and direct about your goals and the nature of the collaboration. Describe your study, establish your expectations, lay out the timeline, and roll out your plans before you begin.
▶ Start small. Design a model that involves a small number of teachers and requires little of individuals other than the collaborators.
▶ Avoid selecting inexperienced teachers and those new to a grade level (unless these variables are inherent to your study).
▶ Select teachers who are willing to devote extra time for collaboration during and following the research initiative.
▶ Select teachers who are supported by their administration and by the parents and community.
▶ Protect the anonymity of the individuals involved (if relevant), and be careful what you say about collaborating teachers, schools, and communities when discussing your work in college classes, school presentations, and so forth. Your conversations and explanations should focus on your research agenda and the learners.
▶ Be careful to give credit to your partners in collaboration by naming them, with their permission, and including them as co-authors when appropriate. The cooperation of students, parents, and administrators should be acknowledged (usually in a note) in any subsequent publications.

Through our collaboration, we have been committed to bringing to early elementary social studies the same components that have proven successful in the research and development of other school subjects: emphasis on teaching for understanding, content networks structured around big ideas and developed with an emphasis on applications, and a focus on domain-specific content and pedagogy. This research and collaboration will continue to deal simultaneously with curriculum, instruction, and assessment issues. This commitment can be realized only through hand-in-glove teacher-professor collaboration.[5]

NOTES
1. A. Guy Larkins, Michael Hawkins, and Allison Gilmore, "Trivial and Non-informative Content of Elementary Social Studies: A Review of Primary Texts in Four Series," *Theory and Research in Social Education* 15 (1987): 299-311; Diane Ravitch, "Tot Sociology or What Happened to History in the Grade School," *American Scholar* 56 (1987): 343-353.
2. Fred Newmann, "Qualities of Thoughtful Social Studies Classes: An Empirical Profile," *Journal of Curriculum Studies* 22 (1990): 253-275.
3. Kathleen Roth, "Science Education: It's Not Enough to 'Do' or 'Relate,'" *American Educator* 13 (1990): 16-22, 46-48.
4. Mary Hoberman, *A House Is a House For Me* (New York: Viking, 1978).
5. Janet Alleman and Jere Brophy, "On the Menu: The Growth of Self-Efficacy," *Social Studies and the Young Learner* 12, no. 3 (2000): 15-19; Janet Alleman and Jere Brophy, "Current Trends and Practices in Social Studies Assessment for the Early Grades," *Social Studies and the Young Learner* 11, no. 4 (1999): 15-17; Janet Alleman and Jere Brophy, "Strategic Learning Opportunities During Out-of-School Hours," *Social Studies and the Young Learner* 10, no. 4 (1998): 10-13; Janet Alleman and Jere Brophy, "Social Studies: Instruments, Activities, and Standards," in *Handbook of*

Classroom Assessment: Learning, Achievement, and Adjustment, ed. Gary D. Phye (San Diego, Calif.: Academic Press, 1997); Janet Alleman and Jere Brophy, "Considering Textbook Limitations and Strategies for Compensation," *Social Studies and the Young Learner* 9, no. 2 (1996): 4-7; Janet Alleman and Jere Brophy, "Is Curriculum Integration a Boon or a Threat?" *Social Education* 57 (1993): 287-291; Jere Brophy and Janet Alleman, *Powerful Social Studies Teaching and Learning* (Fort Worth, Tex.: Harcourt Brace, 1996); Jere Brophy and Janet Alleman, "Elementary Social Studies Should Be Driven by Major Social Education Goals," *Social Education* 57 (1993): 27-32; Jere Brophy and Janet Alleman, "Activities As Instructional Tools: A Framework for Analysis and Evaluation," *Educational Researcher* 20 (1991): 9-23; Jere Brophy, Janet Alleman, and C. O'Mahony, "Elementary Social Studies: Yesterday, Today, and Tomorrow, in Elementary, Middle, and High Schools," in *America: Yesterday, Today, and Tomorrow* (Ninety-ninth Yearbook of the National Society for the Study of Education), ed. T. Good (Chicago, Ill.: University of Chicago Press, 2000).

Teaching Social Studies in an Urban Elementary School: Collaboration for Integration and Inquiry Learning

KEITH C. BARTON
LESLIE A. KREIMER

The Scene

The twenty-four students in Leslie's third grade classroom in inner-city Cincinnati, Ohio, put away their books after Sustained Silent Reading, and Leslie called their attention to a piece of chart paper she had taped to the board. Leslie wrote the heading "Westward Movement," and said she wanted to find out what students already knew about the topic they were going to study. She explained that, today, they would write down what they *knew* and what they *wanted* to know, and as they went through the unit, they would add what they *learned* to the chart. She explained that they would begin by making their own lists for the first two of these categories, and then they would combine them into a single classroom list on the KWL chart on the board. She asked two questions—first, whether they should worry about writing full sentences at this point (students responded that they should just jot down their ideas in brief) and, second, whether it would be appropriate to talk to each other while they were doing this (when students weren't sure, Leslie explained this could be exactly the right time to talk, because that would help them come up with better ideas).

As students began to work on the task, Leslie circulated around the room giving support. She was assisted by a teaching associate from the University of Cincinnati, and by Keith, a professor with whom she has collaborated for many years. When several students had difficulty identifying what they already knew about the Westward Movement, Leslie called their attention to a series of books she had placed around the room from their previous unit on forms of transportation in the past and present. Many of these books had pictures of covered wagons, and some students had done projects on those. When some students still couldn't come up with anything, Leslie assured them that it was okay, because the purpose of doing this was to find out where she should start the lesson.

After calling the class members back together to compile what they already knew (which resulted in a fairly long list of generally accurate observations), Leslie had students develop questions they had about the topic. She asked students to "push yourselves" and come up with at least four or five things "you sure would like to find out." Later, she compiled these questions on the chart.

In the second part of the lesson, Leslie had students bring their social studies notebooks to the reading corner and copy the title of the book they would be reading together, *Cassie's Journey: Going West in the 1860s.*[1] She explained that although the book was a work of historical fiction, and Cassie wasn't a real girl, it was based on the diaries of people who really had moved west, and that the author put these together into a story so they'd be easier to understand. She explained, "As I read to you, jot down any notes, any information you hear, anything you think is important." Several students wrote constantly as she read, while others made only occasional notes, or none at all. Stopping frequently to discuss the details on each page, Leslie emphasized the connection between the information in the book and the questions they had developed together. After reading about half of the book together with students, she had them return to their seats, and she explained the next activity—writing a letter to a friend in the East from the perspective of the book's main character.

The Purpose of Our Collaboration: Improving Social Studies through Integration and Inquiry Learning

The description above highlights many of the characteristics of meaningful social studies instruction—an inquiry orientation, integration of subject matter, activation of prior understanding, scaffolding of students' learning, and an awareness of the features of disciplinary knowledge. But this vignette also demonstrates the importance of collaboration, for without the ongoing links between the two of us (as well as with teaching associates and interns from the university), this scenario might never have taken place—or at best, its impact may have remained limited to one classroom, with no influence on other teachers or on students in the university's teacher education program.

Our collaboration has focused on the use of inquiry-oriented instruction and an integrated curriculum to teach social studies to elementary students in urban classrooms. We have attempted to do this in a way that not only honors children's diverse backgrounds and their developing curiosity about history and other subjects, but also is consistent with local curriculum guidelines and with critically important state testing procedures. This collaboration has helped each of us better understand how to apply constructivist principles of teaching and learning to the "real world" of young children. Undertaking such work as a collaborative effort has had important professional benefits for each of us individually, but we hope it also has improved the quality of learning among both the elementary children and the beginning teachers for whom we are responsible.

Constructivist theories of teaching and learning have dominated the literature on social studies, as well as other content areas, for many years.[2] As most teachers will by now be aware, constructivist perspectives emphasize the creation of situations in which learners can construct their own knowledge. Recommendations for constructivist learning in social studies have often focused on the process of inquiry, in which students undertake investigations of meaningful questions, either those set by the teacher or those initiated by students on the basis of their own needs and interests. Educators often assume that this process is the most effective way of engaging students in authentic activities—the kind of learning people pursue in their lives outside school—and hence is the best way of providing students with the chance to construct their own ideas about the social world.

But successfully engaging children in inquiry requires at least two critical kinds of intervention by teachers. The first involves activating students' background knowledge. Only by addressing what students already know can teachers build on their prior ideas, expand and refine their understanding, or address any misconceptions they may have. This attention to prior knowledge is crucial to any kind of instruction, of course, but it is especially important when students are engaged in inquiry, for young learners may not always see the connections between what they already know and the new information they come across. Without explicit attention to such links, students may have difficulty finding meaningful information during their investigations or drawing such information together into conclusions that make sense to them.

Second, teachers must provide a variety of forms of instructional scaffolding.[3] Particularly when children are new to the process of inquiry, teachers must give them the assistance necessary to complete their investigations successfully. This may involve stimulating students' interest, modeling procedures for them, using probing questions to highlight the meaning or relevance of information, providing critical feedback on students' accomplishments, breaking the overall task down into more manageable parts, or creating graphic organizers to aid in the collection and interpretation of information. Without these forms of help, students are unlikely to be able to carry out an inquiry-oriented project, no matter how meaningful and authentic it may be. In fact, we all probably have had the experience of creating relevant and motivating projects for children, only to find that they had great difficulty once they began their investigations. When such difficulties arise, insufficient scaffolding is often the culprit.

A final aspect of many contemporary recommendations for constructivist approaches to teaching and learning involves the integration of more than one of the traditional subject areas.[4] When students can see the connections among skills or content that are relevant to more than a single field, they may be better able to understand what they learn and apply it in meaningful contexts. In settings outside of school, for example, we rarely encounter math, language, social studies, or any other subject in isolation; rather, we learn what we need to in order to accomplish certain goals, and this learning may involve content or skills from many different areas. Integrating subjects in a similar fashion in school, then, makes students' learning more authentic, more like what people do in other meaningful contexts. In social studies, such integration can also capitalize on the wealth of children's literature that addresses topics relevant to the curriculum, as well as engage students in representing what they have learned in social studies through language, mathematics, or art, all of which are critical features of "authentic" instruction.

It's easy enough to recommend that teachers do all of this while sitting in a university classroom, but in the world of real classrooms and real children, the process is much less simple, and much less obvious, than scholarly recommendations would make it appear. Children may appear unmotivated, it may be difficult to find areas they seem to know anything about, and time pressures may force integration onto the back burner. Often faced with an all-too-apparent mismatch between classroom realities and the admonitions they encounter in course work or readings, beginning teachers (or even experienced teachers new to processes of inquiry or integration) may reject constructivist principles in favor of using textbooks, worksheets, and drill-and-practice in low-level skills, all of which may seem to be what "really" works, rather than the abstract ideas of scholars.

Two other factors encourage this tendency to abandon inquiry-oriented and integrated instruction in favor of more traditional paper-and-pencil routines. The first is the impact of high-stakes, standardized testing programs—or perhaps more accurately, it is teachers' perception of such tests that leads them to avoid these approaches. Without question, statewide testing programs can have a significant impact on both the content and format of instruction. Under pressure to raise scores on tests, teachers often limit their curriculum to a narrow range of topics and present them as isolated subjects for "mastery," interpreted as the ability to recall information for a test. Ironically, though, in our experience, the topics that teachers emphasize may do little to prepare their students for high-stakes testing. In many states (including Ohio, where our own work has taken place), contemporary state tests do not exclusively require the recall of factual information, but instead demand the application of higher-order skills and conceptual understandings, and also require reading and writing in the content areas—precisely the kinds of learning encouraged by integration and inquiry, but not by drill-and-practice schemes.[5] Moreover, local curriculum guidelines in Cincinnati also mandate an emphasis on conceptual understanding rather than factual information, yet new teachers are often adamant in their beliefs that just the opposite is true. Helping them understand more accurately the relationships among local curricula, state testing, and instructional methods is an ongoing challenge both for university professors and mentoring teachers.

A second factor in limiting the range of teaching methods is less often articulated openly, but both of us see its influence in the day-to-day operation of schools and classrooms. This is the assumption that inquiry learning, construction of knowledge, higher-level thinking, and a range of other such admirable educational goals and procedures are perfectly appropriate for some students, but not for others—often, poor and minority students.

In our experience, beginning teachers frequently express their admiration and respect for inquiry learning, but they note that it wouldn't work "at my school" or "with my students." In some cases, they suggest that their students simply don't have enough background knowledge to build on, or that they are so lacking in basic skills that time spent on anything else would be wasted; presumptions of students' lack of interest in learning and low levels of parental support and involvement in education typically reinforce such dismal assessments of the possibility for meaningful inquiry learning with children in urban schools. Although it might be easy to dismiss such beliefs as either open or unconscious prejudice, these beliefs are perhaps more likely to stem from a simple lack of experience with urban children and their families, combined with the absence of teachers who can serve as role models in developing children's intellectual curiosity in such schools. Much of our collaboration, then, has focused on learning how to implement inquiry-oriented learning and integrated instruction with the students for whom "it doesn't work"—including the difficult process of building on their background knowledge and scaffolding their learning.[6]

The Nature of Our Collaboration: Flexible Connections in an Institutional Setting

Our collaboration takes place within the context of a professional development school in the Cincinnati Initiative for Teacher Education (CITE), a partnership between the Cincinnati Public Schools, the Cincinnati Federation of Teachers, and the University of Cincinnati. In this partnership, students in the university's teacher education programs complete two-year field placements in urban schools, as teaching associates one year and paid interns the next. The teachers at those schools serve as supervisors and mentors. This arrangement seeks to alter the balance in the preparation of new teachers, so that schools do not merely serve as "field placement sites" but as fully collaborative partners in educating new members of the profession. The CITE program provides numerous opportunities for collaboration among university faculty, experienced teachers, and students in the teacher education program, including shared supervision and evaluation, joint short- and long-term instructional planning, university courses taught by practitioners, and jointly funded action research projects. Although the program is a highly structured undertaking, with binding contractual arrangements and clearly defined institutional roles, the individual collaborations between practitioner and teacher are very flexible and unstructured.

We work together within the context of a structured institutional partnership, but the focus of our collaboration is not any particular program or project. Perhaps it can best be described as an intellectual collaboration—the chief thing we do is try to learn from each other about teaching and learning social studies in an urban, elementary context, and we try to pass on what we have learned to beginning teachers.

This kind of collaboration involves, first and foremost, conversations between ourselves about how best to teach the subject. The first discussions we had were firmly rooted in the context of the professor-student tradition: The teacher (L.K.) asked how she could improve her social studies instruction, and the professor (K.B.) told her, explaining his ideas on the subject and sharing the rough draft of a book on the topic he had recently co-authored. This kind of interaction could hardly be called collaboration, but over the years the nature of our discussions has evolved into a much more balanced one, as we have set down repeatedly to talk about what makes for effective learning in social studies. These conversations involve a mutual consideration of possibilities. We talk about what topics could be covered (and why), what resources are available, how students respond to instructional activities, what might be done differently, and what problems arise in the course of instruction. These conversations take place in a highly sporadic fashion, whenever we have time; they may be longer conversations after school, or shorter ones during a planning period, and they make take place in person, over the phone, or by e-mail. And increasingly, Leslie is the source of information and insights that are indispensable to Keith as he attempts to prepare future teachers—information on state testing procedures, local curriculum standards, and teacher evaluation guidelines. These kinds of official policies and administrative practices take place outside the realm of the university, and they can be fully understood only "from inside the classroom"—thus the balance of our access to meaningful information has shifted in important ways, so that it is now the university side of the collaboration that has the most to gain from the practitioner.

Another important aspect of the collaboration has been Keith's observation and participation in Leslie's classroom. This initially began simply as an attempt by Keith to get a better sense of how integration and inquiry might work in Cincinnati schools, and these early observations were infrequent and unstructured; they consisted of occasionally assisting Leslie as she engaged students in inquiry projects. Even this brief involvement was an important source of insights because each of us picked up a few practical teaching tips from the other. Eventually, these observations became part of more formal and systematic scholarly projects. The first consisted of an attempt to detail more precisely what is involved in planning and implementing integrated thematic units—specifically, thematic units that have serious academic content and that move beyond a collection of superficially related activities. This involved more frequent observations by Keith, longer and more detailed interviews with Leslie, and her own written reflections and unit plans. The result was a practitioner-oriented article, authored by Keith and another university colleague who had worked with Leslie, using Leslie's ideas and experiences as a way of exploring key features of thematic units.[7]

Our most recent collaboration, involving both discussion and observation/participation, has been a two-year action research project, funded by the university and the school district, to explore how the use of visual images and children's literature affects their understanding of history. In this project, we have worked together to identify and obtain visual and literary resources for teaching about the Westward Movement, immigration to the United States, and Ohio history. Leslie's role in the project has been to plan and implement instruction for her third graders, and she has also kept written reflections on the successes and challenges of her teaching.

Keith, meanwhile, has conducted formal interviews with a sample of students before and after instruction to identify patterns in their ideas about history and to see how those ideas change as a result of instruction, and he has conducted regular observations in the classroom. These interviews and observations have been based in part on the issues Leslie has identified as critical to her attempt to address the curriculum, and in part on issues Keith has derived from the academic literature on elementary children's learning of history. Both of us have shared our observations and emerging conclusions throughout the process in order to make adjustments both in classroom instruction and in the focus of the more formal research component.

Finally, we continually collaborate in the preparation of new teachers. Students who take Keith's social studies methods courses may serve as teaching associates or interns in Leslie's classroom or with other teachers at her school, and thus they have a chance to see the content of their university courses in action. In addition, Leslie occasionally visits Keith's class and shares her experiences with students; because her teaching is so closely aligned with the principles that students are expected to learn in the course, her information matches easily with the course content, and thus her visits are a natural part of the instruction rather than an isolated appearance by a "guest speaker." And, as will be discussed in more detail below, Keith's observations from Leslie's classroom become a constant source of examples for his university teaching.

What I Have Learned from Our Collaboration (L.K.)

As I reflect back on my ten years of teaching, there is one common thread that links the years together: No matter what grade level or group of students I was teaching, I constantly searched for a better way to guide my students through meaningful academic experiences. I would strive every day to plan and execute lessons that excited, inspired, and engaged them. I continually asked myself questions such as, How could this lesson be improved? Did I engage my students? In what ways can I connect this lesson to other academic areas? How can I relate what I'm teaching to my students' prior knowledge? Did my lessons address various learning needs? My desire to improve my own teaching led me, first, to pursue a master's in education, and then to achieve National Board Certification.

As a part of this quest, over the past eight years, I have collaborated professionally with Keith to explore instructional strategies and resources. Over the past five years, I have become involved in my school's leadership team and a districtwide committee that is developing a new teacher evaluation system. This combination of professional development, university collaboration, and leadership responsibilities has brought me to a place in my career where I want to share my knowledge and skills with other professionals in order to improve their quality of teaching.

As I began my teaching career, social studies was not an academic area in which I enjoyed planning lessons. The school district was only beginning to embrace the concept of teaching standards, and the social studies curriculum basically consisted of map skills, timelines, and national holidays. If my students received social studies instruction more than two to three times a week, I was doing pretty well. My opportunity to improve the situation came while I was beginning to work on my master's, when I first met

Keith. He had written a book describing how elementary students learn about history.[8] I read it and then began to apply some of the recommendations to my practice. I presented more content that was related to their personal experiences, as well as challenging activities that permitted student choice. The collection of resources, lessons, and projects required to teach this way called for dedication and commitment to students beyond the school day or school year.

One of my graduate courses addressed authentic ways to integrate academic areas. Being sold in most teacher stores at the time were resources offering "thematic" approaches or "integrated" units of study. Unfortunately, these tended to be full of loose connections, meaningless activities, and lessons not based on local, state, or national standards. I was frustrated because I didn't have time to create my own integrated units whenever I was introducing a new topic. As a result, I began using webs, which I learned about through another book I borrowed from Keith, to link the academic standards for my students with a plan of study.[9] This gave me the basis for a meaningful unit. I looked for ways to connect the experiences my students already had with experiences I could offer them. I would also match literature resources with topics/activities whenever possible. I was particularly interested in the use of read-aloud literature from a combination of historical narratives, realistic fiction, and nonfiction, and this is when I truly discovered the power of the integration of content areas. One of the most essential skills for students' success is the development of strong, well-rounded literacy skills.

Social studies can easily incorporate literacy skills. If students are studying historical time periods or events, writing a report describing, comparing, and contrasting each of them is quite effective. Also, many elementary students have difficulties with historical concepts, such as explaining cause and effect between major events and analyzing these in relation to other events occurring in the same time period. For example, most elementary students know that Columbus came to America; however, they don't necessarily understand that Columbus's voyages to America inspired other Europeans to travel to the "New World" or that these explorers were working on the behalf of governments; they were not just individual adventurers. Or students may know that the Civil War was related somehow to slavery, but may have little understanding of the impact of slavery on individuals and their families until they read books written from the perspective of a child who lived during that time period. Works that focus on the experiences of real people—such as *Across the Wide and Lonesome Prairie: The Oregon Trail Diary of Hattie Campbell* in the Dear America series[10]— are extremely helpful when integrating social studies and language arts, and they are effective at motivating students and getting them interested in the topic.

My coverage of social studies, and its integration with other subjects, has also expanded considerably over the years. My unit on the Westward Movement has now evolved into a study of the migration of people, including not only pioneers moving westward—men, women, and children—as well as the experiences of African Americans, Native Americans, and European Americans, but also immigration to America, the forced migration of slaves, and the settlement of Ohio. This unit also incorporates science in ways that help to define and explain these historical events. For example, it includes attention to the evolution of transportation, settlements by rivers, the use and distribution of resources, and how humans affect the environment. Students have researched various types of transportation, created multitiered timelines, and connected this information to population growth and the migration of people. The completion of the transcontinental railroad, for example, eventually made wagon travel obsolete. But my students didn't make this connection until they were deeply involved in this research project. Similarly, while studying the river systems in Ohio, we plotted all the major cities in that state on a map. Using this information, we analyzed the relationship between the invention of the steamboat, the geography of the river systems, and the early settlement of Ohio.

Another effective way to excite students about history is to use artifacts and historical photos (either loose or in a book). Elementary students have a difficult time with abstract ideas. If they can see it, touch it, or do it, they have a better chance of remembering it. Building on what students already know is especially important, and giving them direct experiences means the new information will be connected to their prior knowledge. When studying the history of Cincinnati, for example, students worked with a book called *Cincinnati, Then and Now*,[11] which contained photographs of the same places one hundred years ago and today. This book was also the basis for many literacy activities. For example, students wrote descriptions for each of the photographs, then discussed their comparisons with partners. Then they created Venn diagrams comparing and contrasting the two photos of the same location, citing specific examples of changes in transportation and technology, changes in landscape, different building materials, and new businesses. It was amazing how this simple tool immersed my students in a challenging reading and writing lesson. It was especially meaningful because the pictures they selected were from an area close to where they lived.

What I've Learned from Our Collaboration (K.B.)

One of the first things preservice teachers want to know of their professor is, Have you ever taught? But because nearly all professors in the field have taught at some point, students also have learned to ask, How long ago was that? These questions are fair ones, for experience in the classroom confers a certain validity to what might otherwise appear to be abstract generalizations. My students probably overrate the importance of recent classroom teaching, seemingly assuming that today's children are vastly different from those of the distant past of the 1980s. I would agree with my students, however, that the ability to draw on classroom examples to illustrate important principles is closely tied to how recently the professor has worked with teachers and children.

When I first began teaching social studies methods courses a decade ago, my years of teaching were so recent it was no problem to remember relevant examples from my own classrooms. As those memories have begun to fade, however, I have found it increasingly necessary to refresh my stock of practical experience by observing and participating in the classrooms of teachers I admire and respect. I need to be reminded that one kind of scaffolding is showing students whether to fold a piece of paper "like a hot dog" (vertically) or "like a hamburger" (horizontally).

But working in Leslie's classroom has done far more for my ability to teach social studies methods courses than providing me with a ready store of examples of what I already knew, for Leslie is such an insightful and reflective teacher that she has significantly extended my understanding of what it means to teach social studies, particularly in diverse urban settings. Watching Leslie's teaching has helped me better recognize the features necessary to developing students' conceptual understanding and their ability to engage in inquiry, and it has helped me more fully appreciate ways of teaching that are different from my own.

The most striking characteristic of Leslie's instruction is her tremendous respect for her students' intellects. Leslie never suggests that her students are incapable of doing a task, that they don't know enough about a subject to investigate it, or that they will not be interested in academic learning. Rather, she continually treats students as though they do know things already, are academically curious and motivated, and have the capability to investigate a new topic.

As seen in this chapter's opening scenario, Leslie makes it appear to students that intellectual curiosity is a natural feature of the human condition. She doesn't tell them that they are completing tasks because they "have to," or because it's part of the curriculum, or even so that they will please her. Rather, she takes it for granted that they engage in learning to have their own questions answered. This is not a perspective beginning teachers always bring to their work, particularly if they have little experience with poor and minority students; they more often believe that children have to be scolded, cajoled, or otherwise "managed" to get them to engage in academic tasks. Leslie, on the other hand, provides a model of someone who respects her students' curiosity. As they come up with questions for their KWL chart, for example, she emphasizes that they're not just trying to get some words down on paper, but instead are recording what they "sure would like to know." Similarly, she explains that the author of *Cassie's Journey* has compiled and rewritten diaries so that we can better understand what they have to tell us, as though wanting to know about the experiences of pioneers in the 1800s is completely unproblematic, something one can't help but wonder about. And Leslie constantly models this intellectual curiosity for her students; *she* wants to know things about the Westward Movement, and *she* finds answers as they read as well.

As the year goes on, students increasingly adopt this perspective as they become more and more adept at developing questions and finding answers. Even in the activity above, which took place near the beginning of the year, many students conscientiously took notes while Leslie read to them because they believed her when she told them it was a good way to keep track of what they were finding out. They weren't taking notes for their teacher; they were taking notes for themselves.

A related aspect of Leslie's teaching is her tendency to assign tasks that seem to me far too difficult, and then to help students complete them successfully. She might, for example, have students look through a variety of difficult reference sources to find information on the changing uses of transportation over time, or assign them cards with descriptions of events from the Westward Movement and ask them to reason out how they should be arranged chronologically, or have them compile budgets for needed supplies for the trip west in 1820.

Rather than prejudging children's abilities—and thus placing an artificial limit on what they will be asked to do—she gives them the chance to rise to the challenges she sets. Not every student completes all tasks successfully, of course, and activities at the beginning of the year can be a particular challenge, but Leslie's belief that her students can do difficult work ensures that none will be doomed to a regimen of low-level basic skills or isolated worksheets.

Leslie helps students rise to the challenge of learning about social studies in several ways. First, she finds a variety of different ways of building on what they know for any given topic. Whereas I might note the importance of doing a KWL chart or web with children as they begin to study the westward migration, Leslie has them interview relatives about the moves they have made in their lives and their reasons for making them; she compares the Westward Movement to previous literature they have read and projects they have done; she focuses on the everyday experiences of people; and she does a KWL chart or web. While she and I both recognize the importance of building on students' background knowledge, her practical experience and her insights into the nature of children's learning considerably extend and refine my understanding of how to accomplish such goals.

And finally, I have been particularly impressed with Leslie's use of probing questions as she circulates around the room to help students with their work. Because she has set very difficult tasks for them, students initially need a great deal of help, and when no adult is near, they frequently get off task. My instinct while circulating is to approach students and tell them to "get to work"—not a very useful strategy. But Leslie maintains order and keeps students on task not by reminding them that they should be working but by engaging with them intellectually. As she circulates, she neither reminds students of behavioral expectations nor answers questions, but goes to each individual, pair, or group, and begins talking to students about the substance of what they are doing. If students are trying to make a decision about which route across the mountains a group of travelers might take, for example, she asks them questions about the relative merits of each alternative: "What do you think they might find if they went this way? What might be the problems with the other trail? Which one do you think would be the most frightening? Do you think they would have had the same fears as you, or different ones?" Her genuine interest in their ideas, and her encouragement for students to become interested in each other's ideas, further supports the creation of a learning community in the classroom. By seeing these features of Leslie's teaching in practice, I have a much better understanding of how integration and inquiry learning can be meaningfully implemented in a practical context.[12]

Conclusion

As noted above, ours is a flexible and largely unstructured collaboration, although it takes place within the context of a highly formal and institutionalized arrangement among the Cincinnati Public Schools, the Cincinnati Federation of Teachers, and the University of Cincinnati. To some extent, these formal structures encourage and support our collaboration—action research grants allow us to purchase materials for the classroom, teacher internships help us link university and school, and the involvement of teachers in the university's education program provide both faculties with a better understanding of the context of each other's work. Yet some of the most meaningful collaboration takes place on a smaller scale, between the individuals involved in these larger institutional frameworks. It is through these ongoing connections—discussions, interviews, formal and informal observations, and regular visits to each other's classrooms—that we have learned how to teach better and how to educate teachers better. We hope that what we have learned through our collaboration will improve the ability of our current and future colleagues in urban elementary schools, and elsewhere, to use integration and inquiry learning as effective tools for teaching social studies.

NOTES

1. Brett Harvey, *Cassie's Journey: Going West in the 1860s* (New York: Holiday House, 1988).
2. Jere Brophy and Bruce Vansledright, *Teaching and Learning History in Elementary Schools* (New York: Teachers College Press, 1997); John Bruer, *Schools for Thought: A Science of Learning in the Classroom* (Cambridge, Mass.: MIT Press); Catherine Twomey Fosnot, *Constructivism: Theory, Perspective, and Practice* (New York: Teachers College Press, 1996); Linda S. Levstik and Keith C. Barton, *Doing History: Investigating with Children in Elementary and Middle Schools* (Mahwah, N.J.: Lawrence Erlbaum Associates, 1997).
3. Barbara Rogoff, *Apprenticeship in Thinking: Cognitive Development in Social Context* (New York: Oxford University Press, 1990); David Wood, *How Children Think and Learn: The Social Contexts of Cognitive Development* (Malden, Mass.: Blackwell, 1998).
4. Christine C. Pappas, Barbara Z. Kiefer, and Linda S. Levstik, *An Integrated Language Perspective in the Elementary School: An Action Approach* (New York: Longman, 1999).
5. Sample items from the state testing program can be found at the web site of the Ohio Department of Education, www.ode.state.oh.us.
6. Our work is similar to the principles of "culturally relevant" or "culturally responsive" teaching as outlined in Geneva Gay, *Culturally Responsive Teaching: Theory, Research, and Practice* (New York: Teachers College Press, 2000) and Gloria Ladson-Billings, *The Dreamkeepers: Successful Teachers of African American Children* (San Francisco, Calif.: Jossey-Bass, 1994).
7. Keith C. Barton and Lynne A. Smith, "Themes or Motifs? Aiming for Coherence through Interdisciplinary Outlines," *The Reading Teacher* 54 (September 2000): 54-63.
8. Linda S. Levstik and Keith C. Barton, *Doing History: Investigating with Children in Elementary and Middle School*, 2d ed. (Mahwah, N.J.: Lawrence Erlbaum Associates, 2000).
9. Christine C. Pappas, Barbara Z. Kiefer, and Linda S. Levstik, *An Integrated Language Perspective in the Elementary School: An Action Approach*, 3d ed. (New York: Longman, 1999).
10. Kristiana Gregory, *Across the Wide and Lonesome Prairie: The Oregon Trail Diary of Hattie Campbell* (New York: Scholastic, 1997).
11. Iola Hessler Silbersten, *Cincinnati, Then and Now* (Cincinnati, Ohio: League of Women Voters of the Cincinnati Area, 1982).
12. For other works on integration and inquiry learning in social studies, see Jere E. Brophy and Janet Alleman, *Powerful Social Studies for Elementary Students* (Fort Worth, Tex.: Harcourt Brace, 1996); M. Gail Hickey, *Bring History Home: Local and Family History Projects for Grades K-6* (Boston, Mass.: Allyn and Bacon, 1999); Tarry Lindquist and Douglas Selwyn, *Social Studies at the Center: Integrating Kids, Content, and Literacy* (Portsmouth, N.H.: Heinemann, 2000); and Michael O. Tunnell and Richard Ammon, eds., *The Story of Ourselves: Teaching History through Children's Literature* (Portsmouth, N.H.: Heinemann, 1993).

Service-Learning and Community-Based Teaching and Learning: Developing Citizenship through Social Action

Three

Sally R. Beisser
Diana Schmidt

The Scene

As the fifth graders in Diana Schmidt's class sat in a circle talking about an idea for their next service-learning project, they expressed an interest in the topic of homelessness. Students asked questions about the actual number of homeless citizens in their community. They wondered how homeless people get by, what they live in, and why they don't just live with family or friends. One student wondered how homeless students complete their homework. Some wondered why we don't just give them homes. They wanted to know their ages, when and how they eat, take a shower, or change their clothes. Another asked if people are happy being homeless. Still others wondered if kids could even do anything about homelessness. Inviting elementary students to understand and empathize with the needs and issues of homelessness in our university community is, indeed, a challenge.

Mr. Vic Moss, the director of the Emergency Residence Project, came in to speak to the class. He told the children that approximately 270 people are homeless in their city, Ames, Iowa, a midsized university city of approximately 50,000 people. "Homeless" includes those staying at the Emergency Residence Project, Women's Crisis Shelter, and the Habitat House for Humanity. In addition, some homeless people live in cars or abandoned properties. Other residents "double-up," which means one family without a home moves in with another family. The fifth graders had many questions.

The fifth graders, along with two college students in Sally Beisser's Service-Learning Independent Study course, did several things to help the homeless families in the community. They contacted the Holiday Inn, which donated soaps, shampoos, and lotion as well as sheets, blankets, pillows, and hair dryers. A local clothing store donated 250 bottles of scented body lotion. The fifth grade students, along with their college student partners, were enthralled with their empowerment to meet the needs of homeless people in their own community.

Conceptualization of Social Studies

> We hold these truths to be self-evident, that all Men [sic] are created equal, that they are endowed by their Creator with certain unalienable Rights, that among these are Life, Liberty, and the Pursuit of Happiness. (*Declaration of Independence, 1776*)

> We, the people of the United States, in Order to form a more perfect Union, establish Justice, insure domestic Tranquility, provide for the common Defense, promote the general Welfare, and secure the blessings of Liberty to ourselves and our Posterity, do ordain and establish this Constitution for the United States of America. (*Preamble of the Constitution of the United States, 1787*)

Effective social studies teachers build understanding of America's history on an action-oriented level and connect history to contemporary issues. For example, in studying America's historical past through reading documents such as the Declaration of Independence and the Preamble of the Constitution, Diana asked her students to analyze what it meant to "pursue happiness" and "promote the general welfare." She used service-learning as a pedagogical bridge between the community and the classroom. This gave students a contemporary framework to analyze social injustices, such as homelessness. They examined individual freedoms, such as gainful employment, and the basic rights to "life, liberty, and the pursuit of happiness."

Service-learning projects involving homelessness encompass deeper social issues such as economic poverty, equality of opportunity, or work as important to a person's independence and pursuit of happiness. Students have an opportunity to become socially responsive to the homeless population in their community, who for whatever reason did not have equal opportunities to obtain an education, employment, or adequate housing.

The study of homelessness connects to the National Council for the Social Studies (NCSS) thematic strand ✪ **CIVIC IDEALS AND PRACTICES**, which expects students to "examine the origins and continuing influences of key ideals of the democratic republican form of government such as individual human dignity, liberty, justice, equality, and the rule of law."[1] Students must practice forms of civic discussion and participation consistent with the ideals of citizenship in a democratic republic.

In this project, students researched the needs and issues of homeless people by speaking with community agency leaders and directors. They made collaborative decisions within the classroom in order to take social action and reach consensus on what could be done at the local level. Such discussions encouraged students to practice civic discussion so they could participate in the ideals of citizenship in a democratic republic. They read library books and journal articles, sent for materials from the state Department of Education, and searched electronic sources to learn about the national and state perspectives on homelessness.

Students also learned that varying levels of service are possible. They could, in fact, address the issue of homelessness on one or more levels of service. For example, a direct level of service brings students close to the personal needs of others in an effort to meet immediate needs of other people. Students might take direct responsibility to supply food and personal grooming items to homeless shelters. An indirect level of service involves organized efforts to channel student efforts. Direct service is intended to approach the problem or issue with an immediate response, while providing indirect service operates on the assumption that a response to a need is channeled in the best interests of the beneficiary. Students might engage in organized efforts to provide food, clothing, funds, or resources to help the homeless. Advocacy levels of service involve political or social activism for students to address the needs of others by lobbying public officials, promoting proclamations, or increasing involvement in local laws and issues. To support the homeless population, students might lobby for the U.S. Census 2000 effort to count and include the homeless population accurately, people who would otherwise not be assessed because they did not have a permanent address.

Investigating homelessness invited students to build "habits of the heart." More than a century ago, Alexis de Tocqueville[2] was impressed by Americans' "habits of the heart," in reference to the civic-mindedness of people who cared for neighbors, joined clubs and organizations, or gathered food for the hungry. Americans created groups to solve problems, undertake projects, and engage in common interests.[3] There is evidence, however, that "habits of the heart" once characterizing American society have given way to the rise in juvenile crime, use of uncontrolled substances, media influence on children and adults, persistence of racism, political distrust, prevailing school violence, and perceived decline in decency and civility.

Schools, in response, have adopted character education and development programs. Former Secretary of Education William Bennett's book *The Book of Virtues: A Treasury of Great Moral Stories*[4] has become a national best seller. He argues that if schools do not provide moral guidance, kids may find television and the confused world of their peers as a source of values. *Educating for Character: How Schools Can Teach Respect and Responsibility*, by educational psychologist Thomas Lickona,[5] is promoted among administrators and counselors. Lickona endorses traditional instruction of specific virtues such as providing caring classrooms and advocating social justice in community schools where consensus can be reached for the renewal process.

Meaningful service-learning in education promotes quality in school-based and community-based service-learning programs. Members of the Alliance for Service-Learning in Education Reform[6] recommend that effective service-learning efforts strengthen both service and academic learning by using concrete opportunities for youth to learn new skills and think critically. Although service activities need skillful adult guidance and supervision, youth need to be involved in the planning process. Indeed, service-learning gives students an authentic opportunity to "promote the general welfare."

Our Process of Collaboration

Our collaboration began with in-service meetings at the university, conducted by Sally through a federally funded grant from the Corporation for National Service: Learn and Serve Higher Education. Teachers worked with student teachers to understand service-learning as a pedagogical strategy integrating the curriculum with a school- or community-based need. Teachers received free books such as *The Kid's Care Book*,[7] a 100-page curriculum resource packet called *Service-Learning in the Core Curriculum*,[8] and a small monetary stipend ($150) for project support. They applied concepts such as "preparation, action, and reflection components" from a nationally recognized training video from the Maryland Student Alliance, *The Courage to Care . . . The Strength to Serve*.[9] Diana participated each semester when she had a student teacher. She indicated an interest in having more university students facilitate service-learning projects with her fifth grade class. She gave Sally possible weekly meeting times, current classroom curriculum themes, and service projects of interest to her fifth grade class. University students had learned about service education through Sally's social studies methods course. In addition, they could take a one-semester-hour independent study if they worked with a classroom teacher who was conducting a service project. Some students volunteered because they were interested in service-learning, others wanted extra experience in a classroom, and still others simply needed a one-credit course.

After Sally solicited university students in class, Diana contacted the students and invited them to her room for an orientation meeting. Education majors did not have to be "experts" on service-learning, but needed to be willing to build a project collaboratively with elementary students and their teacher. Student facilitators needed to understand that process is an important component of successful service education projects. Their commitment included being involved for one semester, keeping a journal, and completing a project summary.

At the end-of-the-semester celebration, the teachers and university students met at the university to share service projects, successes, and challenges. For Diana, the value of the service was the realization that service-learning was a "process," not a "project." She learned the importance of continually modifying and reflecting on the project. Sally learned that teachers have meaningful ways to connect kids to the community to serve others. Although federal money ended after a three-year grant period, teachers such as Diana continued service-learning projects by collaborating with local university students.

The fifth grade homeless project involved two university education majors, Kirsten and Mollie. To provide an "indirect level of service" to the homeless in their city, fifth graders "earned" items that had been previously donated for the homeless shelter. On a gigantic poster board thermometer, kids kept track of their earnings. Points were accrued in a variety of ways, such as keeping individual reading logs to record minutes of independent reading at home. Points for mathematics included keeping a fraction journal, or constructing problems about cooking, measurement, or sports. Together they established a class system to earn points, in lieu of earning dollars. They felt they were serving the homeless on both an individual and a group level. This created a great group giving experience. When they reached a 300-point goal, the class visited the homeless shelter to deliver the collected items. Students were humbled by the shelter visit as they engaged in activity to "promote the general welfare" of the homeless members of their city.

Service-learning projects in fifth grade were better organized and more efficient with the assistance of university students who made phone calls, assisted with the field trips, planned the project details, checked student logs and journals, constructed the "goals" thermometer, created a project bulletin board, and assisted students. In addition, Kirsten and Mollie were excellent role models for the students.

To expand involvement with impoverished families and reinforce the mathematical concept of "percent," students organized a bake sale to raise money to buy groceries for the local food pantry. Each fifth grade student had a list of items requested by the food pantry director. From the bake sale profit, each student had an equal share in the amount of $3.45, to spend at the local grocery store to supply the pantry. The grocery store allowed a 20 percent discount for purchases. The students then determined how much they could spend. Their shopping expedition resulted in essential items such as cereal, peanut butter, soups, tuna, and other canned goods. After shopping, the students delivered the food to the pantry and shelved the items. The shelter director was impressed that ten- and eleven-year-olds could have such an impact at a "direct level" of service on a needy population in the community.

Tangible Outcomes

Students increased their awareness of the issues of homelessness, as well as immediate concerns of homeless people in their community. Students' eyes were opened to their limited scope of family and school within the larger community structure. Although the district has a social skills program called "Character Counts"[10] in place, it was more effective to build these skills in connection to the specific student focus. All six pillars in the "Character Counts" program—respect, responsibility, caring, citizenship, trustworthiness, and fairness—were reinforced through service-learning activities for the homeless. At the conclusion of the projects, reflective activities through writing, poetry, drawing, and public presentations revealed how much the students had learned and grown. One public presentation involved participation in the local hospital publicity campaign with student pictures and reflective comments on the hospital web site. They wrote and presented follow-up letters to the senior citizens about their experiences. Another activity invited the students to write to the next year's fifth grade class describing what they'd learned from their service-learning projects.

Our goal was to advance the causes of others before self-interest. Because most fifth graders are self-oriented, engagement in service helps to expand their scope of thinking by giving them opportunities to build attitudes of caring about their community with the long-range goal of becoming caring citizens. For example, Joseph said that helping others makes him feel good and like he is special. Allison liked to help others because it makes her feel good about herself. Jason liked to help others because his parents liked it when he helped others, while Aquavia said helping others "makes me feel like I've helped the world." Katie summarized, "I've learned that the little people can make a difference."

Overall, students gained leadership skills, interpersonal skills, and the confidence to take action on relevant social issues in their lives. According to Conrad and Hedin,[11] the following are potential outcomes of involvement in service-learning according to the research: academic skills, problem solving, critical thinking, ethical development, moral reasoning, social responsibility, self-esteem, assertiveness, civic responsibility, career goals, tolerance for diversity, and political efficacy.

To some extent, benefits supported in the research have been realized in Diana's fifth grade classroom. For example, students seemed more "assertive" as they volunteered eagerly for the school Safety Patrol. They exercised "civic responsibility" as they volunteered before and after school to ensure that younger students were safe to cross the street and to ride the school bus. While fifth graders typically like to help others, the issue of consistently displaying responsibility for others during a yearlong commitment grows out of the shorter service-learning project efforts. For example, the number of students in the class volunteering for Safety Patrol has dramatically increased. They demonstrated "tolerance for diversity" as they read about controversial or critical social issues in the news with greater interest. For example, students eagerly participated in diversity-related activities such as Martin Luther King community celebrations, openly accepted special education and ESL students in their homeroom, studied issues of acceptance in American history, researched prominent "tolerance-seeking" figures in American history, and identified characters representing diversity in contemporary literature books. Students developed "moral reasoning" by suggesting realistic problem solving strategies for school and playground problems. Specifically, one mother revealed that her fifth grade son, who had a penchant for getting into trouble, was actually mowing the lawn without complaining. The mother attributed his new sense of responsibility to the service-learning focus in fifth grade at his school. Students experienced tangible outcomes from service-learning that couldn't be replicated through other means. For example:

- Students learned and applied content from the curriculum into real-world contexts.
- Process skills were transferred to learning situations in and out of the school setting.
- Students felt a part of the larger community when they analyzed needs and concerns of others.
- Leadership skills and feelings of confidence were nurtured as students took action on issues.
- Interpersonal relationships and enhancement of communication skills were emphasized through listening, speaking, reading, and writing.
- Service-learning activities integrated and reinforced the six pillars of "Character Counts."

A Teacher Talks to Teachers (D.S.)

Working collaboratively, we created service projects that supported higher-level thinking and real-world learning to help children and future teachers reflect on social concerns and issues. As part of my collaboration with Sally, I incorporated *preparation, action, reflection,* and *celebration* effectively into my service-learning activities. First of all, preparation was important to identify a need or issue. Students conducted research through reading periodicals and books, checking web sites, and sending for information. Collaboration with university students was essential. With Sally's assistance, the college students obtained videos and curriculum guides on homeless students from the state Department of Education. Service-learning workshops provided resources and ways to connect to organizations. Fifth graders needed information and insights before starting a service project. They invited local guest speakers to inform them about meeting community needs through service organizations, had group discussions about available assistance from community groups, asked critical questions about how to approach local businesses for help, and completed reflective journal writing activities. Eventually, the class decided on a specific project focus.

The action phase of the project required collaboration with the community. The university provided a Service-Learning in the Core Curriculum Guide,[12] which included sample lesson plans, agency names, addresses, and phone numbers of local contacts. College student facilitators were invaluable as they made and returned numerous phone calls, ran errands for the project development, and assisted the fifth graders. They taught whole class and small-group lessons to integrate the service project in the curriculum through content connections in social studies, reading/language arts, math, and science. Project transportation was a challenge. The university students arranged transportation or parent drivers to our service sites. Project funding was another challenge. Extra help was needed to organize bake sales or pop can collections to finance service efforts.

Reflection was essential to student learning. Through a variety of ways such as discussion, writings, artwork, and public presentations, students shared their perceptions and growth. In an effort to do ongoing assessment, students responded to questions such as the following:

- How is the project going?
- What is working? What would you like to change?
- What problems have you encountered?
- What solutions do you have?
- What have you learned? What did you expect?
- What would you like to share with others about this project and how?

Just as the fifth grade students kept journals about their perceptions and impressions, Sally asked similar questions of the university students receiving credit for their involvement. Kirsten and Mollie prepared a portfolio of their experience including a timeline of activities, a photo essay, journal entries, and children's responses to service-learning. Everyone shared. Everyone learned.

Finally, I learned to celebrate service-learning. Students said "thank you" to participants from the community, the university, and our school. Student effort was honored through news articles and photos in the community newspaper celebrating several projects. Local radio and television stations aired student-written commercials about volunteer service. The students' commitment to service was renewed when they read comments in thank you notes received from the various agencies and organizations.

The school principal recognized the students' civic contributions by participating in the celebrations. School newsletters and parent-teacher conferences included highlights and feedback about service-learning. When the university students left at the end of the semester, they were missed. They valued working collaboratively, as well as learning about service-learning in the classroom.

Learning content in a relevant context made learning come alive for the fifth grade students. Through the university collaboration, students learned about themes of service. Projects were built around four themes that provided both direct and indirect service to the community:

I. PEOPLE IN POVERTY. STUDENTS . . .

▶ Provided groceries and items for the local food pantry.

▶ Supplied items for the community homeless shelter.

II. SCHOOL AS COMMUNITY. STUDENTS . . .

▶ Adopted shelves in the school media center to organize (kids had to know the Dewey Decimal System and use alphabetizing skills).

▶ Volunteered for the school safety patrol (kids learned to provide a safe, secure environment at school and to develop leadership skills).

▶ Learned first-aid techniques to help others in need.

III. ENVIRONMENTAL. STUDENTS . . .

▶ Developed rock trails at local parks and sowed seeds to reestablish prairie land through Environmental Curriculum Opportunities (ECO).

▶ "Adopted" wild animals that have been injured by raising money for the Wildlife Care Center orchestrated by university veterinarians who volunteer their time to save wildlife.

▶ Participated in Be Kind To Animals Week by writing an ad for the local animal shelter in the weekly advertiser. Students also wrote and performed in a local television commercial and wrote and recorded a local radio commercial.

IV. INTERGENERATIONAL. STUDENTS . . .

▶ Wrote books for patients at the pediatrics unit of our local hospital.

▶ Created games for students at the handicapped class to learn their alphabet and numbers.

▶ Interviewed residents at a local nursing home and wrote their biographies; learned about their personal history by interviewing each of the residents; and wrote plays, sang, and did projects together.

▶ Invented modifications for a wheelchair for a handicapped person who had visited our class by writing letters to wheelchair manufacturers about our ideas. We wrote to public officials to change laws for betterment of disabled and handicapped people.

Projects related to intergenerational learning examined issues of ageism and perceptions of the elderly population, particularly in relation to youth culture. Students gained understanding of senior citizens, based on essentiality and commonly shared ideals, such as the basic need for mutual communication. Service-learning projects involving environmental issues examined the larger issues of laws and governance for protection of public parks and facilities, wildlife and plant species, or environmental agencies. Students actively engaged in such endeavors become concerned about the well-being of their community, state, and nation. The projects never end. The students actively and enthusiastically participated in service-learning projects with positive, participatory attitudes.

However, there were "downsides" to service-learning, such as the considerable time, energy, and persistence required to coordinate arrangements and plan integrated curriculum. Service-learning does not work well if a teacher is lock-stepped into teaching separate subjects with a "drill and kill" approach. A creative mind is required to weave a web of instruction that incorporates district expectations with real-world service applications. Service-learning requires good communication among the teacher, parents, and administrators. Goals for learning must be specified. Time is at a premium in classroom instruction as a result of the push for accountability and assessment of student learning. We found that sometimes there was no choice but to take the quickest and easiest path to instruction. There were also problems in making connections with service agencies because there was a turnover in staff or change in location. In the middle of a project, all of a sudden, a contact person may have left the agency. Planning field trips to care centers, shelters, or grocery stores involved logistical arrangements, such as finding drivers or funding for bus transportation. The teacher sometimes needed to fund project supplies, camera film and developing, or treats.

Money was a key issue when donating to a shelter or a wildlife care center. In our state, it is no longer appropriate to ask students to bring money for anything, including field trips. Bake sales are now frowned upon, because of the fear of spreading contagious diseases. Businesses are saturated with requests for donations; therefore, it is increasingly difficult to enlist their help. It takes an enormous accumulation of pop cans to add up to a substantial sum. Several times, I attempted to find a local service organization partner, but the support never materialized.

Although many challenges exist, service-learning projects are limited only by the imagination of the teacher and students, and the availability of resources.

A Professor Talks to Professors (S.B.)

University-to-school collaboration requires professional leadership, joint conversations, and adequate time. Although the initial university in-service opportunities involved a modest monetary stipend, teachers valued the continued help from a professor and her university students.

First of all, professional leadership was fundamental for successful collaboration. Teachers appreciated research summaries and practical journal articles about service-learning. They wanted evidence that service education had value in an already crowded curriculum. Teachers needed print and nonprint materials to build service education into their existing curriculum. Next, teachers appreciated support. Although they could have conducted the service projects without student assistance, it was beneficial to have well-prepared university students support them in these time-consuming projects. Student teachers validated the teachers' service-learning focus in the classroom and shared their skills, knowledge, and attitudes in support of service-learning. Nearly 50 percent of the teachers continued classroom service projects long after the university students graduated. Joint conversations with teachers helped me maintain a classroom connection and observe learning theory in practice, remember what I loved about the classroom dynamics as a former teacher, and watch children making important differences in the lives of others.

Second, joint conversations invited clarification and consideration about what was working well and what needed to improve. For example, in one of these conversations, Diana explored exemplary service activities and the levels of service of her many projects. It was essential to ask what she learned through our collaboration. Conversations resulted in clarifying what service-learning "is" and "is not."

WHAT SERVICE-LEARNING IS
- Researching local needs or issues
- Integrating academic curriculum content with community or school-based needs
- Sustained service activities over time
- Collaborating between school and community
- Using higher-level thinking skills and problem-solving skills
- Understanding real-world content with real-life situations
- Fostering a sense of caring for others

WHAT SERVICE-LEARNING IS NOT
- An additional subject for teachers to teach and for classroom students to learn
- A good deed or a single act of charity

- A one-shot activity
- An isolated learning activity
- Activities disconnected from the regular classroom curriculum or district initiatives

Collaboration requires adequate time. Over three years, we were able to build a trusting relationship and reflect on project development and success. We planned opportunities to share with professional audiences. We did not keep the success of our collaboration to ourselves. We presented at state conferences and local events to room-packed audiences. Diana is now a school coordinator for a $3,000 service-learning grant from the Iowa Department of Education. She had the training, resources, and support to write a sustainable grant. I presented at national, state, and local conferences. Diana and I presented at two state conferences, and I presented nationally at the Association for Supervision and Curriculum Development (ASCD) with one university student. I was invited to present at the National Symposium on Service Learning, which included state directors, chief state school officers, and curriculum directors from more than twenty-five states.

Although university-to-school collaboration is time-intensive, multiple benefits resulted from our endeavors. Regular interaction with master teachers who teach with purpose and enthusiasm reaffirmed my passion for teaching and learning. As preservice teachers returned to campus, I was excited to hear what they had learned. They beamed with a newfound ability to incorporate a service focus in the curriculum content. They felt they made a difference in their community. I felt gratified to receive personal notes from university supervisors who were impressed that student teachers were conducting thoughtfully designed service-learning projects. It seemed that these students were not just teaching to earn a living, but had learned to live a life.

> To give of one's self; to leave the world a bit better; whether by a healthy child, a garden patch, or a redeemed social condition . . . to know that even one life has breathed easier because you have lived—that is to have succeeded. *(Ralph Waldo Emerson)*

NOTES
1. National Council for the Social Studies, *Expectations of Excellence: Curriculum Standards for Social Studies* (Washington, D.C.: Author, 1994).
2. Alexis de Tocqueville, *Democracy in America* (New York: Doubleday, 1969).
3. Walter Parker and John Jarolimek, *Social Studies in Elementary Education*, 10th ed. (Upper Saddle, N.J: Merrill/Prentice Hall, 1997).
4. William J. Bennett, *The Book of Virtues: A Treasury of Great Moral Stories* (New York: Simon & Schuster, 1993).
5. Thomas Lickona, *Educating for Character: How Our Schools Can Teach Respect and Responsibility* (New York: Bantam Books, 1991).
6. *Standards of Quality for School-Based Service-Learning*, Alliance for Service-Learning in Educational Reform (May 1993).
7. Joan Novelli and Beth Chayet, *The Kid's Care Book: 50 Class Projects that Help Kids Help Others* (New York: Scholastic Professional Books, 1991).
8. *Service-Learning in the Core Curriculum: A 100 Page Curriculum Resource Packet*. Contact Dr. Sally Beisser, Drake University, Des Moines, IA; 1-800-44-DRAKE, #4850, or 515-271-4850.
9. Maryland Student Alliance, *The Courage to Care . . . The Strength to Serve* (Baltimore: Maryland State Department of Education, 1992).
10. Josephson Institute of Ethics, *Character Counts!* National Office, 4640 Admiralty Way, Suite 1001, Marina del Rey, CA 90292-6610; 310-306-1868 (phone), 310-827-1864 (fax), or www.charactercounts.org (web).
11. Dan Conrad and Diane Hedin, "School-Based Community Service: What We Know from Research and Theory," *Phi Delta Kappan* 72 (June 1991): 743-749.
12. *Service-Learning in the Core Curriculum Resource Packet*. Contact Dr. Sally Beisser, Drake University, Des Moines, IA; 1-800-44-DRAKE, #4850, or 515-271-4850.

Family/School/University Collaboration to Enrich Social Studies Instruction

BARBARA COZZA
TATA MBUGUA
PATRICIA NOAKES
MICHAEL INTOCCIA
LOU GUZZI
MARY LOU KELLY

The Scene

One preservice teacher e-mailed us (B.C. and T.M.) with a moving message about his experiences in a social studies classroom. Al wrote,

> I am so tired! This is a lot of excitement for one day. Every now and then I am reminded that I am responsible for a lot of stuff when I design lessons and tasks about Mexico and then try to implement these ideas with real children. I even spent preplanning time searching for appropriate Internet sites for the lessons so that children and parents could explore the same lesson ideas at home. I worked hard to teach geography and the concept of environment during a Mexican learning center postcard project task. I asked the children to create a postcard representing geographical locations in Mexico. Everything seemed to be going fine. Children worked in groups to select a place in Mexico. They all decorated their postcards in creative ways. Children even explored a site with parents at home[1] to supplement the learning of geographical concepts. But what exactly am I doing? What exactly are the children learning? Why should parents play an important role in my classroom?

As university professors, we find that the most positive aspect of our work is interacting with our preservice students. E-mail has allowed our students to stay in touch with us during the teaching and learning process in the schools.

Why Does Parent/School/University Collaboration Improve Social Studies Education for Children?

Typically, parental involvement is episodic, involving one-time participation as a volunteer to assist with a trip or to read a book in class. Epstein argues that teachers, parents, and preservice teachers should communicate in writing and talk frequently about the children in order to create meaningful school partnerships.[2]

The family/school/university partnership, the triad of our project, improves social studies understandings for children. We are partners in our children's education, and our collaboration gives children the increased support necessary to succeed in school. Research has underscored the importance of including all stakeholders in education by debunking the common assumption that when children enter the school door, they become the sole responsibility of educators.[3] Our triad emphasizes the idea that a quality social studies program should include respect for parents and the inclusion of family cultures, goals, and needs to enrich children's learning in school.

Buttery and Tichenor insist that schools and teachers must seek parents' cooperation, solicit their support, and maintain a common commitment to the education of their children.[4] Educators need to appreciate the importance of parental involvement and expect varying degrees of participation to maximize the benefits of parental connections.

Our goal in this collaborative project was to use Epstein's suggestions and include parental involvement as an integral part of a semester-long teaching and learning process. Parents were involved in learning projects during the semester through class volunteering, extending school tasks to the home, and integrating technology. Parents from both schools were involved in this collaborative project. We used the following partnership components created by Epstein to develop our project.[5] "Parent workshop" took on a meaning of making information on a unit topic available to parents in a variety of forms that could be viewed, read, or discussed either through technology or paper materials. "Parent volunteer" meant anyone who supported classroom lesson goals in any way and at any time. This approach alleviated families from feeling left out of the learning process because of a limited English background, limited formal education, or just experiencing difficulty in communicating with teachers because of drastically different life experiences.[6] Some tasks that preservice teachers integrated in classroom plans were parents reading books in their native language, sharing cultural stories, values, and artifacts, and participating in discussions on a variety of levels following unit activities.

Using computers to connect the classroom and home was another aspect of our collaboration. Our parents enjoyed using e-mail and the Internet to answer questions about social studies topics. Unfortunately, not all parents and children have computer access at home. We made some accommodations by using paper journals and written notes for this group of parents. In addition, oral reports were accepted as an ongoing dialogue from parents about their views on the unit activities in which their children were engaged.

Our Process of Collaboration and Some Tangible Outcomes

This project began in a social studies methods course. Fifty-two preservice teachers enrolled in this course were required to study a specific culture from Africa, Asia, or Central or South America. Preservice teachers selected Mexico, Kenya, Chile, and China, to name a few. This collaboration evolved from an idea that professors and preservice interns discussed. Our methods course content was enriching but lacked work with children. Our goal was to make this teaching and learning experience appropriate for all stakeholders, and to construct an enriching social studies classroom environment.

The project is implemented in the spring semester. The rationale for this time period reflects three specific reasons: (1) children and parents are well acquainted with their school teachers and school environment, (2) classroom teachers know their children by this time of the school year, and (3) the social studies methods courses are offered during this semester. We used schools where we have already established collaborative relationships.

The selection of the two schools was based on a joint decision-making process among classroom teachers, principals, and university professors. The schools located in the Scranton, Pennsylvania, area were selected with one important consideration in mind: they have two very different student bodies based on socioeconomic status and cultural background.

School A is a private, multiage school setting. Most of the children come from affluent middle to upper middle class families. All of the stakeholders in this school community are on a first name basis. The school has an informal open classroom setting. Children are allowed to move through the curriculum at their own pace. The social studies curriculum emphasizes the study of cultures around the world.

School B is a traditional public school setting. The children come from diverse backgrounds. Many children come from homes that speak English as their second language. The school curriculum follows a textbook series and rarely integrates cultural themes.

GET-TO-KNOW-YOU PHASE

The first activity is a "get-to-know-you" session. Professors and classroom teachers write letters to parents inviting them to be collaborators in the project. Teachers, parents, and children meet the university faculty and preservice teachers during an informal meeting at each school. The university faculty and preservice interns give a brief overview of the project. Teachers present an overview of school population, teaching philosophy, and their ideas of how multicultural and global education issues might be integrated into their social studies programs. Parents are encouraged to discuss ways they might participate in the project. A bonus to this introduction is that children get a chance to meet and greet the preservice teachers who will be in their classrooms for ten weeks.

In the social studies course, preservice teachers develop unit lessons and learning center tasks with a focus on global interconnections. Then, the preservice teachers visit classrooms and implement the developed curriculum. Lessons and learning center tasks incorporate the five content areas of social studies—political science, economics, history, sociology, and geography. The social studies content strands serve as a framework for the design of the lessons and to guide the development of performance expectations regarding the knowledge, processes, and attitudes of social studies.

We encourage our preservice teachers to pre-plan unit ideas with peers, classroom teachers, children, and parents. Unfortunately, this planning stage is a weak area in the program. Preservice teachers need more time to interact with classroom teachers, children, and parents during the planning process. We find that scheduling meetings is difficult within the short time of one semester.

CURRICULUM EXAMPLES

Holly and Melissa, who were preservice teachers, developed a history lesson on Brazil for fourth graders. The children worked in small cooperative groups at computers. They took virtual trips to Brazil.[7] The children explored historical events that took place in the country and constructed a timeline of the events. This activity integrated the National Council for the Social Studies (NCSS) Standards theme of ❶ **TIME, CONTI-NUITY, AND CHANGE**[8] when studying the history of Brazil, and demonstrated how people of different times and places view the world differently.

Taylor and Melissa, working with third and fourth graders, asked their students to investigate the town they live in to learn about Chinese and Kenyan cultures. The children began by collecting information using the telephone book. They counted Chinese family names and determined how many Chinese restaurants were listed in the yellow pages. The children were asked to visit the local mall with their parents to find products that are available from Kenya such as coffee, handicrafts, and animal woodcarvings. Using these data, they drew conclusions about production, distribution, and consumption of goods and services and investigated how each culture influences scarcity and choice within each community. The children used map skills to locate both of the countries and discuss the interaction of human geography—use of land, building cities, and ecosystem changes in global communities. They did follow-up activities with specific cultural lessons to compare how people from China and Kenya think about and deal with their physical environment and social conditions. At home, children talked with their parents about what they had learned at school. Amy, a fourth grader, discussed how she was excited to learn about the migration of animals in Kenya that was necessitated by weather patterns. She was particularly struck by what little knowledge she had about the developments in Kenya, specifically the cosmopolitan cities of Nairobi and Mombasa, until she took the virtual trip to this country.[9] In an e-mail message, Amy's mother discussed how fascinated she was to engage in these tasks with her daughter, so much so that they decided they might plan a trip to Kenya for some time in the future.

The activities made an impact within the communities where the children lived. Cory's mother entered in her paper journal that an activity on China which was sent home earlier in the week gave her courage to visit her neighbor's family who were of Chinese background. This interaction led to a friendship that allowed both families to learn more about each other and exchange artifacts.

We consciously moved away from collaboration characterized by what Dickens[10] defines as imprecise, interchangeable, broad, and inclusive. Instead, our collaboration has taken a more focused approach. Professors and classroom teachers meet to plan together and discuss the logistics of lesson presentations made by preservice teachers. These meetings often take place at the school sites. Preservice teacher lessons are implemented in classrooms during the ten-week semester. Teaching schedules for the preservice teachers are organized around the classroom teachers' needs although the preservice teachers' schedules sometimes make this difficult. As a culminating experience, preservice teachers spend many hours in the school implementing their unit lessons and learning center projects with children, in collaboration with teachers and parents.

Learning centers supplement the unit plans developed by the preservice teachers. Children and parents are invited to participate in collecting artifacts, photographs, and other kinds of information that help children gain knowledge about a culture. For example, in the China center, Ellen, a preservice teacher in a second grade classroom, included books, chopsticks, clothing, and other objects from Chinese culture. The children experimented with chopsticks while eating popcorn. Through hands-on learning center tasks, children developed an appreciation for aspects of that culture. In a second task, second graders compared the American game of Jacks to the Chinese game of *Zhuazi*. They compared the two games to understand the similarities and differences of these two cultures. In a third task, children used a Chinese horoscope book to look up the animal for the year of their birth and brainstorm words about their own horoscope animal. They used this information to create a poem to describe their animal. One child wrote,

> Dragon
> Hot, Fire, Huge
> Screaming, Roaring, Yelling
> Dragon
> Dragon

The goals of these expressive learning center experiences are twofold: to help children understand the similarities of their own culture and that of another global community and to encourage them to see how things are done differently in other parts of the world. Children also have an opportunity to express themselves through play, creative writing, and role-playing. These creative experiences enhance children's interest in learning about other cultures.

Preservice teachers chat on-line with faculty about their lessons and learning center experiences during the preplanning stage and implementation stage. These e-mail discussions focus on the various components of the lesson plans and teaching strategies. Preservice teachers also "chat" about the anxieties they felt before presenting the lesson, and afterwards they reflect on the effectiveness of their teaching. Loren, a preservice teacher, wrote,

> I could not believe how much prior knowledge these six and seven year olds have
> about Mexico. They knew how to count to ten in Spanish and they even knew about
> a family tradition known as the "El Dia De Reyes," a celebration that occurs on
> January 6th to celebrate the Three Wise Men. Since they had a good background on
> Mexico, I decided to teach a lesson integrating a Mexican folktale. I read aloud the
> story *Three Brothers and the Singing Toad*. Children were then asked to work with a
> partner to create a picture storyboard of the main scenes of the tale. Through
> literature they were able to visualize some aspects of the Mexican culture and at the
> same time relate it to their own world.

Parents also participated in e-mail discussions by offering support and acknowledging what the preservice teachers were doing in the class. Some parents expressed their interest in the project and their willingness to work with their child on homework activities. A parent wrote,

We enjoyed baking corn bread and cooking chili. My son and I had an interesting discussion of the variety of crops eaten by Mexican people such as rice, oats, wheat, beans and tomatoes. We also took time to find resources on the Internet about Mexican crops. I particularly enjoyed using the chat room as a form of communication. It allowed for a close relationship between home and the classroom.

It was interesting for professors, preservice teachers, and classroom teachers to read messages from parents expressing excitement and enthusiasm toward the collaboration. This was a "new" way for parents to use home computers to enhance their child's educational achievement. Our next step to increase parental involvement will be to outline the content and concepts in the units and learning center activities for parents.

Some parents felt more comfortable talking and discussing ideas with us rather than using e-mail. We allowed parents to communicate on the level with which they were most comfortable. One parent talked with Sean, one of our preservice teachers, after her daughter and she completed a research problem-solving homework lesson:

> I was delighted to participate in a worthwhile hands-on problem-solving home task about China. My daughter Kim has incorporated research of China's culture in class lessons prior to our home experience. At home, Kim and I began to apply Kim's knowledge about China by simply boiling rice for a Chinese meal. Together we were able to identify what kinds of things might be served at a Chinese meal, what ingredients are used in various dishes, how the foods are prepared and served, and on what occasions they are eaten. Kim knew all the right stuff. She gained all this new information from the research she did in class.

This hands-on home activity allowed the parent and child to apply what the child had learned from her class research. These tasks engaged the children in intellectual discovery and reflection on Chinese culture.

Parents also voiced concerns throughout the project. After two weeks of participating in the collaboration, one parent was concerned about the relevance of the activities. He wrote in a paper journal entry, "I am having a difficult time understanding what all these pre-planned activities have to do with real learning. Why are the children not being taught about America and its diversity rather than inundating them with information about other countries?" Another parent wrote, "How will my own Chinese culture be validated in these activities?" We knew from these comments that we needed to inform parents about our use of the NCSS Standards. We decided that an after-school parents' workshop was needed to introduce the standards and to show how they were reflected in the social studies lessons implemented in the classroom.

In School B, children acted as resource helpers by bringing in oral reports from their parents if they did not speak English. Most of the children who did not have computers at home maximized the use of the school computers by sending e-mail messages about their work and parents' responses to the preservice teachers. One student wrote an e-mail message about how her mother responded to an assignment sent home about current events on Kenya: "That is where the terrorists bombed the U.S. Embassy . . . we are all connected in this global village." The preservice teachers used these kinds of responses as teachable moments to discuss issues about prejudice, bias, and hatred. One parent's paper journal entry expressed interest in participating as a guest speaker: "I see my culture validated at school in a special way. . . . I want to be a part of this experience." One parent made a profound statement that captured the essence of our culminating activity:

Although this experience is confined to our school, I hope it will demonstrate to all who hear about it that global migration is unstoppable and diversity inevitable. Therefore, we all need to learn about, understand, and appreciate one another.

At the end of the semester, university faculty collected data including journals, e-mail messages, unit and learning center projects, and lesson materials to evaluate the strengths and weaknesses of this family/school/university collaboration.

Teacher Perspectives from School A (L.G. and M.L.K.)

Classroom teachers who participate in collaborative partnerships with parents and universities have much to gain. It has been said that a teacher's number one enemy is time. We can always use a helpful hand with unit lessons and creative learning centers, but any help needs to dovetail neatly with a curriculum that has been thoughtfully planned for that classroom. In our multiage classroom setting, this type of collaborative project enhances the teaching and learning process for social studies.

WHAT WE HAVE LEARNED THROUGH THIS COLLABORATION

From the minute we invited parents to become involved, they were very willing to take part in this collaboration. Two important elements stand out from the parents' feedback. They welcomed the ideas that the school curriculum would be integrated into their home situation and that technology could play an important role in their children's learning process.

As classroom teachers, we maintained anecdotal records of the teaching and learning process. The following remarks offer parents' responses to a homework assignment planned by the preservice teacher's lesson taken from my (M.L.K.) teacher journal. During an activity in the social studies unit lesson, Lori, a preservice teacher, asked children to create a survey at home of how parents viewed values of cleanliness, education, family, physical fitness, respect for law, competition, and cooperation in relation to their own family culture. The children brought back to class the parents' ideas and compared them to the values of a Chilean way of life. The parents seemed to be happy to have the opportunity to have an activity that could be done in the home. One parent voiced her opinion saying, "It is so nice to have things to do that are not related to watching TV." Another stated, "The unique nature of activities to be done at home with my daughter gives homework a new meaning."

These parents were responding to a homework activity that required their children to explore the meaning of culture and to talk about their family tree. This is just one of my teacher journal entry examples that depict how preservice interns and parental thinking successfully affected children's social studies learning.

We found that parents appreciated a chance to use home computers to reinforce what was being done in school. One parent wrote, "The fact that everyone is learning together is most desirable. I enjoy our home discussions on comparing and contrasting the Chilean and Mexican cultures with our own culture. We might decide to travel to these countries in the near future." For some parents, it was their first introduction to e-mail discussions.

THE MOST VALUABLE EXPERIENCES

Our elementary students responded well to the preservice teachers who were enthusiastic about their lessons. The opportunity to investigate a variety of cultures informally in unit lessons and learning center tasks contributed to successful situations for all collaborators in the project. This collaboration provided an opportunity for parents to be aware of the content, concepts, and skills that were taught based on the NCSS Standards. Also, this was an opportunity for parents to interpret data with their children in a way that was uniquely suited to the values of the family unit. We found that bringing parents into the learning process not only created meaningful learning for students, but also helped strengthen family ties because the parents were involved.

The opportunity to collaborate with university faculty is also a valuable experience for classroom teachers. Barbara Cozza, a curriculum specialist, interacted with classroom teachers, children, and parents. This assisted the professors and our teachers to understand how theory and practice can be integrated into the classroom. We found through this collaboration that theory and practice are more related than we thought. These professors were not interested in ensconcing themselves in an ivory tower, but were interested in what goes on in the field and in using it to make the learning experiences of children and preservice teachers more meaningful.

Factors Necessary to Make the Collaboration Work for Us, as Elementary Teachers

One of the challenges in the project was to coordinate the units and learning centers with the curriculum plans of the classroom teacher. To do this, we provided the university professors with a calendar that indicated exactly when cultural topics would be discussed. The calendar had a list of content, concepts, and process skills to be covered.

It so happens that for me (L.G.), in March (school week 26) I began a unit on the early modern world with sections on interactions among Europe, Africa, and the Americas followed by sections on Asia. It also happens then that the centers which are most useful to our class would have to do with the topics of Africa, China, Japan, and the Ottoman and Mogul empires, at least regarding content knowledge. The same goes for a unit I began in the last week of March about the changing world from the 1770s to the 1930s. In this unit, we study Latin America and Mexico. Centers about other peoples would be useful only if they were designed to teach a skill or a social studies content or process that happens to be already incorporated into my unit. If the center isn't topical regarding what we are learning in terms of facts, concepts, generalizations, skills, and social studies processes, its use is going to be compromised.

Teacher Perspectives from School B (P.N. and M.I.)

School B is located in a relatively low-income area of Scranton. The student population is reflective of the neighborhood. For the last fifteen years, I (P.N.) have taught in third, fourth, and fifth grade classrooms in this school. The student population has changed over the years from a relatively middle class to low socioeconomic status. The level of parental involvement for the last six years has decreased significantly, and this has implications for my teaching and my students' involvement. The attitude of parents toward education has an indelible mark on their children, and the general view has been that parents have not been active in their children's education in our school. The specifics of this are the following:

▶ Homework rarely gets done, and oftentimes there is no parent's signature.
▶ Parent-teacher conferences do not materialize.
▶ Phone calls made home are not returned, and notes sent home are not reciprocated.

Speaking from the point of view of a classroom teacher at School B (M.I.), it is imperative that any teacher who enters this collaborative partnership be prepared for the time investment and express a willingness to reorganize his or her classroom to accommodate the preservice teacher's presence in the classrooms. I have found that flexibility becomes a central focus in collaboration in order to meet one's objectives for the year and also provide mentoring for the preservice teachers.

Benefits

There are benefits to this collaboration. The presence of a young, energetic, preservice teacher who is willing to learn and teach in the classroom and the extra hands that preservice teachers provide are welcome. Their presence in the classroom alters the dynamics in a significant way, and the assignments that they send home have stirred some interest among some of the parents. During the unit lessons and learning center activities, children are actively engaged and enthusiastic. The presence Professor Mbugua, who is originally from Kenya, offered a unique opportunity for the teachers, children, and parents to experience another culture firsthand. Assuming the role of a cultural consultant, she taught children some Swahili words. Students also tried on some Kenyan clothes like *kitenge* and *kanga*, and tried their hands at some games like *nyama, nyama*. The important reward from the collaboration at this juncture is that the classrooms that participated in the unit lessons and learning center tasks came alive while exploring the social studies concepts of different cultures.

The most important learning experience has been with the integration of technology in the classroom. Although we have computers in our building and probably one of the best computer labs in the district, it has taken the presence of a preservice teacher to get me (M.I.) to a comfort level in using the technology. I now use the computer as a tool for teaching and learning social studies.

Factors that contribute to making the collaboration work include a willingness to take risks and to have others critique your teaching. As classroom teachers, we feel supported in facilitating learning and in contributing to a team approach for the implementation of this project.

A Professor's Perspective (B.C.)

Three years ago, as a professor of education, I set out to tackle a nagging problem. I wanted to create collaboration with schools and my preservice teachers. I wanted to construct a working environment so that teachers at all levels could work together toward common goals and to create a professional community. The outcome of my efforts has been rewarding.

As a university professor, my greatest reward was to see the preservice teachers empowered and knowledgeable about nonwestern countries—becoming experts in these areas and having the confidence to share the knowledge gained with the children, parents, and classroom teachers. We enjoyed every moment. The aim was to create an openness to differences by talking with and learning about others who were different from us. An important aspect of this learning process was that my students participated in discussions that helped them grow as reflective teachers. Input from others made them aware of things that they did not know and led to an expansion of their understandings. Many times my students were exposed to ideas that contradicted their beliefs. For example, they realized that the basic needs and wants of other cultures were very different from their own. Factors that influenced cultural differences were based on geographical location and human values. This caused them to examine their own beliefs and perhaps restructure them. The need to communicate their ideas to others forced them to articulate those ideas more clearly to the children and parents. This learning process also sharpened the preservice teachers' conceptions. An important element that the preservice teachers learned was that it is sometimes difficult for children to study objectively those things to which they are are very close—their family, language, and customs. Children need to study other cultures and compare and contrast these new cultural ideas with their own way of life. Preservice teachers always emphasized the children's cultures and then compared them to new cultural understandings.

The study of different cultures provided a basis for contrasting unfamiliar behaviors from another culture with what children already knew about their own culture. Thus, when children studied the Mexican, Brazilian, Kenyan, Chinese, and Chilean ways of family life, the information from these cultures helped them to become more aware of the day-to-day behaviors and structures of American families.

I think that this collaboration is a beginning that will assist parents, teachers, and preservice interns in growing more comfortable in dealing with the demands of social studies teaching and learning. One major challenge in this program is the energy that goes into putting a collaboration together. Participants have many schedule demands that often cannot be met by all of us. The second weakness of this program is time. It takes many months, if not years, to establish a collegial attitude and professional rapport with all participants in order to implement a successful program. A third challenge was doing global education in a ten-week block. The teachers and I discussed the dangers of creating stereotypes associated with the cultures we were studying—for example, chopsticks and the Chinese culture. Such stereotypes are pervasive in American society, and teachers need to help children get beyond these simple images of other cultures. No group escapes these images. Our goal was to examine stereotypical images critically during classroom discussions to help children understand cultures in more complex ways.

A Professor's Perspective (T.M.)

The collaborative partnership has been a tremendous learning opportunity for me. There was a remarkable level of synergy that emanated from the collaboration with all of the participants offering a unique voice to the project from inception to implementation.

In effect, new roles and opportunities were created for all the participants: the classroom teachers were mentors to preservice teachers and liaison persons with parents; the preservice teachers were resource persons in the elementary classroom and experts on specific global communities; parents had multiple roles as volunteers, decision makers, active participants, and resource persons; and university professors wore many hats—as instructors, mentors, facilitators, and resource persons.

Throughout this project, I reflected on my personal cultural experiences. I was born and raised in Kenya, East Africa, a country that is diverse in languages, races, and classes. I have also had the opportunity to study and work in Europe, Asia, and North America. As a result, I have had extensive cross-cultural experiences that have contributed to a personal interest and commitment to issues of diversity in general, and an integration of global perspectives in education.

During the spring semester discussions in the social studies methods class, I tried to model competencies that are necessary and meaningful for the preservice teachers prior to their going out to the elementary schools. I have used pertinent personal experiences to counteract myths about Africa, in general, and Kenya, in particular. One of the ways I have done this is by taking on a role of a preservice teacher "expert" in a learning center that focuses on Kenya. I also contribute ideas while exploring the social studies concept of "culture," and underscore the importance of emphasizing the similarities and validating the differences without value judgments. My experience teaching a variety of courses has been that students often confuse cultural differences with developmental deficiencies. The important point is that of creating a balance between what the students know and get through media coverage with what is reality in most nonwestern countries. For example, I bring into class my own photos, videos of Kenya, and web sites that we explore as a class. The aim here is to help students recognize, understand, and critique current social inequities in both Kenya and the United States.

From the outset, I realized that real-life experiences were crucial in providing children with authentic learning tasks. The main question I had was, How do I go beyond my "accent" that captured the interest of the children and some of the parents, and inculcate meaningful learning experiences? I sought to use practical examples and personal experiences to amplify and clarify content and concepts that were taught in the Kenya unit. I provided firsthand information as a primary source. When children asked, "Dr. Mbugua, how do you say government in Swahili?" I responded, "serikali." I also acquired the role of a resource person by providing books in Swahili language, games, and artifacts to be used in the learning center. I even demonstrated how to play musical instruments and games that were in the learning center.

Where Do We Go from Here?

Given the demographics of our preservice teacher populations, middle or upper class white females from a relatively homogeneous region of northeast Pennsylvania, we found it necessary to model specific competencies and behaviors that would help students learn about people different from themselves. Our team of participants for this family/school/university model continues to work. We discovered early that we all need constructive feedback and support on a consistent and frequent basis. We gained insights into how important it is to have access to computer technology at school and to maximize its use even though the technology might not be available at home.

There are many differences across the populations of our two schools in addition to the many cultures we studied. The diversity in our schools and in the global curriculum we develop and teach provides enormous possibilities for enriching the school culture of all participants—university professors, preservice teachers, parents, classroom teachers, and children.

NOTES
1. See info.er.usgs.gov/education/teacher/what-do-maps-show/index.html.
2. Joyce L. Epstein, "A Checklist for an Effective Parent-School Partnership: The Six Types of Parental Involvement" (Baltimore, Md.: Johns Hopkins University's Center on Families, Communities, Schools, and Children's Learning, 1996). Available on-line at members.aol.com/pledgenow/appleseed/chklist.html.
3. Lynn Malarz, Marcia D'Arcangelo, and John Checkley, *Involving Parents in Education* (Alexandria, Va.: Association for Supervision and Curriculum Development, 1992).
4. Thomas J. Buttery and Mercedes Tichenor, "Parent Involvement and Teacher Education," *SRATE Journal* 5 (1996): 42-50.
5. Joyce L. Epstein, "Challenges and Redefinitions for the Six Types of Involvement," *Phi Delta Kappan* 5 (1995): 705.
6. James P. Comer, "Educating Poor Minority Children," *Scientific American* 259 (1988): 42-48; O. C. Moles, "Collaboration Between Schools and Disadvantaged Parents: Obstacles and Openings," in *Families and Schools in a Pluralistic Society*, ed. Nancy Chavkin (Albany: State University of New York Press, 1993).
7. See www.brazil.com. This site allows children to explore historical and cultural events of Brazil.
8. National Council for the Social Studies, *Expectations of Excellence: Curriculum Standards for Social Studies* (Washington, D.C.: Author, 1994).
9. See www.kenyaweb.com. This site includes several links to information about people, land, history, and government.
10. Cindy Dickens, "Too Valuable to Be Rejected, Too Different to be Embraced: A Critical Review of School/University Collaboration," in *Collaborative Reform and Other Improbable Dreams: The Challenges of Professional Development Schools*, eds. Marilyn Johnston, Patti Brosnan, Don Cramer, and Tim Dove (Albany: State University of New York Press, 2000).

Connecting Family and State Histories: A Teacher Educator and Classroom Teacher Collaborate

AVA L. MCCALL
THELMA RISTOW

The Scene

Today, students are sharing their family history projects during our focus on multicultural Wisconsin history in Thelma's fourth grade classroom. Everyone has completed a simple project with the assistance of an adult member of his or her family. At the beginning of the school year, we shared our family histories with the students and met with at least one parent from each child's family. We explained the different options the children could choose for their family history project and requested help from an adult member of the family as the student completed the project.

Maria (all students' names are pseudonyms), a Mexican American, stands in front of the class and quietly explains parts of her father's Air Force uniform and Vietnamese money he saved during his military service in the Vietnam War. She also reads from an interview she did with her mother in which she learned that her mother's need for a job caused her to leave Mexico and settle in Wisconsin. Next, Jake, a Polish American, proudly shows many documents related to his great-great-great-grandfather who served in the Civil War, including copies of $13 to $15 paychecks for "fighting in the army." Rameen, whose family immigrated from India in 1992, smiles broadly and holds up a large poster with several pictures of his family arranged and labeled for everyone in the class to see. Rameen says that his family moved to this community from India because family members could live with an uncle who had already settled here, and his parents were able to find jobs. The class remains attentive while Hua, one of the four Hmong students, seriously explains her family tree and shows the class detailed pictures she has drawn of objects used or worn in Laos. The rest of the class finds the bracelets the most fascinating as Hua explains they are used to "keep bad spirits away and have good luck."

For the next two days, the students share family photographs and artifacts, family history timelines, summaries of interviews done with family members, and family trees. The class listens respectfully to each presentation and asks questions to learn more. These family history projects illustrate a few of our goals for this collaborative project: (1) teachers and students are actively involved in teaching and learning Wisconsin history, (2) students make personal connections with historical topics, and (3) students develop knowledge of and appreciation for their own and others' cultural backgrounds.

Throughout the project, we observe the students' progress in meeting these goals. As Hmong, Mexican American, East Indian, and European American students investigated their family history and presented their findings to the class, they connected family history with Wisconsin history and became more at ease in sharing special cultural traditions. Although one Mexican American boy was very knowledgeable of his heritage and willing to share it with the class throughout the semester, not all students were. The four Hmong students especially grew in their willingness to talk about their family histories, traditions, and special celebrations as the semester progressed. By the end of the unit, all students increased their knowledge about their family histories. They learned what countries their ancestors emigrated from, why they emigrated, how they traveled to the United States, who their special relatives from the United States or from their ancestors' homeland were, where they first settled in the United States, why they moved to Wisconsin, what special artifacts belonged to their family, what their ancestors' life-styles were like, and which family members had experiences in war activities or notable occupations. Most students also learned important ideas from their classmates' family histories. One fourth-grader explained, "It's important to know about others' family histories because if you think about it, all of our family histories are joined together."

By joining our classroom and university teaching experiences, Thelma's students directly benefited. They were interested, involved, and learned about the history of Wisconsin. We also hoped to meet the school district's curricular requirements, address significant goals in social studies and multicultural and anti-racist education, and use collaborative action research methods to investigate which teaching strategies were most effective in promoting learning.

Improving Social Studies Education: Standards, Constructivism, Multicultural Education, and Action Research

We believe good social studies education often includes juggling students' diverse needs, school district expectations, recommendations from social studies research and professional organizations, and our own values and commitments as teachers. During our collaborative curriculum development, teaching, and action research project, we first wanted to help students learn significant social studies content, especially about Wisconsin's history, but also discover how interesting and relevant social studies is for their lives. The ten thematic strands from the National Council for the Social Studies (NCSS) Standards[1] provided valuable guidance in our selecting important concepts and ideas.

For one of our units on the significance of family history as representative of different cultural groups who immigrated into and settled in Wisconsin during the nineteenth and twentieth centuries, we integrated the themes of ❶ **CULTURE**; ❿ **PEOPLE, PLACES, AND ENVIRONMENTS**; and ❾ **GLOBAL CONNECTIONS**. We wanted students to learn about their own cultural backgrounds and family histories as well as the backgrounds of others through the Culture thematic strand. After inquiring into the students' cultural backgrounds, we focused on the most prevalent students' cultures: German Americans, Irish Americans, Polish Americans, Mexican Americans, and Hmong.[2]

For the ❿ **PEOPLE, PLACES, AND ENVIRONMENT** thematic strand, we strove to help students understand the effects of the physical and cultural environments of the immigrants' homelands, which precipitated their emigration from their homelands, as well as the physical and cultural characteristics of Wisconsin, which attracted them to the area. Closely connected to this theme was the ❾ **GLOBAL CONNECTIONS** theme as students explored how war or lack of economic opportunities in one part of the world led to mass migration of some cultural groups to another part of the world, including Wisconsin. Students investigated reasons why different cultural groups left their homelands, such as the potato famine and lack of jobs in Ireland, low-paying jobs and limited farmland in Germany, and war in Vietnam and Laos, and what attracted them to Wisconsin, including the promise of land, jobs, educational opportunities, and freedom from war.

Our curriculum reflected a multicultural, social reconstructionist,[3] and anti-racist[4] approach to education. This approach affirms cultural diversity, fosters equal opportunities, and challenges social stratification. It addresses social issues such as racism, sexism, and classism; integrates the experiences and perspectives of women and men from different cultural groups; includes students' life experiences, especially regarding issues of oppression; and encourages students to think critically and analyze different perspectives. It focuses on the process of racial identity among different groups and engages people in strategies to admit and resist white dominance and privileges.[5] Educators dedicated to this approach use anti-racist educational practices such as empathizing with the perspectives of people of color, teaching "Whites" about "White" dominance and privileges, admitting racial injustices, speaking out against racism,[6] and serving as advocates for students of color and anti-racist role models for European American students.[7]

During our unit on family history, we affirmed the cultural diversity among students here in Wisconsin. We examined the different experiences among women and men through family history projects and guest speakers. Topics included the role of women in India and motivations for leaving India and settling in Wisconsin, why different cultural groups immigrated to Wisconsin, and everyday life among nineteenth century immigrants. As students shared their research on the forces that led to their families' and their cultural group's immigration to Wisconsin, we modeled and encouraged the students to empathize with different people's experiences, especially the Hmong and other people of color who have frequently been the targets of prejudice and racism. Although no Hmong students initiated descriptions of experiences of prejudice, discrimination, or racism they had after moving to the area, we introduced the issue. We described experiences with people's prejudice against the Hmong because of their lack of understanding of Hmong history. Many people are unaware of the Hmong alliance with the United States during the Vietnam War, which precipitated the need to flee their homeland and move to the United States after the war. We encouraged European American children especially to become more knowledgeable about and recognize their own cultural backgrounds as distinct from other cultures and not the "universal" or superior culture often attributed to European Americans. Issues of sexism and racism were raised when we read about everyday life among nineteenth century European American immigrants in *Little House in the Big Woods*.[8] We asked students to analyze the text for the significance of women's and men's contributions to family survival and for racist depictions of Native American people.

When we taught collaboratively, our goal was to use social constructivist teaching methods, which recognize that students' cultural knowledge is part of their prior knowledge and assumes that students construct shared meanings and interpretations through interactions with others.[9] Our role as teachers was to act as leaders, pose divergent questions, promote sustained dialogue about a topic in-depth, elicit students' thinking, emphasize higher-order thinking about authentic issues and problems, and share responsibility for learning with students.[10] We strove to make our own cultural backgrounds explicit, learn more about students' cultural backgrounds, and encourage students to share their cultures as part of the teaching and learning process.[11] Closely connected to social constructivist pedagogy was our use of culturally relevant pedagogy, which is grounded in students' class, race, ethnic, and gender backgrounds and their prior knowledge, and which uses culturally familiar strategies to help students construct new knowledge, but also exposes students to a variety of ways of learning.[12]

To provide opportunities for students to construct knowledge together, we organized students into small groups in which they researched reasons for Germans, Irish, Poles, Mexicans, and the Hmong to emigrate from their homelands and immigrate to Wisconsin. Students helped each other. They read sources and recorded important ideas in notes. They used words and pictures to illustrate the most significant findings on large charts, and then verbally explained their findings to the class. The Hmong students, with our encouragement, often spoke in their first language as they worked together completing their research and creating their chart. We guided the students in identifying main ideas, explaining these ideas in their own words, and then representing the concepts through words and pictures. Students drew on their different strengths and talents in reading, writing, drawing, and speaking while we supported the involvement of all group members throughout the activity in order to practice all skills.

Students also worked in small groups to investigate different aspects of everyday life among immigrants to Wisconsin during the nineteenth and early twentieth century through artifacts and photographs. Students analyzed and speculated about the identity and function of artifacts dealing with making food and clothing. They analyzed photographs for additional insights into how early immigrants built their homes and barns, prepared and stored food, made cloth, and sewed and washed clothes. We encouraged the students to use these objects and photographs to generalize what everyday life might have been like for some early immigrants. These small-group activities not only provided opportunities for students to construct knowledge together but also built on Hmong and Latino/a cultural groups' values, which emphasize cooperation and the well-being of the group over individual accomplishments.[13]

The family history projects provided opportunities for us to share our cultural backgrounds with the students and for students to share their cultures with each other through presentations and the preparation of a class book on our family histories. Our cultural backgrounds also became more explicit as we compared our family backgrounds to the Wilder family activities portrayed in *Little House in the Big Woods*.[14] We encouraged the Hmong students to explain similarities and differences in gardening and caring for animals in Laos with how the characters in the text engaged in these important activities. Those students with farming in their family histories made similar comparisons.

Critical literacy was also part of our curriculum and pedagogy, including the challenge of recognizing the link between language and power and how language learning and use are connected to both individual experiences and societal position. We tried to be aware of how systems of domination are part of reading and writing, classroom interactions, and texts. We also invited students' interpretations of texts as well as raised social issues suggested by texts, but ignored by students.[15] We strove to select books dealing with students' distinct gender and cultural experiences as well as those depicting commonalities among different cultures. We encouraged students to analyze texts critically as they read them.[16]

We asked students to make personal connections between texts and themselves and share their interpretations. Our goal was to affirm all students' responses to texts and encourage them to elaborate on their thinking. Additionally, we encouraged students to analyze texts for verifiability of information, biases, and point of view. We raised those issues in discussions of *Little House in the Big Woods* if students did not. We used different strategies to encourage all students to speak and be listened to during class discussions, including the more quiet Mexican American and European American girls and the Hmong students.

Part of the reality of collaboratively teaching within a school district was the expectation that we would focus on the social studies curricular goals and objectives from Thelma's school district. We not only agreed to address these curricular objectives during our project but also to integrate these objectives with the NCSS Standards. We found enough "wiggle room" within the local curricular objectives and national standards to transform them with multicultural, anti-racist concepts and themes. These were integrated in the five curriculum units we created and taught during the semester.

Finally, we believe that good social studies education includes reflection on one's teaching in order to examine how our teaching methods match our goals and which teaching strategies help students learn. We chose to reflect more formally through collaborative action research. We worked together to investigate systematically our own teaching and students' learning in order to improve our educational practices and the quality of our students' learning experiences.[17] We regularly collected data (lesson plans, observation notes, videotaped lessons and classroom activities, students' work samples, and interviews with students) about the curriculum we were teaching, the teaching strategies we used, students' responses to our curriculum and pedagogy, and what students learned. We met regularly while we taught to discuss which teaching strategies promoted learning and those that needed modifications, and to consider additional methods to support all students' involvement and learning. The actions we took were modifications in our teaching to improve our teaching and students' learning.

When Two Experienced Teachers Collaborate: Multiplying Our Strengths and Accomplishments

Our collaboration began during early fall 1996 when Ava asked Thelma to work with her. Ava was interested in developing social studies curriculum that integrated national social studies standards, school district social studies and literacy curriculum objectives, multicultural, anti-racist educational ideas, and critical literacy, then teach it in Thelma's classroom and study what students learned from it. Ava wanted to discover if the multicultural, social reconstructionist,[18] anti-racist[19] approach she used in her university social studies methods course would engage and help elementary students learn. During the past ten years, Ava had continuously developed and applied this orientation at the university level with varying levels of success with preservice teachers. However, she had not yet experienced teaching elementary students from this approach. Ava was aware of Thelma's extensive teaching experiences, confidence, and willingness to take risks because they had both supervised clinical students placed in Thelma's classroom, and Thelma, for her master's degree, had completed a graduate educational issues course that Ava taught.

The possibility of opening her classroom to a professor willing to come out of the "ivory tower" to test ideas she was teaching her preservice teachers and find out what an elementary classroom of today was like interested Thelma. She also wanted to know more about action research and hoped she would learn more effective ways to guide students in their learning. Ultimately, Thelma believed her students would benefit from two teachers in the classroom.

Although Thelma was concerned about the time commitment she was making, she agreed to the project. Ava then prepared a proposal to obtain funding for curriculum development work for each of them for the summer of 1997; Ava's funding came from the university's Faculty Development Program while Thelma's school district paid her for curriculum writing hours. Ava then prepared another Faculty Development Program research proposal to fund her half-time release from university teaching responsibilities for the fall of 1997 to enable her to teach and conduct research with Thelma in Thelma's classroom. Ava also requested funds for a research assistant to help gather research data and prepare instructional materials for the project.

After we were notified that our curriculum development and research proposals were funded, we spent the summer collecting resources to plan five Wisconsin history curriculum resource units. Thelma collected materials from her school and her own professional library while Ava gathered materials from her professional library as well as the university's library and educational materials center. We also reviewed catalogs and the many resources from the Wisconsin historical society to integrate with our curriculum units. We met weekly or biweekly at each other's homes during the summer to share resources and rough drafts of the curriculum resource units.

After discussing Thelma's prior experiences in teaching Wisconsin history and Ava's interest in including Native American history and culture within the curriculum, we decided to focus on five main components of Wisconsin history and created a curriculum resource unit for each topic:

1. The significance of family history as representative of different cultural groups that immigrated into and settled in Wisconsin during the nineteenth and twentieth centuries
2. Traditional life-style and cultural beliefs of indigenous people who lived in Wisconsin before the immigration of other cultural groups
3. Cultural conflicts among indigenous people, European Americans, and the U.S. government over land, cultural identity, and sovereignty
4. Different perspectives on the region's becoming a territory and state and who enjoyed voting rights from statehood to today
5. Major industries in Wisconsin including the evolution of the lumber industry into the paper industry and the transition from wheat farming to dairy farming

Ava offered to prepare the curriculum resource units following the format she asked students to use in the social studies methods course. Each curriculum resource unit contained the following:

1. A definition of the topic
2. A rationale for teaching the unit
3. Unit goals
4. NCSS thematic strands
5. School district social studies and literacy curriculum objectives
6. Multicultural concepts and themes
7. Background knowledge on main ideas
8. Activities for teaching main ideas
9. Family involvement activities
10. Overall assessment strategies
11. Resources

Because Thelma was more familiar with the school district's social studies and literacy curriculum, she proposed which curricular objectives fit with each resource unit. Ava suggested NCSS social studies thematic strands and multicultural concepts and themes appropriate for each resource unit.

At the beginning of the school year, in early September until the end of the first semester in January 1998, we developed and taught in Thelma's classroom formal lessons based on our resource units. We discussed plans for lessons in advance and collaborated on teaching lessons, although Ava prepared the formal written lesson plans as one record of our teaching. Our research assistant prepared instructional materials and bulletin boards and assisted students during classroom activities. Simultaneously, we used collaborative action research methods[20] to study students' constructed meanings and to modify our teaching based on students' learning. We each recorded our observations and reflections on our teaching and students' work in field notes and shared these notes with each other. A research assistant videotaped selected lessons, interviewed students at the close of each unit about what they learned, and copied students' work samples. The research assistant transcribed selected videotapes while Ava summarized each videotape in her field notes. Throughout the fall semester, we regularly met on "research days" to review and plan lessons, discuss what students were learning, and share concerns about students' learning and development. Our research assistant, who was a licensed teacher and full-time graduate student, served as the substitute teacher in Thelma's classroom on these days.

The "research days" were important opportunities to step away from the hectic pace of classroom teaching to think more deeply about specific teaching activities and students' responses. We noted fourth graders who had difficulties working in small groups or appeared uninvolved in whole class activities. Our research days helped us pool insights about the students, their learning, and the effectiveness of our teaching. We discussed how we might improve our teaching by brainstorming additional teaching strategies for engaging all students in whole class discussions and small-group activities.

During the spring semester of 1998, after we finished teaching the units, we continued to meet to analyze and summarize student interviews. Ava returned to a full, twelve-credit teaching load at the university, and Thelma continued her full-time teaching responsibilities. The school district, however, provided a substitute for Thelma to be away from her classroom one-half day a month for this data analysis while Ava used professional writing time. We developed categories of main themes that students learned from each unit and the teaching strategies that appeared most effective in promoting their learning. During the following summer, we met weekly or biweekly in Ava's home office to finish analyzing all data and write a report based on initial findings for the school district and the university's Faculty Development Program. Beginning in the spring and continuing throughout the fall, we made several professional conference presentations about the project, sharing our experiences and resources with other social studies teachers.

When each of us returned to her "regular" teaching responsibilities during the 1998-99 school year, we each integrated the results of the project into our work: Ava into her social studies methods course and Thelma into her fourth grade classroom. Thelma continues to use family history projects, simulations, and children's literature when she teaches Wisconsin history. Ava integrates inquiry activities with artifacts and children's literature when students explore Wisconsin Native American nations. Both of us now have three thick binders containing our Wisconsin history curriculum resource units, written lesson plans, and supporting lesson materials. The resource units themselves are regularly extended as we find new resources for teaching Wisconsin history. Ava shares the curriculum resource units with her social studies methods students, and students who teach Wisconsin history in their clinical placements often use these materials in their teaching.

Our latest work is cooperatively preparing a book proposal and sample chapters about our collaborative project. We also have shared copies of the curriculum resource units with other fourth grade teachers responsible for teaching Wisconsin history in the local school district. We hope our work will be helpful to other social studies teachers in the local school district as well as nationally.

Opening My Classroom: Collaborating with a University Professor (T.R.)

Each of us contributed our expertise to the project. As a classroom teacher, I had knowledge of fourth grade students—their capabilities, developmental levels, what they should be learning, and different strategies that might be effective to guide their learning. Another contribution I brought to the project was the understanding that learning was a more meaningful experience for students if they are actively involved in their learning. Having taught Wisconsin history for many years, sometimes we had discussions in which I acted as facilitator, and sometimes students did projects, reports, and plays to show what they learned. I brought additional books into the classroom from the media center as resources for the students to use when preparing their projects and reports. We learned about Wisconsin government, physical resources, manufacturing, farming, and service jobs, as well as the early history of Wisconsin. Children learned about explorers, Native American experiences, and geographical reasons for the location of cities and industries. Still another contribution I made to the project was knowing what was important to teach, based on the school district's curricular goals in both social studies and literacy. I also was aware of the teaching resources available at the district and building levels.

Another insight I gained as a result of the project was learning about action research and the importance of taking good field notes. Writing field notes, which are a documentation of what happened in each lesson, is an important and beneficial component of action research. As I looked back on the notes that Ava wrote, I was able to relive each lesson. In this new role as researcher, I found out how challenging it was to record what was being taught and students' comments and behaviors. I was more comfortable in the teacher role and found myself engrossed in the lesson, both with Ava's teaching and the students' interactions. I had to learn to discipline myself. Writing notes about what was going on got in the way of watching the children and their enthusiasm for learning. Writing the notes seemed such a distraction. As a result of my involvement in this action research project, I became aware of different ways to observe more closely just which teaching strategies worked most effectively with the students. Observing and listening to the students work in their groups provided me with insight into what they were learning. Having more than one teacher in the classroom offered more opportunities for me to do this intensive observing.

Working with Ava on this project also gave me the opportunity to learn more about constructivist theory and a social reconstructionist approach to teaching social studies. Having the students participate in simulations of Native American-U.S. Government treaty negotiations and the moving of Native Americans to reservations provided opportunities for the students to gain a sense of what it may have been like for Native Americans. Likewise, by having the students participate in an Ellis Island simulation, I believe most students gained a deeper understanding of what it was like for immigrants entering this country. Because I saw the value of these simulations for the students, I have continued to use them in teaching Wisconsin history. I also realized the benefits of students learning about their own family history before we talked about why people immigrated to Wisconsin. By learning why their own families left their homeland and came to Wisconsin, students could better understand different reasons for immigration. I continue to encourage the students in my class to share their family history.

One piece of advice I would give any teacher considering a collaborative project would be to find a university professor who is open to your ideas and has something to contribute to elementary students. This person should be knowledgeable in social studies and should respect the classroom teacher's knowledge and experiences. In a team-teaching situation, both the university professor and classroom teacher must be willing to negotiate and compromise to use teaching strategies that are most beneficial for elementary students. It can be scary to try out new teaching ideas in front of another experienced teacher, but when we agreed to criticize the ideas rather than each other, it was easier to take the risks.

Classroom teachers also need support at both the building and district level for working collaboratively with universities. I was fortunate to have a principal who encouraged and supported me in this collaboration, which she saw as a growth opportunity for me and a valuable learning experience for the students. It was her enthusiasm for this action research project that led to the school district's support.

My principal showed her interest by frequently inquiring how our action research was progressing. The deputy superintendent was eager for teachers within the school district to do action research and whole-heartedly endorsed our project. He approved one day per month release time for me to work with Ava to evaluate our teaching and student learning and to plan the next month's lessons. The school district also provided teaching materials, including sets of trade books that we requested to use in our project. These materials became permanent resources in my building and are now used by other teachers.

Classroom teachers need to be mindful of the time element involved when doing a collaborative action research project. There is a commitment of time, particularly the writing of field notes. I suggest writing notes at the end of each day. If one waits longer, there is a tendency to forget. I recommend staying focused and not attempting something too "grandiose." Had I not had any other responsibilities, I might have had more time to devote to the project and still have a personal life outside of the classroom. My involvement in professional organizations and school district committees has always taken a huge amount of my time. There were also parts of the curriculum that were not integrated with the Wisconsin history lessons that needed to be taught in order to meet state requirements. An additional demand on my time was the need to become familiar with a new curriculum on social skills and values that my school had adopted. I needed to become familiar with this curriculum, prepare lessons, do additional reading, and find resources. Even though it was a time-consuming collaborative project, I was thrilled to be a part of it. I learned a great deal and at the same time was given the opportunity to share my expertise and knowledge with Ava.

Benefits and Challenges of a Teacher Educator Returning to the Elementary Classroom (A.M.)

This collaborative project has enriched my teaching at the university level as well as affirmed my commitment to teach to create a more caring, just world. One important insight I gained from this experience was that fourth grade students are open to learning about multicultural concepts. We discussed racism and sexism inherent in the treatment of Native American people by European immigrants. The students' strong sense of justice was evident as we discussed the implication of treaties, the movement of Native American people to reservations and their children to boarding schools, and the exclusion of voting rights based on gender, race, and property. When I encourage preservice teachers to infuse multicultural concepts and themes within their social studies teaching, some preservice teachers claim that elementary children are not ready to deal with issues of oppression related to race, gender, and class. I now have evidence from my experiences with the fourth grade students that such issues can be raised for discussion. Children are ready to question why groups of people have been treated unfairly and how individuals and groups have fought for equality. I also share my experiences with social studies methods students and explain how teaching social studies often involves juggling school district's expectations, national standards, and a professional commitment to multicultural teaching.

The project provided an opportunity for me to understand the significance of including the students' family and cultural history into the social studies curriculum, which not only helped the children to learn more about their cultural backgrounds but also helped them develop a sense of pride in their culture. Although I have often encouraged preservice teachers to incorporate students' family histories and cultural backgrounds into the social studies curriculum, sometimes the social studies methods students are hesitant because of the diversity among families and their fear of excluding some families. I now share the experiences of how Thelma and I encouraged all students to participate in investigating and sharing their family histories and the benefits for children when they connect their family and cultural background with social studies.

The project also helped me experience to a certain extent the many pressures on elementary teachers today to participate in special school activities and schoolwide programs in addition to teaching the basic curriculum. It was very challenging to find the teaching time we wanted for this project as well as meet the additional demands on instructional time. We discovered midway through the project that we needed to communicate more clearly about all the pressures Thelma was experiencing in everything she needed to teach as well as work with me three days a week. We decided to reduce our joint teaching time from three days to two and one-half days a week to allow Thelma more time to teach the other areas of the curriculum. I also share this insight with preservice teachers as we discuss ways to address time constraints in elementary classrooms and the importance of integrating social studies with other areas of the curriculum as one avenue to make the most of limited time for social studies.

For teacher educators considering collaborative projects with classroom teachers, it is important for both classroom teachers and teacher educators to have support from the school district and university. Without this support, what we could have achieved on our personal time would have been significantly reduced. Thelma's school district supported her summer curriculum development work and released her from classroom teaching responsibilities for a monthly research day during the 1997-98 academic year. On these days we planned lessons, discussed possible changes in our teaching to address students' needs, and analyzed and summarized data. These days were crucial in giving us the opportunity outside of the usual teaching day to work on our teaching and research. My support from the university's Faculty Development Program was necessary for the summer curriculum development work and the two and one-half to three days a week I needed to spend in Thelma's classroom during the fall semester. The Faculty Development Program also funded the hiring of a research assistant who supplied crucial support in videotaping lessons, interviewing students, and transcribing the videotapes and audiotapes. Without a research assistant, we would have invested less time in teaching in order to complete these research tasks. We both had support from the university and school district to spend time completing our initial data analysis and writing a final report during the summer of 1998. The school district and university also contributed funds to purchase additional trade books and other teaching resources needed in teaching the curriculum as well as research materials such as videotapes and audiotapes. Our accomplishments were due not only to our hard work and students' responsiveness to our teaching but also to significant institutional support.

NOTES

1. National Council for the Social Studies, *Expectations of Excellence: Curriculum Standards for Social Studies* (Washington, D.C.: Author, 1994).
2. A number of Hmong people prefer the Hmong identification rather than Hmong American.
3. Christine E. Sleeter and Carl A. Grant, *Making Choices for Multicultural Education: Five Approaches to Race, Class, and Gender*, 3d ed. (Columbus, Ohio: Merrill, 1999).
4. Gary R. Howard, *We Can't Teach What We Don't Know: White Teachers, Multiracial Schools* (New York: Teachers College Press, 1999).
5. *Ibid.*
6. *Ibid.*
7. Sandra M. Lawrence and Beverly D. Tatum, "Teachers in Transition: The Impact of Antiracist Professional Development on Classroom Practice," *Teachers College Record* 99 (1997): 162-178; Sandra M. Lawrence and Beverly D. Tatum, "White Educators as Allies: Moving from Awareness to Action," in *Off White: Readings on Race, Power, and Society*, eds. Michelle Fine, Lois Weis, Linda C. Powell, and L. Mun Wong (New York: Routledge, 1997), 333-342.
8. Laura I. Wilder, *Little House in the Big Woods* (New York: HarperTrophy, 1971).
9. Geoffrey Scheurman, "From Behaviorist to Constructivist Teaching," *Social Education* 62 (1998): 6-9.
10. Jere Brophy and Janet Alleman, *Powerful Social Studies for Elementary Students* (New York: Harcourt Brace, 1996).
11. Peter W. Airasian and Mary E. Walsh, "Constructivist Cautions," *Phi Delta Kappan* 78 (1997): 444-449.
12. Valerie O. Pang and Roberta H. Barba, "The Power of Culture: Building Culturally Affirming Instruction," in *Educating for Diversity: An Anthology of Multicultural Voices*, ed. Carl A. Grant (Boston, Mass.: Allyn & Bacon, 1995), 341-358.
13. Jo Ann Koltyk, *New Pioneers in the Heartland: Hmong Life in Wisconsin* (Boston, Mass.: Allyn & Bacon, 1998); Carrie Rothstein-Fisch, Patricia M. Greenfield, and Elise Trumbull, "Bridging Cultures with Classroom Strategies," *Educational Leadership* 56 (1999): 64-67.
14. Wilder, *Little House.*

15. Carole Edelsky, "Education for Democracy," in *Class Actions: Teaching for Social Justice in Elementary and Middle School*, ed. JoBeth Allen (New York: Teachers College Press, 1999), 147-156.
16. Donna C. Creighton, "Critical Literacy in the Elementary Classroom," *Language Arts* 74 (1997): 438-445.
17. John Elliott, *Action Research for Educational Change* (Philadelphia, Pa.: Open University Press, 1991); Richard Sagor, *How to Conduct Collaborative Action Research* (Alexandria, Va.: Association for Supervision and Curriculum Development, 1992).
18. Sleeter and Grant, *Making Choices*.
19. Howard, *We Can't Teach What We Don't Know*; Beverly D. Tatum, "Teaching White Students about Racism: The Search for White Allies and the Restoration of Hope," *Teachers College Record* 95 (1994): 462-476.
20. Elliott, *Action Research*; Sagor; *How to Conduct Collaborative Action Research*.

Middle School

Students Reclaim Their Community's History: Conducting Interdisciplinary Research with Technological Applications

Six

Marsha Alibrandi
Candy Beal
Anna V. Wilson
Ann Thompson
Betty Mackie
Neville Sinclair
Virginia Owens
Rita Hagevik

The Scene

On the last day of school in June 1998, bulldozers making way for a new addition felled the school's two historic oaks. They were downed before the last bus pulled away. Two veteran teachers rushed out asking that slices of the trees be saved. Seeing those icons of school history downed, the teachers felt their sense of place and history disappearing. Was this how it had felt in 1971 for the black community to lose this neighborhood school to integration?

One year later: Echoes of the fallen trees moved teachers, students, and the community to recapture the rich stories of this place. What were we thinking? Who in her right mind would schedule a culminating extravaganza for the last week of school? Weren't there grades to get out, books to collect, assemblies and activities to run? But the media center was abuzz with preparations for the exposition. Soon parents and community members would arrive. For the first time, everyone who had worked on the yearlong interdisciplinary project researching the history of this formerly segregated high school (now an integrated middle school) would be able to see all of its parts together in one room. The scope of the effort was mind-boggling.

Each middle school teacher worked with her own group of students participating in the project and focused on helping them to present their research. They had conducted oral histories, prepared prototype digital maps, researched key local history events linking them to tree rings, and become sensitive to Raleigh's Jim Crow years. Bringing their own perspectives and current technologies to the task, students had created books, displays, digital maps, archives, and web sites to preserve the stories of people they had come to know, respect, and admire. June 3rd had arrived.

"Oh my gosh, it's the governor!" remarked one student.

A parent was overheard to say, "It's all I've heard all year. You just can't get them to stop talking about it." Another confided, "I just cannot believe how much the students have learned and how much they have taught me."

A student shared with her mother, "The alumni couldn't thank me enough for writing their stories and kept introducing me as the author of their story. How cool is that?"

Was this project exhausting? Yes. Was it invigorating? Yes. Did it address social studies standards? Absolutely. Did it enhance students' understanding of history? We believe so. Are the student outcomes testable? Not easily. Are they demonstrable? Yes. Has it enhanced the community? Yes. Finally, has it enriched the lives and characters of the students who participated? Please read on.

Toward Improving Social Studies
INSTRUCTIONAL TECHNOLOGY TEACHER AT LIGON GT MAGNET MIDDLE SCHOOL (A.T.)

How often do social studies teachers get to teach social studies as a "lab course" in which students do research, interview people who made history, examine primary source material, and then document that history? That's exactly what happened in this collaboration of J.W. Ligon High School alumni, middle school teachers and students, university professors and graduate students, and community partners. This was not traditional social studies taught from a textbook. These students wrote the book and produced the web sites. In the process, the middle school students and the adults learned history, geography, culture, and politics while they acquired skills in research, reading, writing, communication, science, and the use of technology resources.

The Ligon History Project's unique feature was that the current Ligon GT Magnet Middle School occupies the building that served as J.W. Ligon Junior Senior High School (LHS) from 1953-71. LHS served all of the African American students in the city of Raleigh, and it served as the center of a thriving, close-knit Black community. Consolidation and integration robbed the community of its core school. The resulting diaspora sent African American students to schools all over the county, contributing to the decline of the community around the school.

Although the Ligon History Project emphasizes social studies, it gained depth and richness from its interdisciplinary components. Using a constructivist approach, students designed their investigations. The project evolved to reflect the interests of the students and the availability of resources. They documented historical information that might otherwise have been lost with the deaths of those who lived it.

The journalism class conducted oral history interviews, assisted by Professor Wilson and graduate students in a historiographic methods class. Transcripts of these interviews became the basis of a first volume, *Capturing the Past to Guide the Future*, written by students and edited by their teacher, Betty Mackie. The interviews served as a resource for students in other classes participating in the project. From these interviews, students learned what it was like to live as an African American under Jim Crow. This information spawned investigations of history, culture, and politics by the journalism students and by the other classes that used the interviews as resource information.

Using Butchart's *Nearby History*,[1] students in the Geographic Information Systems (GIS)[2] science/technology elective, Satellites, Computers, and Mapping, generated geographic questions that directed research for their digital history products. They studied interviews gathered by the journalism students and researched primary source materials, library resources, and the Internet to glean background information for their computer maps.

Sixth grade science students participating in the Ligon History Project studied tree-ring dating (dendrochronology) using tree slices preserved from the sixty-foot willow oaks felled during building renovations in 1998. This scientific study evolved into a multifaceted project with implications for social studies. One preserved tree slice serves as a "timeline" that links events of the school's history with those of local and national importance in marked tree rings.

Students in a Wake County History elective researched historic buildings in the area and wrote reports on two patriarchs of the African American community, religious leaders and educators John Ligon and John Chavis. Because traditional resources were limited, the students turned to references retrieved from state and other archives by graduate students.

Several classes in the project explored the city's landmarks on the "Great Raleigh Trolley Adventure." Partner and Professor Candy Beal, author of *Raleigh: The First 200 Years*,[3] conducted the tour on a vintage trolley—an important field trip for grasping the big picture. Starting at the City of Raleigh GIS office, director Colleen Sharpe, a community partner, showed students an annexation map of the city. These digital maps displayed how Raleigh had grown by annexation over time.[4]

Students and teachers were instantly able to visualize how the project could be organized and developed into a GIS model. Colleen also provided annexation, street, and land parcel data for the project.

Next, the students visited the state archives where archivist Ed Morris displayed historic maps of the city in sequence.[5] Students were fascinated by the development of the city and the mapping technology. Sanborn Insurance maps (1923-49) vividly illustrated racial segregation with their "colored" and white areas of the city. Students were startled by the reality presented. After viewing current and historic maps of the city's growth, students toured the city and saw the features represented in the maps. They returned to school eager to share this historical information with others. With their new understanding and motivation, students persevered through the technical challenges required to create a variety of GIS representations.

Students were infuriated to learn that many of the public records needed to tell the story of LHS had been destroyed when the county and city systems consolidated to integrate the schools. They also learned that printed maps showed the city from the perspective of those in power. Therefore, they had to research and conduct interviews to find geographic information important to the African American community.

The GIS class conducted three in-depth interviews with a 1955 LHS graduate, Mr. Leonard Hunter. The final GIS product, "Mr. Hunter's Life Map of Raleigh in the 1950s," shows the city from an African American perspective.[6]

GIS students quickly realized that the data necessary to create historical maps had not been entered into "official" maps. They had to adjust digital information to show the locations and names of streets, landmarks, schools, and parks. The base layer for the project was a digital annexation map of the city. The original annexation data accurately portrayed the land as it was annexed, but some of the associated data were inaccurate. We corrected several data tables and conducted some ground "truthing" to ensure accuracy, checking and cross-referencing "actual" (ground) and "virtual" (digital map) features. The corrected data were returned to the city GIS office; thus, the project contributed a valuable public service to our collaborative partner and community.

As we researched the history, new understandings of place inspired new representational methods. As we faced our first test of collaboration, merging African American oral history with GIS technology, we used John Pickles's *Ground Truth: Social Implications of Geographic Information Systems*[7] to understand how GIS data are useful to represent multiple perspectives. Because "official" data excluded African American perspectives and landmarks, we needed different approaches to represent our historical findings. Technology helped us to represent the interpretations of history we had constructed.

MIDDLE SCHOOL SOCIAL STUDIES METHODS PROFESSOR (C.B.)

As a local historian, I am very interested in the development of a "sense of place" in both individuals and cultures. For middle school students, conducting local history engages them as active participants in both their own learning and in their communities, constructing not only a sense of place but also a sense of identity. The new ground unearthed in terms of African American local history is critically important in the renaissance of the "New South" that integrates all of its history. Most important to me as a middle school social studies teacher educator is the entrusting of students as the agents and "keepers" of the history. In *Service With a Smile*,[8] we suggested that conducting social studies through community service projects is sound in theory and practice.

Through this project, students:

▶ Understood that they could make a difference and that others valued what they are doing. They felt empowered by their accomplishments.

▶ Developed "people" interaction skills through interviewing, collaborative problem solving, and decision making.

▶ Practiced leadership, cooperation, and democratic process. Their group efforts illustrate that together they can accomplish more.

▶ Engaged in meaningful work coupled with new skills that increased the adolescents' sense of personal competence and self-esteem. This is critical to identity development.

▶ Gained empathy and broadened perspective through community service-learning enabling them to appreciate better those who are unlike themselves.

▶ Developed character and sound values, exercised responsibility, and engaged in work that challenged them to make judgments about goodness and justice.

SOCIAL STUDIES METHODS AND GEOGRAPHY PROFESSOR ON CONDUCTING SOCIAL STUDIES (M.A.)

The Ligon History Project emerged out of mutual interests, among them the aim of expanding across interdisciplinary horizons through conducting community-based social studies. Conducting social studies is applied original research by students for their communities. Students conducted oral and architectural history, archival research, and geographic and dendrochronological (tree-ring) inquiry, presenting them in technological applications.

The idea of conducting social studies as community service-learning moves beyond simple historical research to applied research with deeply rooted connections and service to the community.[9] This applied research is intended to develop and strengthen institutional capacities among students, schools, and local agencies. What these students reclaimed was new historical ground in which they actively constructed community history. In the process, they collaborated to develop new documents, audio and videotapes, and digital history products such as web archives, maps, data bases, and virtual field trips that continue to instruct future generations. A new genre of historical representation was developed in the historic African American community GIS map, possibly the first of its kind.

Through this project, the students and community began to see their history and historic places anew. It was as if students had cleared debris and thorny thicket to release a new landscape. In talking with and interviewing alumni, they constructed new understandings of the past. This history was hidden until the energies of young and old were brought together to remember and record it.

In this project, we see the conduct of social studies as an applied discipline. If citizenship is a goal of social studies education, let us engage social studies students with the agents and offices of history, government, and public service. If students are to learn history, let us have them practice the skills of historical research purposely for their own communities. If technologies are to be used in education, let us use appropriate technologies that contribute new knowledge to that community toward its own health and sustainability.

Our Process of Collaboration and Some Tangible Outcomes

In contrast to more traditional school/university collaborations focused on teacher education, our project situated middle school students at its center. With the high school alumni, community partners, three professors, five middle school teachers, eight graduate students, four undergraduates and some 125 middle school students, organizational issues were both problematic and intriguing. But the project developed a vibrant life of its own energized by our meetings. Key to our commitment was continual interaction with high school alumni. Hearing their stories and feeling their love for the school and their determination to keep its memory alive inspired all of us to persevere.

Keeping the alumni's concerns foremost, our primary team (teachers and professors) developed a framework for the project. Our goals were (1) to collect previously undocumented history and present it in digital formats via the Internet, (2) integrate existing official data with archival and oral histories to tell a story, and (3) coordinate this effort into an interdisciplinary middle school curriculum.

This project evolved from preexisting collaborations in technology-based education, GIS education, and local history and community service-learning initiatives. Collaborative technology projects generated by the university had provided local schools with web project opportunities, web space, and technical assistance. Ann and Rita had published web articles and projects as part of College of Education initiatives.[10] These collaborative relationships supported the development of our yearlong grant-funded intergenerational, interdisciplinary school/community project. Plans for extended grant support are being developed to reach further into the community for preservation and education, and several co-authored projects have ensued.[11] One of the project's web sites links to many interdisciplinary aspects of the project.[12]

▶ On-line versions of oral histories[13]
▶ Biographies of two Ligon alumni[14]
▶ A tree slice with labeled aspects of Ligon High School history[15]

Early in the project, teachers and professors set goals and target dates. For each of us, there was initial hesitation and trepidation about committing to that long stretch of butcher paper unfurled across the classroom floor. Each month represented additional work and commitment, but we listened to one another's plans in order to coordinate efforts.

A partnership project of this magnitude required effective communication between collaborators. Meetings of the middle school teachers, students, and principal with the university professors and graduate students were held monthly and were audiotaped. Teachers described the meetings as critically important. At each meeting, participants described and updated their research, and university faculty and students asked teachers how to support them best.

Various tensions emerged over purse strings and products. More tensions arose as each teacher and professor had to stretch beyond already full schedules and curricula. Inevitable crises of faith alternated with the quiet joy of changing race and community relations. Nonetheless, we pushed on, familiar with the necessity of creative tension in developing innovative curriculum.

In our meetings, middle school teachers, students, the principal, graduate students, and professors all had equal time to speak as we went around the room "talking stick" style. In listening to one another, we gained a deeper respect for differences in perspectives, and different avenues of research evolved as we shared information. More than just sharing information, each "go-around" was powerful in developing from each of our voices a collective voice. Most of us essentially worked in our own settings, or periodically in pairs, but when the large group gathered as a whole, the exchange of ideas, progress, and contributions inspired us all. The meetings were necessary, useful, helpful, synergistic, and central to our continued progress as we reconnected with the project as a whole.

Teachers Talking
INSTRUCTIONAL TECHNOLOGY TEACHER, LIGON GT MAGNET MIDDLE SCHOOL (A.T.)
Documenting the history of a school is an excellent collaborative project that allows educators and students to do significant research, experience history through the eyes of those who lived it, and express their creativity in communicating the information to others.

To conduct this type of study in your school setting:

▶ Assess the school's unique features to find aspects of the school's history that will excite students.
▶ Assess the historic resources available (yearbooks, collections, documents, archives).
▶ Find colleagues with complementary skills who are interested in the project and are willing to invest time and energy in it.
▶ Explore community resources that are available in local government, businesses, civic groups, and/or higher education.
▶ Locate alumni and find out how they are willing to invest in the project.
▶ Celebrate completion of the project with a public display of the products.

Due to the complexity of the project and its "bleeding edge" nature, it would have been easy to let the project languish incomplete. The culminating exposition motivated us to complete products. Parents, alumni, school and university officials, and grant funders were invited. Tension mounted prior to the exposition as the last-minute details were added and technological problems were solved. Students, teachers, and professors were determined not to disappoint anyone, especially the alumni. In many ways, the project's success can be measured by the students' burning desire to share the school's history accurately and effectively. Then the magic began when someone asked a student, "Please tell me about your project."

English/Journalism Teacher, Ligon GT Magnet Middle School (B.M.)

The students make all the difference. Teachers, professors, graduate students, and student interns can meet "until the cows come home," but the true test of an educational collaboration is whether or not the students benefit from the project. We were lucky because we had immediate feedback from our students as to whether or not our plans were working.

It helps if students are genuinely interested in the topic. Racial segregation is a topic students had read about in history books but had never experienced firsthand. The face-to-face time spent between students and the dozen alumni interviewed made lasting impressions on us all. It also helps if the students are as devoted to the production of the product as you are. My students put in many hours above and beyond the forty-five-minute class period. I had two- to three-year relationships with all of my students, and they knew my standards from the beginning. This saved time when it came to the production of our volume, *Capturing the Past to Guide the Future.*

Having clear goals from the beginning is essential. My students and I wanted to publish an alumni oral history because the Ligon High story had not been told. We were enthusiastic about the collaboration because it could make the oral history collection a reality. Collaboration tends to snowball; remember that. The round-table discussion/sharing groups kept all members informed of all phases of the project. This format ensured that no one was duplicating anyone's effort.

The experience I valued most was the interviews. Collaborating with Ligon alumni was eye opening for me because I had grown up in the same county and because of segregation had limited contact with the African American community.

Social Studies Teacher, Ligon GT Magnet Middle School (N.S.)

The architectural history project involved researching the history of Ligon and the surrounding area. Students were excited about the project and wanted to find out more about the subject, but there were some problems in getting the project off the ground and keeping it going once we got started. Easily accessible information was limited, and time restraints prohibited routine research at the archives.

In working with middle school students, establishing relationships is one of the most important components for a project to be successful. They especially enjoyed the night when Ligon parents and alumni came. This gave students an opportunity to explain all they had learned about the area's history. They were interested in the history of the area and of their school.[16]

Science Teacher, Ligon GT Magnet Middle School (G.O.)

Collaboration is enhancing. Our periodic meetings became especially important as we carried out our separate paths of inquiry. I think it was beneficial to meet at both middle school and university settings. This variety provided insights into our professional environments and a feel for the community settings from which the project was evolving.

It was helpful to have a collaborative timeline where we set deadlines for our goals. Additionally it was beneficial for group members to prioritize what we wanted to accomplish. We committed to a realistic set of objectives with deadlines and developed wish lists of objectives to accomplish if time permitted. The wish lists helped us to envision ways we could further enrich and explore, and guided graduate students' research to aid us in our separate aspects of the project.

It is important to allow autonomy among the participants in deciding goals. Each of us had a measure of control over what we did and could accomplish within the framework of our schedules. In my case, work on this project was in addition to my normal school duties. Grants can be very time consuming.

I think that the value of an integrated collaboration is that it welcomes people with many different interests. Some students and teachers were lured by the oral history component. To others, GIS was the spark that drew their attention. Dendrochronology was of interest to others. After the initial draw, we couldn't help but learn from other facets of the project.

One of the joys of teaching is the learning that takes place. Although the initial goal was to prepare the tree slices for an exhibit, the study of the annual rings led to the discovery of the science of dendrochronology. A world of tree-ring research opened up with an Internet site. I recommend making use of the Internet to explore the topics involved. It is important to allow time for both teacher and students to wander down those paths of inquiry and journey into those windows of virtual exploration. The University of Arizona's dendrochronology lab laid out the principles of dendrochronology and its numerous applications.

Dendrochronology turned out to be a hot topic in academia, where the science of tree-ring dating is being used in archaeological dating, tracking changes in global climate conditions, and other problems related to history and earth science. How fascinating! We discovered that tree cores could be used as another method of dating. What a thrill to have several professionals in our community visit our school and show us how to take cores from our Ligon trees using a tool called an increment borer. It was fun to see the students engaged in activities designed to explore this field. What impressed me in the collaboration was the variety of ways in which history could be conveyed though books, GIS maps, human interactions, computers, and natural history's own tree rings.[17]

It was worthwhile to have various community partners visit our school and discuss dendrochronology with the students. They not only provided expertise but brought with them the message that the community cared about students' education. We are fortunate to have three universities open to community involvement nearby.

Local, state, and federal agencies were of invaluable assistance. The North Carolina State University College of Forestry, the North Carolina and U.S. Forest Services, the Forest History Society, exhibit designers, and the North Carolina Division of Forest Resources all offered information, ideas, and suggestions. NCSU's Hodges Wood Products Lab machined, finished, and transformed each unfinished tree slice into a "looking glass" of history. Oiled and waxed, the tree's annual concentric lines represented each year of Ligon's story.

It is important to document and date ideas and happenings as the project unfolds. I recommend keeping a list of contacts with phone numbers and taking pictures. I used a loose-leaf notebook to keep all information about the project in one spot. Of course, it has now overflowed to a Ligon History box.

Science/GIS Teacher, Ligon GT Magnet Middle School (R.H.)

Educators and their students are isolated in their classrooms even though the world happens around them. This can be very frustrating as well as comforting to educators. The Ligon History Project launched us all into a new, real-world situation in which the teachers, students, school community, and larger community embarked on an ambitious learning project. We all wanted our students to feel more connected to the world around them, and they were asking to become more involved. So when the trees were cut down in front of the school, it served as a catalyst for this type of learning. The Ligon teachers generated ideas, but we quickly realized we needed help to turn the ideas into reality. NCSU had strong ties with our school. It became obvious that the help we needed would come from those ties. When the teachers asked for a project and Marsha responded by asking, "What would you like to do?," it all began to happen.

The next barriers were funding and administrative support. If funded, the principal agreed to offer his full support. The teachers and Marsha wrote the first two grants that funded the project. This process was important because people began taking ownership of the project. Writing the grants helped us to identify the stakeholders and separate the project into its components. All of the teachers participated in grant writing so everyone was aware of what the project would involve.

This was the first collaborative partnership of this type at the school. We were amazed that the number of community partners continued to grow as the project moved forward. Our collaboration with the community was the key to the project's success. Many individuals with diverse interests and knowledge gave the project life and moved it along at a speed we couldn't have imagined.

Perhaps one of the most interesting collaborations was between the Ligon alumni and the students. At first, the students were unsure about communicating with these "older" strangers from the community, but as they discovered their common interests and goals, relationships flourished. The teachers also developed relationships with the alumni. We all could see history unfolding before our eyes. We realized that by learning about our past, we were discovering our present as well as directing our future. The project was energizing and grew to take on a life of its own. The excitement was contagious. Even though we were all very tired by the end of the year, we wanted to continue. Later, I remember thinking to myself that this was the first school year ever that I wished could have been just a little bit longer.

With any new endeavor there are expectations that cannot be met. This was frustrating to the teachers because we all wanted to do the best job we could. Sometimes deadlines could not be met or we would have to wait longer than expected for a component from one of our partners. We all had to learn to be flexible. There were also many unknowns, which is sometimes difficult, especially when planning for so many students. We had to be willing to adapt and change as the project progressed. For these reasons, the monthly collaborative meetings were the key to the project's success and the overall feeling of well-being for participants.

No matter what the barriers or the problems, the outcomes of this project made the process worthwhile for all of those involved. History came alive for all of us, and we realized that it was our own history we were discovering. This could not have been accomplished without the many collaborative efforts of the entire group. Everyone enjoyed and loved this project including the students and their parents. It was truly amazing to see everyone pull together to work toward a common goal. As one participant put it, "I feel a part of a community I never knew existed."

Professors Talking

MIDDLE SCHOOL SOCIAL STUDIES TEACHER EDUCATION PROFESSOR (C.B.)

I looked at this collaboration for the opportunity it gave adolescents to investigate a period of history that many of their parents experienced as adolescents. In the south, we still feel a hesitancy to question or discuss the Jim Crow period of our history openly. Old wounds of injustice heal slowly, if at all, and for those of us identified with the oppressors, there is a profound regret for the actions as well as a respect and admiration for the victims. We have come to understand that the hurt experienced is long lasting. It speaks of missed opportunities and questions of what might have been. Today, we cannot fathom how the Jim Crow racial injustices could have been perpetuated.

It is not surprising that those who had been maligned would want to have their story told, but who would have the sensitivity to be able to feel and appreciate the story they were telling? The teachers who were their contemporaries felt the weight of the issues that were being examined. There was a lingering awkwardness about asking questions about this time in history. No matter how supportively we might have asked them, we felt as if we were prying. Perhaps that is why this project could have been successful only with students questioning adults. It was not so much a black/white issue among contemporaries as it was an intergenerational learning experience for students who had the rare opportunity to consult with those who had lived the history. Students saw themselves as "keepers of the history." They felt the weight of their responsibility to tell the whole story. The Ligon graduates appreciated the students' honest responses to their story. There were looks of compassion and astonishment on the students' young faces. The alumni knew that their stories would be told with compassion.

I provided Raleigh's historical context for the students. We toured Raleigh by trolley and learned about the city's early history until the present day. I told little-known stories gleaned from the diaries and speeches of original source documents. History came alive for the students. The firsthand accounts helped them understand the power of narrative. They realized researchers using eyewitness accounts had to be responsible and faithful recorders of the stories.

For a collaboration of this sort to work, all of the adults must believe that the students are the keepers of the history. I was fortunate to work with teachers whose expectations were high. They had no need to dominate the process. My faith in their understanding and commitment to a student-centered project and their faith in their students' abilities to deliver proved well founded.

CURRICULUM HISTORY AND HISTORIOGRAPHIC RESEARCH PROFESSOR (A.W.)

I approached this project from a slightly different perspective than my fellow collaborators. My research has focused on segregation and desegregation for the last five years.[18] Although others were surprised and dismayed to find that artifacts of the African American high school were destroyed, I was not surprised. Nonetheless, everyone in this project was committed to identify, to frame what happened in the Ligon High School community during and after desegregation. In fact, through this project, we created a safe place where students, teachers, parents, and alumni reworked the histories of segregation and separation. In this way, we all were empowered to deconstruct the marginalization discourse encountered by African Americans during the era of Jim Crow.

Particularly exciting for me was the involvement of my graduate historiography class in this project. My students learned not only how to gather historiographical data but also how to involve middle school students in that process. At the same time, we were faced with the hegemony of white privilege through the writings and artifacts of those in power making decisions about those not in power. Students learned about textural artifacts made of gestures, words, symbolic objects, and practices of all kinds, and how those were woven through everyday conversations and practices. We came face to face with the ferocious intensity of segregationists who supported resistance to school desegregation. At the same time, we heard the multilayered and multivocal narratives of African Americans who quietly but strongly denounced their marginalized representations. We learned how this African American community acted as a collective whole, with a collective will during a collective struggle for educational equality. Of most importance for my students was our responsibility and honor in participating in both gathering and presenting historical and personal interpretations of African American high school students during desegregation. We all emerged from this project committed to continue to help students connect more authentically with their history and surroundings. By doing so, we honor the struggles of those who fought for educational equality in the South.

SOCIAL STUDIES TEACHER EDUCATION AND GEOGRAPHY PROFESSOR (M.A.)

Having met Ann and Rita while conducting research on teaching and learning with GIS, I had greatly respected their work. When they decided to apply for partnership funding, they approached me and I was thrilled. Ann mentioned her desire to expand on the digital alumni archive project. To me, the possibilities were a social studies educator's dream. With another funding source, more partners—teachers, professors, and community partners as well—came toward the ideas. It all happened quickly and suddenly; there we were, having to plan and coordinate activities in five middle school classes and two or three university courses.

We couldn't have predicted, the first fall day we met to coordinate our efforts, just how much work this project would be. But because we had made plans with one another, we couldn't turn back; so it goes in collaborations. We survived competing interests, limited funds, overworked and disempowered teachers, and unintended workloads.

The technological applications have yielded many more digital history products than could otherwise have been accomplished, and these have contributed greatly to the community. The students in these classes learned far more than we ever imagined they would by contributing their generation's unique gift for generating digital products. The value of digital history is its accessibility to the community for many years to come. Hundreds of hours were devoted to developing meaningful products. By the final exposition, everyone had stretched beyond previous limits—it was the end of the school year, all of the pieces were just coming together and they had to be pulled into presentation formats.

This was new ground. Ann, Rita, and their students had not only pioneered uses of GIS in middle school but also in historic representation. There were many challenges to overcome—sheer time issues and technical GIS problems that any professional GIS technician would face. Betty and her students had conducted, audiotaped, videotaped, and compiled a dozen oral history narratives into a volume. She and her students organized and coordinated the exposition event. Ginny was pioneering dendrochronology as an interdisciplinary scientific/historical study, and Neville was writing a curriculum for the Architectural History course elective from scratch. Each of us may have felt we were shouldering the entire burden at one time or another. I have come to call these "crises of faith." But our faith and impetus were always restored by the alumni's stories, the next person's discovery, shared needs, or the excitement of new ideas. Our "take-home message" is "keep collaborating." A tree fell in the school yard and somebody heard.

NOTES

1. Ronald Butchart, *Local Schools, Exploring Their History* (Nashville, Tenn.: The American Association for State and Local History, 1986).
2. A Geographic Information System (GIS) is a suite of integrated electronic technologies: data bases, graphic representations, and spatial representations (digital maps) that can be used to coordinate and present immense amounts of information. Features in a GIS are "geocoded" to coordinating references such as a latitude/longitude or a street address, and associated with information in a data base. GIS is seen daily on TV weather reports, and is used in city and regional planning, transportation and distribution, utilities mapping and management, and in hundreds of other ways.
3. Candy Beal, *Raleigh: The First 200 Years*. Published under the auspices of the Raleigh Bicentennial Task Force, 1992.
4. See www2.ncsu.edu/ncsu/cep/ligon/about/history/esri/P7317.htm.
5. *Ibid.*
6. See www2.ncsu.edu/cep/ligon/about/history/esri/P7318.htm.
7. John Pickles, *Ground Truth: Social Implications of Geographic Information Systems* (New York: Guilford, 1995).
8. John Arnold and Candy Beal, *Service With a Smile* (Raleigh: North Carolina Middle School Council Monograph, 1994).
9. James Percoco, *A Passion for the Past* (Portsmouth, N.H.: Heinemann, 1998).
10. Ann Thompson and Rita Hagevik, "Using Technology Resources and Collaboration to Empower Students" (electronic middle school journal) (Raleigh: North Carolina State University, 1998). Article available at www2.ncsu.edu/ncsu/cep/ligon/anntemp/meridianarticle.htm.
11. Other products from the project include a new collection of African American history and literature at the Middle School Library; a project uniting the efforts of author and archivist Linda Simmons-Henry of the Historically Black St. Augustine's College, to develop a permanent Ligon High School History exhibit; Linda Simmons-Henry and L. Edmisten, *Culture Town, Life in Raleigh's African American Communities* (Raleigh, N.C.: Raleigh Historic Districts Commission, Inc., 1993); a cover article, Marsha Alibrandi, Candy Beal, Anna Wilson, and Ann Thompson, "Reconstructing a School's Past Using Oral History and GIS Mapping," *Social Education* 64, no. 3 (2000): 134-140; a chapter on the use of GIS in the project, the first book to date on that subject in G. Ludwig and R. Audet, eds., *GIS in Schools* (Redlands, Calif.: Environmental Systems Research Institute, 2000); and a Power Point presentation, developed collaboratively between NCSU faculty and Ligon teachers that has gained attention in national settings that may be developed into a CD product.
12. See www2.ncsu.edu/ncsu/cep/ligon/about/history/esri/P7311.htm.
13. See www2.ncsu.edu/ncsu/cep/ligon/about/book/intro.htm.
14. See www2.ncsu.edu/ncsu/cep/ligon/about/history/interviews.htm.
15. See www2.ncsu.edu/ncsu/cep/ligon/about/history/dendro2/sld001.htm.
16. See www2.ncsu.edu/ncsu/cep/ligon/about/history/ah/ah.htm.
17. See www2.ncsu.edu/ncsu/cep/ligon/about/history/esri/P7319.htm.
18. Anna Wilson and William Segall, *Teacher Narratives During Segregation* (Albany: State University of New York, 2000).

Global Connections Project: Collaboration among Middle Level Students and Teachers and University Teacher Education Students and Faculty

Seven

Helen Carlson
Carol Holm

The Scene

Standing in a classroom at the University of Sydney in Australia prior to the beginning of the international social studies conference, we (Robert, a middle level teacher in Sweden; Carol, a middle level teacher in Minnesota; and Helen, a university professor in Minnesota who also taught in Sweden) talked about how the collaboration had started so many years ago through teacher exchanges and formal and informal conversations. We looked at the children's materials spread out before us, materials that we would soon share with conference participants. It was an emotional experience when we looked at the answers to the question, What do children in each country need to live happy, healthy lives? Our responses were the rights to education, the love of a family, safe and healthy places to live—the answers were the same in different countries. We thought about how the dreams of students and instructors had come to life through the friendships and learning developed over the past seven years.

We were halfway around the world in Australia. Here were the graphs and summary charts of the traffic counts conducted in Växjö and Duluth, Minnesota. Helen remembered walking down the road to Furutåskolan while Robert and the teacher education students guided the middle level students in counting the bicycles, cars, trucks, and buses going past the school. Carol remembered how her students reviewed the Växjö and Duluth data, and discussed the environmental impacts of energy consumption in the extensive car use around Woodland School. The students demonstrated their awareness of energy consumption and patterns of travel in the two countries.

And here were the records of the on-site interviews the middle level students, with support of teacher education students, conducted with business and government leaders in their areas. Carol and Helen reflected on the small-group debriefing meeting after the interviews and looked back on the information gained by both levels of students. The middle level students were amazed at the history of the power company and how technology had changed in making newspapers while the teacher education students were astounded at the amount of information the middle level students accessed without turning to print or textbooks. Robert and Carol thought about the enthusiasm of their students in doing research in the community, how they just would not quit, digging up facts and teaching their teachers.

And over there were the videotapes and maps that middle level students had made of their own schools and shared with each other after they had gotten to know each other through pen pals and key pal letters. We talked about how these were connected with the learning centers made by university students about the culture, geography, and language of the countries. How excited the middle level students were to participate in cultural events and learn about the diversity in each country, how the refugee children in Sweden wept during the United Nations Celebration Day, and how Native American children in Minnesota shared stories about their spring pow wows after maple sugaring. The middle level students went on to make learning centers about the history, geography, and customs, and related to topics about where their ancestors (native, migrant, refugee, and immigrant) were born.

We thought about how we got to this place. What had happened over the years? What were our dreams for the future? What formed the base of our work?

Our Process of Collaboration and Some Tangible Outcomes

Our collaboration began seven years ago when a retired principal from the Duluth Public Schools gathered together several people from the public schools and university who were interested in international experiences and global education. We talked long into the night, dreaming about a global charter school. From this initial meeting, we developed a small resource center filled with materials (books, maps, software, posters, art prints, culture kits) for future and practicing teachers and called it the Children's Center for Global Understanding. Eventually, the project involved middle level students, teachers, university teacher education students, and faculty in several countries as they sought to infuse global outlooks and inquiry learning into their social studies curriculum and methods courses. The schools involved in the project initially included Woodland School, Furutåskolan, and the University of Minnesota-Duluth (UMD). Woodland School in Duluth, Minnesota, is a middle school with grades five to eight, which includes approximately 750 students and thirty-five teachers and staff. Teams of teachers at each grade level focus on language arts and social studies while others concentrate on math and science. There are constant efforts to build relationships, coherent philosophies, and goals across all grade levels. The school attracts students from both high- and low-income neighborhoods and has a full range of athletic, music, and language programs.

Furutåskolan is a compulsory school (grades one to six) with six hundred students and twenty teachers in the Telleborg section of Växjö, Duluth's sister city in south central Sweden. Like other compulsory schools, there is a full range of academic subjects, including English as a Second Language (ESL), with grade level teaching teams assuming different responsibilities. Teachers also stay with the same group of children for three years, thus teaching the curriculum for grades four, five, and six in three-year cycles. Creative expression in music, handicrafts, creative dramatics, and environmental studies are emphasized.

The University of Minnesota-Duluth has 8,500 students with 1,000 students studying to be teachers at the early childhood, elementary, and secondary levels as well as special education. Students have a full year of field experiences connected to methods before student teaching. The education department has a learner-sensitive teaching model with emphases on diversity, collaboration, technology, reflection, and empowerment.

In thinking about the types of collaboration that have occurred over the last seven years, three main phases emerge: synergy, understanding, and extension.

INITIAL SYNERGY PHASE

During the initial synergy phase, our collaboration consisted of joint brainstorming and sharing of ideas leading to the development of goals and objectives, grant writing, and joint planning of curriculum for both middle level and university students. We held monthly meetings during which the excitement was so generative that everyone was talking at the same time. Goals were written that included the following (for both teacher education and middle school levels):

▶ Improve the learner's awareness of the world through geographical understanding.
▶ Increase understanding of technology's potential to open doors to the world.
▶ Support learners as they become more caring global citizens.
▶ Promote friendships with learners in other regions and countries.
▶ Facilitate students' understandings of themselves and their own cultures through enhanced perspective taking.
▶ Develop skills in problem solving and analytical and creative thinking.[1]

We incorporated global perspectives into the ongoing curriculum as middle level students developed pen pal relationships and took virtual Internet field trips guided by teacher education students in the university computer lab (this was prior to middle level schools having access to the Internet). For example, teacher education students were paired with two middle level students, and they searched the Internet for sites related to Duluth's sister cities. They found maps (physical, political, product) and discussed why cities were located in particular places. They learned about customs such as All Man's Land in Sweden, where all the land is held in common and anyone can use it with respect. This was in contrast to the private property and no trespassing signs in the United States. They found historic sites near Petrozavodsk, Russia, and Thunder Bay, Canada. On occasion, the teacher education students helped the middle level students create key pal (pen pal letters through e-mail) letters and send them to their counterparts in Sweden.

Middle level students heard guests from different countries talk about the geography, history, culture, and economy of their respective countries. They posed questions that connected the standard social studies concepts with the information presented.

We developed country culture kits, compiled with resources from community members who had been involved with sister city and international exchanges, as well as purchased materials. The kits included books written in the language of the country, music compact discs and audiotapes, teacher resource books with suggested lessons, lessons sent by teachers in the other country, language charts, menus from restaurants, artifacts, maps, flags, money, and videotapes of celebrations and life across different cultural groups within a particular country. For example, in the Australian culture kit, there were gum seeds and didgeridoos while in the Japan kit there were unique pop bottles, fans, and samples of and materials for writing Japanese letters. In the Sweden kit, there were hand-crafted items like the Dalarana horse, materials related to Santa Lucia, and maps of various geographic and political regions. Students used the resources in the teacher-developed lessons to learn about life in different countries. Lessons included water studies across several countries, conversion of U.S. dollars to foreign currency, art experiences, and reenactment celebrations from other countries. The culture kit materials provided real examples to complement other print and multimedia materials. Teacher education students used the culture kits for developing plans they taught in their field experiences.

Teacher education students also developed, implemented, and evaluated social studies learning centers that included global connections related to geography, history, culture, and language. For example, teacher education students from Sweden created learning centers focused on the Vikings and their trade and settlement patterns. American teacher education students studying in Sweden developed learning centers based on input from children in Sweden; handicrafts like embroidery and woodworking for both boys and girls were included.

In turn, the middle level students created their own learning centers about the countries (native or foreign) from which their ancestors came. In a huge community celebration, the middle level students provided a program of music and dance from other countries and then used their learning centers to teach their parents about the countries' history, geography, economics, culture, and political systems using the artifacts, maps, posters, photographs, and other information they had gathered. One example of a learning center focused on Finland; there were maps of the country, drawings from Helsinki's historic area and Olympic center, traditional clothing artifacts, and a menu (in Finnish) from a restaurant in Helsinki.

Middle level students came to the university to engage in folk dancing taught by people from different countries and to engage in art experiences designed by an art educator with the help of teacher education students. Kits of art prints and slides from different countries illustrated basic art concepts as well as the cultures of the artists and the countries. For example, there were folk art from northern Sweden, paintings of the Canadian mounted police, fish prints and origami from Japan, and Matrushka nested figures from Russia. Teacher education students used these and the culture kits in creating social studies curricula.

In a university folk festival celebration, the middle level students sang songs and developed a display highlighting their work. The middle level students interacted with university students from Malaysia to Russia, from Sri Lanka to Pakistan, from Brazil to Tanzania, raising questions, hearing other languages, and talking about leisure time and music from the different countries.

During the initial synergy phase, there were many global learning experiences infused into the social studies curriculum. In turn, the curriculum strands from the social studies became the organizing structure for the block-scheduled integrated learning experiences connecting social studies concepts with research and creative expression (see Chart 1).

INITIAL SYNERGY PHASE	Writing pen pal letters to students in other countries
	Taking virtual (Internet) field trips to other countries
	Engaging with materials in culture kits
	Developing internationally focused learning centers
	Teaching parents using child-created learning centers
	Learning dances and folk music from other countries
	Creating art experiences based on art processes from other countries
	Participating in university folk festivals
	Learning from international guests invited to classroom

DEEPENING THE PROCESS PHASE	Establishing relationships with students in another country
	Posing questions about individuals, families, schools, community, nation, and global issues
	Gathering primary source information related to questions posed
	Writing topical and ongoing pen pal letters
	Conducting interviews with elders and community members
	Making videotapes of typical school days
	Creating school maps
	Observing, recording, and graphing traffic flows
	Recording types of houses in school neighborhood
	Conducting environmental audits and surveys
	Conducting human rights surveys
	Summarizing and synthesizing information in varieties of formats
	Exchanging information with classrooms in another country
	Comparing and contrasting information exchanged
	Drawing overall conclusions

EXTENDING THE COLLABORATION PHASE	Presenting the Global Connections Project at conferences
	Writing articles about the Global Connections Project
	Expanding to additional classrooms and countries
	Developing service-learning projects
	Creating culture kits for younger learners

DEEPENING THE PROCESS

The collaboration moved to the development of a framework that allowed more depth of understanding about both the local and global environments. A social constructivist inquiry approach included posing questions; finding, analyzing, and summarizing information; exchanging information with middle level students in another country; and comparing and contrasting the information and drawing conclusions. This was done at the personal, family, community, national, and global levels (see Figure 1).

To develop the in-depth inquiry that occurred during this phase, it was helpful to begin with teachers from the two countries who knew each other. In this case, Robert and Carol had been exchange teachers in each other's schools; Helen had an ongoing collaboration with Växjö University and was an exchange professor there. Contacts such as these can often be established through Sister City organizations as well as exchanges arranged through the United States Information Agency. The middle level students did not travel because we wanted full participation of all students in regular public education settings. Instead, they completed in-depth inquiries in their own settings and then exchanged this information. The information was timely and authentic, and presented by people from the country and culture (rather than secondary sources).

The middle level students then moved beyond their introductory pen pal messages and the experiences noted above to sharing information about their families across countries. For example, the middle level students realized what a diverse background many Americans have as they looked at the records people kept about their ancestors. Many middle level students inspired their family members to write down their stories from their past. Middle level students using *Growing up in My Family*[2] made a family history book. Students conducted interviews with elders attending the University for Seniors. Questions related to leisure, school, family composition, shopping, games and toys, personal histories (driving a car, dating), and historical events like World War II, the depressions, and the development of technology were included. Family histories by teacher education students increased the middle level students' exposure to diversity. For example, Hmong students shared their stories of life in refugee camps, moving to the United States, and the customs and celebrations that hold their community together today. Videotapes of a typical day in school and maps of the physical setting were shared and compared across countries at the middle level and reviewed by teacher education students as part of their social studies methods course. One of the key differences in school life focused on the lunchroom. In Sweden, glass dishes and cloth napkins were used on round tables with floral

Figure 1: **Levels of Investigation and Process of Investigation: A Matrix**					
LEVELS	QUESTION POSING	INFORMATION GATHERING	INFORMATION SYNTHESIZING	INFORMATION EXCHANGE ACROSS COUNTRIES	COMPARE/CONTRAST DRAWING CONCLUSIONS
Individual					
Family					
School					
Community Life					
Global Issues					

and candle centerpieces where teachers and students conversed together for an hour. Woodland students questioned their lunch environment, which seemed rushed and more like a warehouse.

Questions for community leaders were generated by the students and included the following:

▶ What is the history of your business/organization?
▶ How has your business changed over time?
▶ How do you use technology?
▶ How do you protect the environment?
▶ How many people work in your business/organization?
▶ How do workers use basic skills in their work?
▶ What does your organization do to help build good relationships with the community?

Data from the on-site interviews of community leaders, facilitated by teacher education students, were completed, shared, and compared, as were things like traffic counts, housing surveys, recycling options, and the needs of children in each community. Again, the information was exchanged across countries and in the teacher education course as based on the National Council for the Social Studies (NCSS) Standards dealing with global connections and the geography standard of human-environment interaction.[3] Some of the conclusions, after comparing the information from the two countries, included the following comments:

▶ In Sweden, there is cleaner air without so many cars or industries. At Woodland, we cannot ride bikes because of the heavy traffic, whereas in Sweden everyone rides bikes (teachers, too).
▶ Packaging is different in the two countries—there are more returnable glass bottles in Sweden than we have at Woodland.
▶ There is much emphasis on recycling in both countries. Furutåskolan has a pig that eats the scraps from lunch.

We used this approach for local/global comparison as a model for curriculum generation, assessment, and evaluation at both the middle and university level. It provided opportunities for students to investigate, share, synthesize, and evaluate their learning. Students developed friendships, intellectual understandings, and critical reflections about alternatives and possibilities for dealing with issues such as environmental protection and human rights.

Extending the Collaboration

After the local/global framework was developed and assessed, there were extensions of the collaboration in three ways: (1) presenting at conferences and writing articles, (2) connecting to additional countries and educational levels, and (3) developing service-learning projects. Each of these has involved different types of collaboration.[4]

Additional classes and resource people in other countries have become involved in the project. After Helen said "yes" to the Ibura Primary School in Tanzania, the school implemented a local/global investigation model there. Middle level students began exchanging letters about their lives and sending information about their school and community to Woodland School. In Bukoba, Tanzania, only 5 percent of the homes have electricity and many people are learning to build cooking cones to save fuel and conserve energy. The middle level learners and university students like to participate in choral singing groups and plays. There are very few cars or bicycles, and most transportation is by foot. The new information led to broader conclusions and understandings about life where the economic rewards are few. Teacher education students are exchanging and comparing information about educational programs and parent attitudes in other countries. We also have developed an ongoing relationship with colleagues and students in Australia, Saudi Arabia, Russia, and Latvia.

A service-learning project grew out of the relationships with middle level students in Tanzania. After establishing beginning relationships and understandings, the Duluth middle level students decided to collect school supplies for the school in Tanzania. Other classes in the building found out about the project, and they wanted to participate. Even the mayor's wife sent some school supplies. The university students collected funds for mailing ten boxes of supplies. The high point came when the middle level students came to the social studies methods course to share their reflections about this project in a new role as teachers. In essence, the middle level students became instructors for the teacher education students. This middle level student teaching will continue as these students share global understandings with younger elementary children and early childhood teacher education students. Some of the comments from the middle level students included the following:

▶ Sharing is a very important thing. I learned that we have a lot and that there is great poverty in other countries, but children still have fun.
▶ It means a lot to me because I feel the happiness that they (the children in Tanzania) feel when they get things we collected.
▶ When we started collecting, the rest of the kids wanted to help us. Even the kids in the seventh and eight grades brought things. The whole school helped.
▶ I felt happy that we could help people to learn and know more. . . . I'm also proud we can help people if we try.

During this phase, the teacher/faculty collaboration meetings were less frequent and more focused on the investigation process and its meaning at both levels. The interactions of the middle level students and the teacher education students sometimes involved face-to-face learning experiences. Sometimes the investigation process took separate but parallel paths. And sometimes the work of the middle level students served as models and information sources for analysis and reflection by the teacher education students (see Chart 1, p. 74).

These three phases have each yielded different challenges and outcomes. As life circumstances and professional responsibilities of the collaborators change, new opportunities for working together emerge. Change in the collaboration tasks has happened and will continue to happen, as one would expect in any long-term project.

Our Conceptualization of Improving Social Studies

The theoretical underpinnings of our work connect global dimensions, broad social studies curriculum standards, and social constructivism and inquiry. These three areas were interwoven in the project. For example, the global and diversity perspectives permeated the goals of the project when they were developed and influenced the learning experiences during the initial synergy phase. The social constructivist and inquiry skills formed a base for the "deepening the process" phase in which students across countries were active constructors of understanding as they posed questions and collected, synthesized, and compared evidence. Social studies curriculum standards formed a framework for the learning experiences offered in all three phases with service-learning and civic responsibility emphasized in the "extending the collaboration" phase (see Figure 2).

GLOBAL DIMENSIONS

Global dimensions encompass human values, including universal and cultural values, practices, and interconnections, as well as global systems, including patterns, issues, problems, and history. In selecting global issues, we could examine the following areas: political, cultural-social, development, and economic.[5] More recently, there has been an emphasis on multidimensional citizenship, multinational curriculum, deliberation, and ethical questions in educating world citizens.[6] Goals for global studies can be structured through delineation of skills in three areas:

- Cognitive (making distinctions, demonstrating conceptual understanding, stating problems, forming hypotheses, exploring consequences, collecting and analyzing data, making and applying generalizations)
- Participatory (observing, proposing, mobilizing, organizing, bargaining, negotiating, voting)
- Affective (grounding a position, empathizing, promoting equality, applying justice, demonstrating cross-cultural awareness)[7]

Cultural theorists have emphasized open-mindedness, resistance to stereotyping, inclination to empathize, social transformation and advocacy, and antibias attitudes. It is essential to move toward a transformation curriculum where diverse voices across nations have equal contributions to the story line of the curriculum.[8]

SOCIAL STUDIES CURRICULUM STANDARDS
Of particular importance in this project were the NCSS strands related to culture:

- **❶ CULTURE**
- **❷ TIME, CONTINUITY, AND CHANGE**
- **❸ PEOPLE, PLACES, AND ENVIRONMENTS**
- **❹ INDIVIDUALS, GROUPS, AND INSTITUTIONS**
- **❼ PRODUCTION, DISTRIBUTION, AND CONSUMPTION**
- **❽ SCIENCE, TECHNOLOGY, AND SOCIETY**
- **❾ GLOBAL CONNECTIONS**
- **❿ CIVIC IDEALS AND PRACTICES**

These standards incorporate civic practices in which students locate, access, analyze, organize, and apply information about selected public issues, such as recognizing and explaining multiple points of view, and participating in social actions consistent with ideals of human dignity, justice, equality, and rule of law.[9]

SOCIAL CONSTRUCTIVISM AND INQUIRY
We wanted to involve students in active and meaningful learning experiences. The construction of authentic, accurate, and up-to-date concepts is a major interest as countries move to standards for performance. Social constructivism involves communities of learners posing questions and considering and analyzing varieties of information, deliberating about commonly accepted tenets, and uncovering values and interests together.[10] Group participant observation, investigation, and discussion offer new avenues for learning.

Thus, these three legs—global and diversity perspectives, broad social studies curriculum standards, and social constructivism—guided our work in this project.

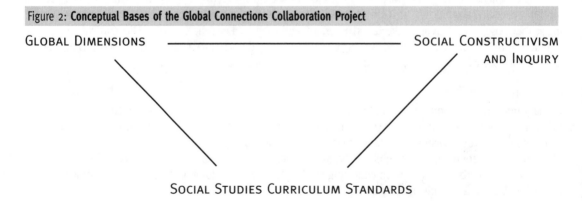

Figure 2: **Conceptual Bases of the Global Connections Collaboration Project**

GLOBAL DIMENSIONS ——————————————— SOCIAL CONSTRUCTIVISM AND INQUIRY

SOCIAL STUDIES CURRICULUM STANDARDS

A Teacher Talks to Teachers (C.H.)

I first met Helen Carlson at a meeting that was set up by my building principal, Mavis Whiteman. There were teachers and faculty. We met to discuss the possibility of starting an international charter school. At that point, my building principal had several foreign students working in our school, and she had just completed a principal exchange with a school in Denmark. The charter school idea was too big a project for us to accomplish but it set the stage for the work that Helen and I continued.

Memorable Moments and Outcomes

We decided to start working on a global project that paired middle level students with university students. It was a plus for my students to be able to interact with university students and provide them with the resources available at the university. Helen looked at it as a way for university teacher education students to work with children.

The students on my team at school made several visits to the university during the school year. It was easy for us to get there because we are within walking distance. We made some very cold trips across the parking lot in the wintertime, but it saved us the expense of using school buses.

On our trips, we visited the university art gallery, the displays in the science wing, and the planetarium. We also had some of Helen's students work with our students in the university computer lab. At that time, we did not have Internet access in our building. The university students showed our students how to access the Internet and took them on a trip to Sweden, where our pen pals live. The students visited museums and points of interest for tourists on their electronic field trip. Helen also set up a time for our students to work with the university physical education students so that we could learn folk dances from around the world.

Those of us interested in the charter school began to have regular meetings. We kept notes and assigned tasks for each other to accomplish between meetings. The meetings kept us focused on global studies in our classroom. We used the time to write grants and track our spending. We decided then to have a Children's Center for Global Understanding. Helen arranged to have it housed in a room at the university. We wanted it to be a place where teachers could go to get resources or a place where we could bring our middle school students to work on projects with the university education students. We wrote some grants and got money to purchase resource materials. We ordered materials during our monthly meetings. Mavis kept track of the finances for us and made sure all of the bills got paid. We spent several Saturdays cataloging materials and organizing all of the resource materials that we ordered.

Helen and I became good friends. We discovered that every time we met, we rejuvenated our enthusiasm for global studies. We "fed" off of each other. We were both excited about starting new projects. I relied on Helen as a resource person and a mentor. I discovered that it made me a better social studies teacher to have someone who could discuss ideas with me and help give me direction in my teaching of social studies. The people on my team change on a yearly basis. That makes it difficult to keep any continuity in our program. Each of the teachers on my team was responsible for certain components of the global social studies that we did. It was hard to teach new teachers about the components, and some of them were not willing to give up the class time to do it. Mavis became busy doing other projects at the university, but Helen and I, along with Robert from Sweden and Mary from Tanzania, have continued to keep our students working together.

We have done service projects together. Helen has visited the classroom of our pen pals in Sweden. She got pen pals from Tanzania for us when she went to visit there. We have presented at several conferences. We have had our students meet to discuss projects we have done together. We have worked together to set up art lessons (related to culture standards) for students in the Tweed Art Museum at the university.

Benefits and Frustrations

I believe the benefits of working together with the university are twofold. We not only have the opportunity to work with older students and benefit from the projects that they bring into my classes, but my students get the opportunity to use the resources that the university has to offer. I believe it also motivates some of my students to want to attend a university when they get older. On one of our first visits to UMD, I overheard one fifth grader tell his mom that he wanted to go to college because the kids there get to wear hats to school and chew gum if they want to. On another of our trips, the father of one of my students arranged for us to have cookies and Kool-Aid in the cafeteria with the university students. It made a big impression on my students.

Students also have become attached to local university sports heroes. On several occasions, we have had some of those students working with us on projects. The university students were wonderful role models for my students. I feel that exposing my students to the university is a big benefit for all of us. I think it is important for university students planning to be teachers to be exposed to school children as much as possible. It is often difficult for them to work in a classroom as much as we want them to, so bringing my students to them seems a logical thing to do. On one visit, Helen had her university students meet with mine to discuss the service-learning projects we had done. We had several groups work together, consisting of five middle school students and five university students. My students told them about their project, their goals for the project, and how they accomplished it. On the walk back to school, we discussed how the groups went, and several of my students asked me why the university students were afraid of them. When I was a student at the university, I, too, remember feeling afraid of being in charge of a group of elementary students. It seems to benefit university students just as much as my students when we get them together.

I have learned to use our university as a valuable resource. Not only have we connected with future educators at the university but we also have met with the University for Seniors. They are senior citizens who take classes at UMD. We have discovered that they have a wealth of historical information, and most of them have time to spend with us. I learned about this resource through my connections at the university.

Personally, the biggest drawback with our collaboration is frustration in trying to share the things I have learned with colleagues. As classroom teachers, we are all very busy. Not everyone is willing or able to give up time to plan trips or to coordinate class times with the university. I think the key is to find a friend to work with because the two of you become committed to helping each other.

A very important aspect of collaboration with the university is to have the support of the administration. The principal that I currently have is very supportive of what we do. My biggest downfall is not keeping him as informed as I should. He is new to the building and not always aware of the programs we are doing, and that is my fault. I recommend making sure that teachers document everything they do and making a copy for the principal. I have not been very good at doing that, and it is something I need to work on.

I teach the social studies component in four rotations in a middle school. A huge challenge for me is knowing where to fit the global emphasis into the sixth grade curriculum. Today, I am responsible for covering certain curriculum requirements in the sixth grade; the pace set by our school district is very demanding. We have the Minnesota graduation standards and must prepare students for standardized testing, which makes the curriculum narrower than before. I believe this is part of the reason colleagues aren't as receptive as I might want them to be. There isn't enough time. I have resolved that problem. I have learned to understand that social studies (with its national curriculum standards) is the study of life and life is global. If we are working on a project for Tanzania, Sweden, or Australia, I know the importance of what we are doing. My students do also. In addition to global standards infused within social studies periods, the social studies standards can provide a framework for and be integrated into all subject areas.[11] I use literacy standards related to data gathering and research and focus them on students' local/global inquiry in social studies. Conclusions drawn from information that is gathered and compared are connected to the social studies curriculum standards. I think my students have done a good job of helping university students understand that also. My hope is that when they start teaching, they will remember the importance of this global infusion.

My advice to other teachers is to get involved with a university and find a friend to work with. The rewards are numerous. Try not to get frustrated . . . and if you do, talk to your friend and keep your administrators informed about what you are doing. It helps to bring a new perspective to all you do in the classroom. It's also a good idea to lobby for monies for teacher travel. Also, I recommend that teachers get on the

Internet. The benefits and rewards of the university and its students are tremendous. This collaboration is one of the most rewarding components of my teaching career.

A Professor Talks to Professors (H.C.)

When the collaboration began, the educational movement in our area schools was toward holistic approaches to teaching and learning. There were classrooms in which children were engaged and learning experiences that recognized the learners' voices in the design of curriculum. At that point, I had had the opportunity to be involved in several international experiences. These included an international collaboration project with student and faculty exchanges and joint research projects with Sweden, an international lecture and research project in Russia, and a teaching and research experience with the Study in England Program available on our campus.

There were also efforts to develop egalitarian partnerships between teachers and university faculty that would more directly connect theory and practice. Many universities were developing school-based connections ranging from action research to jointly created curriculum. I believed that university teacher education programs often started with theory and research information, which is not connected to any teacher education student's experience. Instead of this, I hoped to develop opportunities for practice in exemplary classrooms followed by opportunities to develop socially constructed knowledge about effective social studies teaching practices.

MEMORABLE MOMENTS AND OUTCOMES

When Carol and I first began discussing the possibilities of infusing global perspectives into our university and middle school classes, I was eager to begin. Our basic philosophies and beliefs about teaching and learning were similar. We first generated ideas and traveled together to Thunder Bay, Ontario, Canada, to collect new materials for our resource center. I remember standing in a store in Thunder Bay looking at books, one of which contained a saying that symbolized our work: "A snowstorm begins with a single snowflake."

As the collaboration deepened and the teacher education students in my social studies methods course became engaged with the middle level students, the constructive processes came alive. Some of the reflections of my students (from qualitative analysis of their reflections) reveal some of the impacts of the collaboration:

▶ I feel that having a variety of needs and cultures addressed in learning about social studies will help the world. One way to do this is through intercultural pen pals. I'm using this in my learning centers.
▶ In my class, like in the Woodland class, I will use the Internet to explore social issues and world relations. Students will pose questions and visit businesses and organizations. They will go to nursing homes and interview the elderly. The students will contact key pals in another country and learn another culture from the perspective of a student their own age.

They will follow the inquiry process:

▶ In order for the students to become familiar with people of different cultures, use different sources, and then people of different races, cultures, and ethnicities won't be thought of as "us" and "them."
▶ When teaching elementary social studies, I plan to use a variety of global sources. I believe the more sources that I bring in from different cultures and countries, the more the students will see different and multiple points of view.

More recently, the teacher education students have engaged in threaded discussion linked to my online course syllabus. After the middle level students came to my methods class, they wrote:

▶ I was so impressed by how much the fifth graders knew about Tanzania in Africa. And how excited they were about service-learning. They obviously had learned facts and developed friendships with the children in Bukoba.

▶ The middle level students' work was often thought-provoking: "Do you wish you could live forever? I don't. I think it would get boring. What do you think? Are there many people in Sweden that use drugs? In the United States, there are a lot." (An American student to a Swedish pen pal)

▶ "For everyday wear, we have the same kind of clothes, but more people live in apartments. . . I interviewed my grandmother, and she described the celebration of the New Year in the Hmong culture. Now we also celebrate Christmas. We bring in the tree two days before the holiday." (Conclusions from family interviews)

▶ "Today we made up questions to ask in businesses and organizations. Then my group went to MPL (Minnesota Power and Light). I found out things about technology, the jobs they have, the history, and how they save the environment. They use recycled paper for reports." (Student report from community interviews)

Several teacher education students have returned after graduation to share examples of global and social studies projects that they completed as classroom teachers. They did family history and community books and made connections with schools in other countries as well as different schools in the United States. To complete their books, they conducted investigations using primary sources and resources on the Internet.

The collaboration has improved social studies teaching and learning in the elementary and middle level settings. Yet we are continuing to work to strengthen our collaboration. Peer teaching and service-learning are now the foci of our efforts.

SUPPORTS AND CONSTRAINTS FOR COLLABORATION

Two supports have been most significant to me—shared beliefs and practices about effective social studies teaching and learning and international experience and connections. One of the most positive parts of this collaboration has been the excitement of sharing ideas with Carol, my teacher colleague and friend. No matter what unusual idea we devised, she was always enthusiastic and willing to give it a try. If we were going to conduct interviews with the elders, she helped to locate participants. If teacher education foreign exchange students needed a placement, she offered her classroom for learning experiences. Our enthusiasm for this collaboration has multiplied our energy levels and fed our need for our own professional development and interest in innovation. We have co-created curriculum for both middle and university level students.

Second, international experiences and connections were important in our collaboration. It is very important for teachers to actually visit and live in other countries. The power of living in places where worldviews and life-style practices are very different from one's own creates dissonance and then a deeper ability to understand the perspectives of others. Being in another setting is an excellent backdrop for bringing openness about other peoples and cultures to students.

Two constraints have been challenging—scarcity of resources for travel and changes in professional responsibilities. Although grant monies seem to be available for buying resource materials, it has been difficult to secure adequate funding for travel to other countries. We were able to secure a grant to purchase culture kit materials from Australia; however, this same funding agency would not agree to fund travel expenses. We use e-mail, listserves, chats, and video-conferencing, and they are certainly helpful. However, we continue to believe that teachers' first-hand experience is an important base for virtual experiences.

Because our collaboration has continued over many years, we are now faced with changes in our own professional responsibilities. In both settings (university and public school), we feel pressured to spend more time on mandated learning templates and prescribed learning activities. Nevertheless, we continue our collaboration. We are beginning an extension with sixth graders who are preparing global culture kits and learning experiences for younger learners, materials that will be used by early childhood teacher education students in their social studies teaching. So the next collaborative phase is just beginning. Stay tuned.

Words of Advice

Our work has been well worth the energy expended on it, and we close with some last words of advice:

Helen: Our collaboration has been one of the highlights of my work in teacher education. I wonder why . . .

Carol: I have found that over the years, working with you and the university rejuvenates me. I get all excited when I ask you if something will work, and you tell me, "Sure, let's try it."

Helen: We've done so many things and even created a local/global investigation model out of our work together. I think it's more profound when it grows from our lives as teachers . . .

Carol: I have discovered through our model what the "heart" of social studies education is and the benefits of the local/global investigation and exchange.

Helen: What advice should we give to others who would like to create such an adventure?

Carol: Use the resources that are available to you. Future teachers at the university have wonderful, creative ideas. They can add the spark and you can add the experience. Together, it is a wonderfully explosive situation. Let everyone know how important it is to provide monies for teachers to experience global situations. Every experience comes back into the classroom with tremendous benefits to our educational system. Get on the Internet and meet some other teachers!

Helen: And have fun together constantly creating and critiquing new ways of teaching and learning social studies including dialogue with teachers and students in other countries.

NOTES

1. Helen Carlson and Carol Holm, "Children's Center for Global Understanding," *Southern Social Studies Journal* 23 (1999): 3-10.
2. Helen Carlson, L. Grover, and D. Anderson, *Growing Up in My Family* (Duluth, Minn.: Duluth Children's Museum, 1994).
3. National Council for the Social Studies, *Expectations of Excellence: Curriculum Standards for Social Studies* (Washington, D.C.: Author, 1994).
4. Helen Carlson and Carol Holm, "Children's Center for Global Understanding," *Southern Social Studies Journal* 23 (1999): 3-10; Helen Carlson and Carol Holm, "Diversity and Global Studies: Elementary Children's Investigations, *Social Studies and the Young Learner* 11, no. 3 (1999): 6-10; Helen Carlson, Carol Holm, R. Krook, and M. Whiteman, "Promoting Effective Citizenship: A Local Interactive Investigation Model," *The Social Educator* 15 (1997): 26-29 (also a paper presented at the International Social Studies Conference, Sydney, Australia); Helen Carlson, "Technological Catalysts in Understanding Culture" (Paper presented at the National Council for the Social Studies Annual Conference, Cincinnati, Ohio, 1997).
5. Merry M. Merryfield and Connie S. White, "Issues Centered Global Education," in *Handbook on Teaching Social Issues*, NCSS Bulletin 93, eds. Ronald W. Evans and David Warren Saxe (Washington, D.C.: National Council for the Social Studies, 1996): 177-188.
6. Benjamin R. Barber, "Challenges to the Common Good in the Age of Globalism," *Social Education* 64 (2000): 8-13; John J. Cogan, David Grossman, and Mei-hui Lei, "Citizenship: The Democratic Imagination in a Global/Local Context," *Social Education* 64 (2000): 48-52; Walter C. Parker, Akira Ninomiya, and John Cogan, "Educating World Citizens: Toward Multinational Curriculum Development," *American Educational Research Journal* 36 (1999): 117-145.
7. Carlos F. Diaz, Byron G. Massialas, and John A. Xanthopoulos, *Global Perspectives for Educators* (Boston, Mass.: Allyn and Bacon, 1998).
8. James A. Banks and Cherry A. McGee Banks, *Multicultural Education: Issues and Perspectives* (New York: John Wiley, 1999).
9. National Council for the Social Studies, *Expectations of Excellence*.
10. M. Cochran-Smith and S. L. Lytle, "Relationships of Knowledge and Practice: Teacher Learning in Communities," in *Review of Research in Education*, eds. A. Iran-Nejad and P. D. Pearson (Washington, D.C.: American Educational Research Association, 1999), 249-306.
11. Virginia A. Atwood, Margit McGuire, and M. Pat Nickell, "In the Soup: Integrating and Correlating Social Studies with Other Curriculum Areas," *Social Studies and the Young Learner* 2 (1989): 19-22; Janet Alleman and Jere Brophy, "Is Curriculum Integration a Boon or a Threat to Social Studies Elementary Education?" *Social Education* 57 (1993): 287-91.

Developing a Service Ethic Together: A Middle School/University Partnership

Eight

ANGELA M. HARWOOD
CRISTINA ALLSOP
LYNN HERINK
CALLIE HART

The Scene: Lisa Finds a Reason

CAST OF CHARACTERS

▶ Lisa, an unmotivated eighth grade student
▶ Callie, her enthusiastic core teacher

LISA'S BEDROOM, 7:00 A.M. IN JANUARY
The alarm cracks the gray silence of the Pacific Northwest winter. Groaning, Lisa slaps the snooze button, rolling to bury her head under the covers. "Ugh! I can't believe it's time for another boring day. Why do I have to go to school, anyway?"

FAIRHAVEN MIDDLE SCHOOL, CALLIE HART'S CORE CLASSROOM
Callie (in her chirpy morning voice) says, "Listen up class! Today I have some big news—it's time to begin our Project Connect service-learning unit. We will start by defining service-learning and brainstorming ways we can help our community . . ."

Lisa raises her head dreamily, giving her teacher a skeptical look. "Hmm, I'm sure this won't be that great." Later, in her journal, she writes, "I don't really see myself as a community servant outside of school because I have a busy life, I'm lazy, and I don't feel a very strong need to go out and clean up in my spare time."

LISA'S BEDROOM, FIVE MONTHS LATER
The alarm rings out on a bright June morning. Lisa slaps the snooze button out of habit, then remembers that it is Wednesday, the day she visits Mt. Baker Care Center and her friends there. She explodes from bed, now looking forward to school. Her final journal entry reflects her change of attitude:

> I guess this experience has helped me understand how lonely old people are that are
> in nursing homes, and to understand what it must be like for them. I think it may
> have made me a little happier, giving me something to do. Also, it's given me a
> reason to go to school on Wednesdays. Before it was just like every other boring,
> pointless day, and I didn't want to get up in the morning.

Although the narrative scenes above are an extrapolation of one student's experience, the reflection entries and the changes we observed in this young woman are authentic. Her experience, and those of her peers and the university students who worked with them, have convinced us to continue our collaborative service-learning approach. In this chapter, we describe an ongoing project in which an education professor and her preservice teachers at Western Washington University work with eighth grade core teachers and their students at Fairhaven Middle School. The project features strong academic components for both university and eighth grade students that are designed to meet state and national learning standards while students provide sustained, needs-centered service to community organizations. In this truly collaborative effort, we think of the students at both levels as "ours"—and share responsibility for the learning of each of our groups jointly. In the following sections we share our perspectives on how this approach improves social studies education, the process of our collaboration, student outcomes, and our individual perspectives on our collaborative journey.

How Collaborative Service-Learning Improves Social Studies Instruction

Educators who teach kindergarten through college levels are expressing interest in service-learning as a promising teaching strategy. Our particular interest in this approach is based on our belief that service-learning can improve social studies instruction by offering students the opportunity to practice "hands-on" civics. By engaging our students in the study of real issues in community-based settings, we are providing them with relevant and exciting learning experiences that serve to strengthen their capabilities as civic beings.[1] Furthermore, by including key elements of the service-learning approach in our classes—including reflection and other assignments that encourage our students to process and apply their learning—we help them to engage in critical thinking and decision making. An emerging body of research identifies the power of service-learning for both middle school students and preservice teachers and provides compelling reasons for engaging our students in service-learning projects.[2] In creating our collaborative service-learning approach, we join other educators who are motivated by reasons that directly coincide with social studies objectives. According to the U. S. Department of Education,[3] educators use service-learning to "help students become more active members of the community" (53 percent), "increase student knowledge and under-standing of the community" (51 percent), "meet real community needs and/or foster relationships between the school and community" (48 percent), "encourage student altruism or caring for others" (46 percent), "improve student personal and social development" (26 percent), and "teach critical thinking and problem solving skills" (19 percent). Each of these goals fits nicely with our own personal goals for both our middle school students and preservice teachers.

Through our collaborative service-learning project, we have been able to meet the goals outlined by national organizations and our own state curriculum standards. Service-learning provides the ideal frame-work for curriculum that addresses citizenship guidelines outlined by National Council for the Social Studies (NCSS) and the Center for Civic Education.[4] Additionally, service-learning can address the goals set forth in the National Middle School Association's publication *This We Believe*,[5] as well as goals outlined at the local level by many middle schools.[6]

Having a direct impact on the education of current eighth grade students is only one focus of our collaborative effort. We also believe that by engaging preservice teachers in service-learning and giving them an opportunity to experience the instructional approach firsthand, they may be more likely to try innovative instruction in their future classrooms. This coincides with a growing interest nationally in service-learning as a transformative pedagogy for preservice teachers.[7] Recent publications of professional standards of teacher education emphasize the importance of providing teacher certification candidates with extended opportunities to work with youth.[8] Several other rationales for using service-learning in teacher education programs have been developed, including helping students question existing policies and assumptions about classroom practice, providing experiences with learning strategies consistent with educational reforms, and developing sensitivity to multicultural populations and societal needs.[9]

Our Collaborative Process

Our collaborative service-learning project, titled "Project Connect," has been growing now for almost three years. We initiated our formal collaboration on this project during the fall of 1998, although several prior events led to its development. During the fall of 1997, Callie Hart completed her student teaching internship under the direction of Angie Harwood. During her internship, she designed and implemented a similar service-learning project in her classroom with the support of her cooperating teacher and supervisor. The following year, Tina Allsop was placed at the same school, where Callie had now obtained a full-time position, and they decided to implement an extended version of the same project together. The idea for the collaboration was initiated (en route to the NCSS conference in Anaheim, California) when Tina expressed interest in implementing a service-learning component and Angie identified this as an opportunity to engage her preservice teachers in the project.

During the spring of 1999, 145 eighth grade students from Tina and Callie's classes engaged in this project with sixteen preservice teachers; during the spring of 2000, a third student teacher, Paula Liburd, teamed with Callie, and their 135 eighth graders worked with thirty-five preservice teachers. Lynn Herink has also joined the collaborative team in assisting with the details of the project addressed at the university. An overview of the project specifics and how our team has worked together to implement them follows.

The university students involved in this project enroll in a course titled "Seminar in Service-Learning," and the eighth grade students attend a two-period integrated social studies and language arts core class. In both university and public school classrooms, we identify community problems, research current events, gather varying perspectives on issues, and explore public policy using print and Internet resources. Students choose to focus their service-learning experience in one of five theme-based areas: (a) working with the environment, (b) working with youth, (c) working with the elderly, (d) working with animals, and (e) working in social service settings. Students then establish service action plans and spend one two-hour block of time in community agencies each week for six weeks. We have worked with more than twenty community agencies and organizations throughout the course of this project. Preservice teachers transport eighth grade teams to their service sites and engage in service activities along with them. Reflective discussions are held on the return trips to school, and are followed with journal writing completed by both groups. The preservice teachers read and respond to the journal entries written by the eighth graders and use them as formative feedback in deciding how they will handle instruction on site each week. The eighth grade students complete a final project comprising both individual and group components.

The specifics of the project emerged through continuous collaborative planning. We met together as a planning team frequently during the months preceding the project to work out the details of curriculum for both middle school and university courses. During the weeks when our students are doing service in the community, we meet at the school weekly to trouble-shoot and discuss project details. We have learned that clear communication and a clear definition of the timeline and task structure are absolutely essential. The following chart provides a summary of the individual and shared responsibilities required to make this collaborative approach workable.

Since the pilot project, which occurred from January to June of 1999, the collaborative team has continued to work together. We have been selected as partners to work on a federal Contextual Teaching and Learning Grant issued to the University of Washington, and will be working to refine our model for dissemination through that group. We have conducted an in-service training program for the local school district based on this project, and have presented it at the annual meetings of the National Middle School Association, NCSS, and National Youth Leadership Council.

Student Outcomes Resulting from the Collaboration

We began collecting evidence of project outcomes during our collaboration last year. To assess the outcomes, we relied primarily on an analysis of the written reflections from both the eighth grade students and preservice teachers and pretest and post-test questionnaires given to the preservice teachers. We found that the eighth grade students gained a knowledge of issues, learned about the responsibilities of citizenship, increased their communication skills, and absorbed "unintended" knowledge as well. Preservice teachers learned about community issues, teaching and the pedagogical approach of service-learning, and eighth graders.

Eighth Grade Outcomes

Throughout the project, eighth grade students responded to different weekly questions in reflection journals. Many of the journal entries included comments about how much the students were learning about the issues related to their specific service sites. In addition, by learning about the issues related to their service category, students were able to see how they could fill a need, both now and in the future: "My experience made me more aware, in many ways, that there were problems going on in Bellingham" (Nicole). "We have learned a lot about what makes a healthy stream so we have the knowledge and appreciation to keep streams healthy when we grow up" (Dylan).

Chart 1: **Project Connect Timeline and Responsibilities Chart**

DATE	FAIRHAVEN MIDDLE SCHOOL RESPONSIBILITIES
JANUARY	• Identify essential learning requirements to be met • Meet with district service-learning coordinator • Administer pretest to eighth graders • Introduce service-learning in core classes • Brainstorm issue topics with students and identify student interest areas • Identify theme areas • Begin current issues discussions
FEBRUARY	• Continue current events discussions • Plan congressional simulation
MARCH	• Do congressional simulation • Research service-learning topics on the web • Host guest panel of experts in topic areas • Identify parent volunteers to chaperone at sites
APRIL	• Begin service-learning field activities • Do weekly reflective writing • Create final project rubrics • Identify and work on final project topics
MAY	• Continue service activities and reflection • Present final projects • Administer posttest • Celebrate!

SHARED RESPONSIBILITIES	WESTERN WASHINGTON UNIVERSITY RESPONSIBILITIES
• Define project goals • Meet with Center for Service-Learning (CSL) to describe project • Call potential sites; work with CSL to identify and contact others	• Meet with Center for Service-Learning to initiate project contact • Construct pretest • Visit potential sites • Create packet to distribute to sites describing project • Create curriculum for Seminar in Service-Learning course
• Continue contacting sites	• Research web sites to use with eighth graders • Pre-visit sites
• Begin mapping site chart with times and students who will go to each site • Distribute and collect district volunteer forms • Create master schedule of volunteers, sites, and students • Create individual site sheets with names of contact people, students, driver, driving directions, and emergency phone numbers • Identify and contact potential guest speakers	• Promote service-learning opportunity in university classes • Identify university student participants • Confirm with sites • Begin service-learning seminar, spring quarter • Administer pretest to university students
• Greet volunteers and help them find the classroom • Introduce drivers and students; coordinate departure from school • Visit sites	• Continue seminar • Transport students to and from sites and provide debriefings • Do weekly reflective writing • Troubleshoot and problem solve • Check progress with sites • Read and respond to eighth graders' journal entries • Create post-tests
• Plan final celebration	• Continue service activities and reflection • Attend project presentations and celebration • Administer post-tests

Overwhelmingly, students expressed a sense of responsibility for their part in the community: "This service-learning experience has changed me by helping me to recognize when and where people need help. I have a different view of our community" (Emily). Lindsay echoed Emily's comment:

> I have learned that I can help those who need it. I have also learned that what one person can do, really will make a difference. My help will always be needed if I am willing to give it.

Not only did students learn about their community, but they also wanted the community to learn about them: "I want people to realize that not all kids are self-centered and troublesome" (Betsy).

Students also discovered firsthand how necessary communication skills are. Working with those both substantially younger and older than themselves challenged many of our students to develop new ways of communicating. Dan, a student who worked with young children at a community day care center, learned a whole new language of "Littlekidspeak," while another student reported the challenge of communicating with nursing home residents:

> I believe that this service-learning group takes a lot of patience. I say this because you have to be able to sit still and keep interest in what the resident you are talking to is saying. Because of their old age it takes longer to get it out, and it's a dramatic change because all teenagers tend to talk extremely fast (Megan).

The students themselves recognized how their communication skills changed through their experience at various sites. "I also learned that I know how to converse with people and can run a conversation in a way that I never thought possible" (Andrea). "Through service-learning, I have developed a higher level of communicating to strangers. It is easier to make conversation with people I'm unfamiliar with" (Jacob).

Some of the most inspiring growth fell into the "unintended learning" category. For instance, students broke down stereotypes that could not be adequately addressed inside a classroom. "I learned that we aren't much different from homeless people. I learned that I have thought of homeless people as below normal society and not just economically but in all ways. I learned that this simply was not true" (Justin).

The advantage of journals was that they showed growth over time. For example, a handful of students began the project as skeptics. By the end of the six weeks, almost all of those skeptics were believers:

> My view of my service-learning project before I started was that it was a waste of time. After a couple of weeks though, I realized that our class made a dramatic effect on the slope of the hill. I will continue to volunteer because I enjoyed the experience and I found it to be fun. When I look back on my life, I want to be able to say that I made the world a better place (James).

The students of Project Connect say it best: "All in all, service-learning is something everyone should participate in" (Jenny).

Preservice Teacher Outcomes

The preservice teachers also exhibited a broad range of learning as a direct result of this collaborative experience. An analysis of pre- and posttest questionnaires and preservice teachers' weekly reflections revealed that they learned many valuable lessons. Preservice teachers involved in this project learned about community issues, and increased their use of a variety of media sources, including newspapers, radio, and computers for news of current events. Post-test responses indicated that students were able to articulate more clearly their understanding of issues in a variety of topic areas. For many, the issues were brought to life by their experience:

Salmon becoming an endangered species seems very real now. We could see the importance of our actions and how each person that contributes makes a difference. Also, that
it is important for each of us to help out and be active in these issues. (Kyle)

Our hope is that this increased knowledge of issues and their impact on the community will contribute to future teachers' ability to teach their students about the importance of current events.

Students also reflected on what they learned about teaching as a result of the service-learning project.
Some of the lessons were about how to engage students in discussion; others learned about the logistics and
preparation involved in administering a community-based learning program. Many gained a greater
understanding of the complexity of service-learning, and about the power it holds as a pedagogical approach. One student was straightforward in her statement: "The main thing I gained was an understanding
of service-learning, both in theory and practice, and how to implement it in my own classroom in the
future" (Ellen). Another expressed feelings shared by other students:

I have learned the most about what a huge impact this type of project can have on the
students, their long-term education, their outlook on life and attitudes towards those in
need, the community's perceptions of youth, and myself. (Marcie, final reflection)

Finally, working intensively with students at service sites and having conversations while traveling to
and from those sites gave the preservice teachers a wonderful opportunity to learn more about middle
school students. Many were pleasantly surprised to find that middle school students were generally happy-
apparently, this contradicted what they remembered about their own experiences from that age. The
following quote is an example:

Honestly, the most important thing I learned is that middle school is not that bad. I have some
of the absolute worst memories of middle school, the eighth grade in particular. This experience helped me see eighth graders as real people and not demons! (Adam, final reflection)

Collaborating Teachers' Perspective (C.A. and C.H.)

The decision to embark on the journey of service-learning was one that we as teachers made because we
wanted to provide our future students with relevant learning experiences. The cry of "Why do we have to do
this? This is boring!" was not one that we wanted to hear in our classrooms. The idea of giving students an
opportunity to make a difference in their community while applying their new knowledge of issues to
classroom curriculum was one that we found exciting and worthwhile. This initial excitement provided the
foundation for a project that could have collapsed had we not had a three-fold commitment to the program
we were developing. First came a commitment to honoring the core philosophy of service-learning in our
planning. Second was a commitment to our collaborative relationship. Finally, and perhaps most important,
was a commitment to the details.

The foundation of any service-learning project should be a commitment to the basic tenets of the
methodology. Service opportunities should be organized with the intent of serving a real need in the community, while at the same time allowing for students to share in the planning process. Giving students the
freedom to serve in an area that they find interesting and worthwhile creates an immediate willingness on the
part of the student to participate. We recommend encouraging students to brainstorm potential service sites
and discuss with them the need for service in these areas. Teachers need to give students time to think about
their choice of a site, reminding them that the choice should be based on their interests and not on the
interests of their friends. As students see that their ideas are valued, their enthusiasm will continue to grow.

Just as students should be involved in the planning process, they must also be given a variety of
opportunities to reflect on the journey upon which they have embarked. Oftentimes, students may be

experiencing things in the field that are new and exciting but possibly uncomfortable as well. It is important that students have a place to make their voices heard, both verbally and in writing.

Talking with classmates and preservice teachers about what they've seen and heard is an appropriate verbal reflection. A journal allows for quiet and unedited written reflection. Carefully selected reflection prompts provide students with focus and guide them through their experience. In our project, the reflection prompts varied from week to week and allowed students to recount what they had done at service sites, as well as consider career opportunities, think about what their actions meant to others, and further explore issues related to their sites. We found that open-ended questions ("What five things stuck in your mind about today?") gave students freedom to express what they were thinking and feeling, and more directed questions ("What have you learned about career opportunities related to your site?") encouraged students to focus their thinking on more specific topics. Reflection opportunities ensure that all students are able to bring closure to their weekly visits and to prepare them for the next set of adventures.

A commitment to the collaborative relationship is the scaffolding that keeps the program standing. Because collaboration requires commitment to partners, it is necessary to carefully consider the people with whom you may be working before you take on the project. Without trust, frequent and open communication, and the ability to delegate responsibility, a program will fall under the weight of an incompatible working team. Indeed, one of the most rewarding elements of our project was the opportunity to collaborate. Working with a team made the task seem surmountable and brought vitality to the planning that is missing when working independently.

Partnerships formed within the educational world are vital, but service-learning programs also necessitate partnerships with community agencies. When working with site coordinators, we recommend that teachers encourage them to consider that young people need structure. Both the agency and the students' experience will be more successful if there are organized tasks waiting for the students upon arrival. As your project progresses, ask for comments and suggestions from site contacts. Likewise, students can be a valuable source of feedback. Teachers can use the information garnered from both sources to evaluate whether the partnership is a viable one.

A program built with a commitment to service-learning and partnerships is completed with a commitment to the details. This commitment is one that requires time and patience. As planning begins, all logistical details must be considered. Inquiries must be made into your district's approval processes. Field trip permission forms, private vehicle insurance waivers, videotaping releases, and fingerprinting for parent volunteers were all things we needed to consider.

As these details are accomplished, teachers need to begin trouble shooting potential problems. Programs that rely on a variety of people face a myriad of potential problems. For example, if a driver cancels at the last minute, it is necessary to have plans for finding a back-up driver immediately. It is a good idea to consider having one teacher who "floats" and does not have a specific commitment during each time period and can drive if needed. This plan also frees up that teacher to travel from site to site checking in on students when all the drivers are available.

Another potential problem is student misbehavior in the field. Teachers need to remind students that when they go out into the community, they are not only representing themselves but also their class, their school, and the public's perception of teenagers in general. If a student is behaving inappropriately, teachers need to decide quickly how to handle the situation. We arranged to have one teacher in a classroom back at the school who would supervise students who were unable to control themselves in the field. Fortunately, this wasn't a regular occurrence, but provisions need to be made nonetheless.

Once these commitments have been made, teachers can prepare to embark on a journey that is rewarding, exhausting, and motivating. The program must have a strong foundation, sturdy supports, and careful planning. Just as the commitment made to the program must be threefold, ultimately, the rewards are threefold as well. Students will succeed both in the classroom and in the community as they apply what they have learned through the experience. Community agencies will appreciate the work of the students.

Teachers will be reenergized by the program's success, making the endless planning sessions, frantic calls to missing drivers, and countless other adventures worth it in the end.

University Collaborators' Perspective (A.M.H. and L.H.)

In the course of our collaborative venture, we have learned many lessons about supporting teachers in their instructional efforts and how to manage a project as unwieldy as this one successfully. Working with the team on this project and refining and redeveloping curriculum for it each year has given us extra motivation to reflect on our practice as teacher educators and to discuss it with the team. We have learned a lot about the collaborative process, important elements of teacher education programs, and the means for building support for collaborative ventures through our work together.

If we had to choose one element that was critical to our success, it would be the shared goals we hold for our students. In developing your own collaborative relationship with K-12 teachers, a primary consideration should be finding teachers who share your educational philosophy and agree with the instructional techniques you will use to carry it out. Our collaborative team was dedicated to providing real-life experiences to help our students learn, and we individually and mutually had chosen service-learning as an approach that can provide a deep and rich set of experiences for our students. Although we have specific goals related to K-12 and teacher education learning outcomes, we all agree on the goals for both levels. This agreement contributes to our students' mastery of those goals and gives us a centering focus that has enabled us to carry on through rough spots in the collaborative process. In addition, similar working styles among our team members helped us to work together effectively.

Another essential thing we have learned is the power of exposing preservice teachers to professional development opportunities while they are in their education programs. Although both Callie and Tina had learned about service-learning through studying it in education courses, it was taking them to professional conferences where they were exposed to different models of service-learning that encouraged them to try it in their own classrooms. These former students have now presented their work on this project at national conferences-and we are firmly convinced that the early exposure to state-level conferences and opportunities to present their work locally led to this further professional development.

A third lesson for us is the need to support preservice teachers throughout their participation in the project. Working with small groups of eighth graders at sites very different from school classrooms proved to be a challenging venture for some of our students. They needed a lot of time to process the experience as a group and to work through questions and concerns they had about the project, themselves as teachers, and working with middle school students. The reflective writing and seminar discussions worked well for this, but individual conferencing time for students who were experiencing difficulty was also vital.

For those who would like to establish similar collaborative projects with K-12 teaching partners, there are many issues to think about. You need to garner support from both your university and school district for the projects. Developing this "buy-in" initially will help you when the inevitable challenges to innovative approaches are mounted. In our case, we had the support we needed when parents questioned taking their children out into the community, when we were challenged about having university students transporting eighth graders, and when the value of service-learning was questioned. Without supportive administrators, it would have been much more difficult to address these challenges.

Finally, any collaborative relationship necessitates clear lines of communication and carefully outlined task structures if it is to be successful. We met frequently, used charts and graphs to outline what needed to be done and who would do it, and communicated often over the phone and by e-mail. Following through on team commitments is a must for those who want to work collaboratively, and doing so will help the team to develop a sense of trust in each individual.

Summary

We learned a tremendous amount in these two years of our collaboration. Making the collaboration work for both levels of students required careful and thoughtful planning and a high level of attention to detail.

Because service-learning always presents logistical challenges, we found that our collaboration improved our ability to think through the many details required to make the project successful. We found that the learning for both groups of students was enhanced through their interaction with one another-each group brought a unique perspective to the project and helped the other to reflect on events and experiences from a different vantage point. The preservice teachers provided positive adult role models for eighth grade students, and the actions of the eighth grade students gave the preservice teachers a heightened appreciation for and understanding of the capabilities of middle level learners. Either of us could have conducted service-learning projects without the other, but we found that our collaborative effort yielded richer rewards, gained from the interaction of our students.

NOTES

1. Rahima Wade, "Beyond Charity: Service Learning for Social Justice," *Social Studies and the Young Learner* 12, no. 4 (2000): 6-9.
2. Dan Conrad and Diane Hedin, "School-Based Community Service: What We Know From Research and Theory," *Phi Delta Kappan* 72 (June 1991): 754-757; *Service-Learning: Every Child A Citizen* (Denver, Colo.: Education Commission of the States, 1999); Diana Hess, "Violence Prevention and Service-Learning," *Social Education* 61, no. 5 (1997): 279-281; Susan Siegel, "Teachers of Service-Learning," in *Community Service-Learning: A Guide to Including Service in the Public School Curriculum*, ed. Rahima Wade (Albany: State University of New York Press, 1997); Rahima Wade, "ProSocial Studies: Curriculum Concerns," *Social Studies and the Young Learner* 8, no. 4, (1996): 18-20; Rahima Wade and David Saxe, "Community Service-Learning in the Social Studies: Historical Roots, Empirical Evidence, Critical Issues," *Theory and Research in Social Education* 24, no. 4 (1996): 331-359.
3. U.S. Department of Education, *Service-Learning and Community Service in K-12 Public Schools* (Washington, D.C.: Author, 1999).
4. Center for Civic Education, *National Standards for Civics Education* (Calabasas, Calif.: Author, 1994); National Council for the Social Studies, *Expectations of Excellence: Curriculum Standards for Social Studies* (Washington, D.C.: Author, 1994).
5. National Middle School Association, *This We Believe: Developmentally Responsive Middle Level Schools* (Columbus, Ohio: Author, 1991).
6. C. E. Fertman, G. P. White, and L. J. White, *Service Learning in the Middle School: Building a Culture of Service* (Columbus, Ohio: National Middle School Association, 1996).
7. J. A. Erickson and J. B. Anderson, eds., *Learning With the Community: Concepts and Models for Service-Learning in Teacher Education* (Washington, D.C.: American Association for Higher Education, 1997).
8. National Middle School Association, *NCATE-Approved Curriculum Guidelines* (Columbus, Ohio: Author, 1994).
9. Rahima Wade, "Service-Learning in Preservice Teacher Education," in *Community Service-Learning: A Guide to Including Service in the Public School Curriculum*, ed. Rahima Wade (Albany: State University of New York Press, 1997).

Resources Supporting Service-Learning

Close-Up Foundation
www.closeup.org
800-CLOSE-UP

Constitutional Rights Foundation
www.crf-usa.org
213-287-5590

Corporation for National Service
www.nationalservice.org
202-606-5000

National Service-Learning Clearinghouse
www.nicsl.coled.umn.edu
800-808-SERV

National Youth Leadership Council
1910 West County Road B
St. Paul, MN 55113-1337
www.nylc.org
651-631-3672

Alliance for Service-Learning in Education Reform
One Massachusetts Avenue, NW, Suite 700
Washington, DC 20001
202-336-7026

Community Service Learning Center
333 Bridge Street, Suite 8
Springfield, MA 01108
413-734-6857

Public Achievement: Collaboration, Action, and Civic Education

Nine

JOSEPH KUNKEL
CLARK JOHNSON
HEATHER BAKKE
JASON MILLER

The Scene

As Thursday lunch ends at Dakota Meadows Middle School in North Mankato, Minnesota, hundreds of seventh and eighth graders tumble back to their afternoon classes. A large van pulls up and out jump a dozen university undergraduates and their political science professor. After a quick check-in at the office, they disperse throughout the building. For the next forty minutes, each university student will coach a team of middle school students. Even though they call themselves coaches and teams, this is no game; the activity is practical democracy. The university students head teams of middle school students who are participating in a civic organization, Public Achievement (PA).

The professor travels throughout the building checking in quickly with each team. In one classroom, Teens for the Environment meets with a custodian to plan a lunch waste-recycling program. In the computer center, a teen pregnancy team works on its abstinence web site. In the teachers' lounge, loud boys who want to legalize fireworks critique their letters to the local newspaper. In a hallway, the Tobacco Hackers design a certificate to award to nonsmoking restaurants. In the lunchroom, three teams meet trying to figure out how to realize their dream of a new teen center. The child abuse prevention team finishes a poster advertising Abuse Awareness Day. The End Racism teams is with the principal videotaping a TV public service announcement. The Pet Patrol is disappointed, wondering why no one is bringing items for its Humane Society supply drive. The Paper Pixies group is creating a school newspaper in a school that had none.

The bell rings and the period ends. The weary university students straggle into the conference room for a thirty-minute debriefing meeting with the professor. Today, a teacher sits in, listening, offering suggestions, and encouraging students to reflect on issues they studied in their Tuesday seminar. They write a few notes in their journals and head for the van. Some are quiet and worn, while others are giddy, laughing about "their kids" as they ride home from another day in the toughest course they've taken so far.

At Dakota Meadows Middle School, students form citizen action teams around issues of their choice with Minnesota State University students serving as coaches. The university undergraduates study democracy in a political science course that provides a reflective, theoretical, and practical context for a rich mix of experiences with democratic action. Together, the middle school and university students create an incubator for community organizing and action. They adopt internal rules, write mission statements, set goals, and research their particular issue or problem. They try to implement actions or projects to address their issue. They evaluate and learn from their experience.

Center for Democracy and Citizenship

The Center for Democracy and Citizenship is part of the national Public Achievement network whose headquarters is eighty miles away at the University of Minnesota's Center for Democracy and Citizenship. The center publishes a coaches' guide for PA. It connects us with visionary activists and educators trying to implement and improve PA at thirty to forty sites in the Midwest. Its university students attend at least one coach conference at the center, and some organize workshop sessions. Its middle school students also have attended the large kickoff events, youth conferences, and year-end celebrations organized with the center. In this way, students experience PA as a national movement and share stories with people of various ages and backgrounds.[1]

Improving Social Studies and Civic Education

A variety of surveys show high levels of distrust in government, disinterest in political events, and lack of attention to the news. The Final Report of the National Commission on Civic Renewal produced a particularly thorough discussion of these developments and also some signs for hope, for along with anti-political attitudes, there are stirring examples of youthful idealism.[2] Many youth are involved in service through schools, churches, and other organizations. Let's take a look at three models of citizenship education and how they relate to these trends.

I. CIVICS

Civic education usually means that students learn about the Constitution, the legislative process, and the role of interest groups, parties, and elections. Typically, this learning is done through a textbook-based curriculum, and may include in-class or extracurricular simulations such as Boys' State, Girls' State, or Youth in Government. This model conveys valuable information, but its limitation is the implication that democracy is the work of public officials and a few hard-core political activists.

II. SERVICE

An alternative vision of citizenship is volunteer or public service.[3] Scouts are encouraged to "do a good turn daily." Church groups do service projects and go on mission trips. Many schools require service or offer service-learning courses. All of these efforts aim to overcome the selfishness in our culture and generate a spirit of empathy, involvement, and caring. They teach the valuable lesson that the good citizen is responsible and caring. The limitation is that while involvement is encouraged, it avoids politics and controversy.

III. PUBLIC WORK

A third model conceptualizes citizenship as public work.[4] When citizens work collectively to build and maintain their communities, they are taking charge of their future. It is work because it is important and difficult, and requires skills that can be learned. The work is public in that it is visible and open, concerns the larger population, and is done by the public, not just by public officials and political elites.

Democracy is more than a way to elect government officials or demand rights and services. Learning about democracy involves more than rote memory of government structures. It requires both the development of skills and a change in consciousness that comes from practical experience and theoretical reflection. The public work approach recognizes self-interest as a powerful motive to participation. With self-interest comes the controversy, differences, and need for compromise that citizens bring to the public arena.

Neither of the first two models adequately conveys the value of politics. Students of civics may still identify politics with deceit and manipulation. Service is virtuous involvement, but may not confront power and controversy. The public work model bridges the gap between government courses and service-learning experiences, teaching the value and idealism of politics and the pragmatism and craft of public problem solving.

Public Achievement is based on this conceptual model. Students don't simply study the founding fathers; they become the founders of their own small, democratic groups. Students choose public issues and problems that arise out of their own experience and interests. They are not pretending or practicing; they are doing real public work. Because of this, they show a remarkable degree of passion and are usually highly motivated. What students do feels real and important. They make a difference.

Public Achievement and Social Studies

According to National Council for the Social Studies (NCSS), "The primary purpose of social studies is to help young people develop the ability to make informed and reasoned decisions for the public good as citizens of a culturally diverse, democratic society in an interdependent world."[5] The learning objectives of PA make real the aims of social studies as defined by NCSS. The objectives of PA are the same for both university and middle school students. Participants do the following:

- Become more motivated, get involved, and develop an increased civic responsibility.
- Feel a sense of empowerment, thus becoming more optimistic about their potential to influence public events.
- Develop political skills and become more able to use practical techniques of influence.
- Better understand political concepts such as citizenship, power, democracy, diversity, and interest.

Public Achievement is perhaps most powerful in its authenticity. When students experience educational opportunities that are real and valuable to them, they hold onto what they learn. With authentic learning, students not only retain content material but also experience a challenging thinking process. They struggle to resolve complex issues that have no clear cut answer.[6] Once students in PA decide what issues to address, they start planning and working toward solutions. The solutions may not even be attainable by the team, but students experience the challenge of following that elusive pathway to a personally important political goal.

While working toward their goals, students become engaged in a variety of activities through which they practice and refine their public skills. By year's end, our students are able to name a diverse set of skills that they have acquired as a result of PA. In a written evaluation of the program, middle school students state that they have learned how to:

- Speak in front of people.
- Cooperate with other people.
- Plan a long-term project.
- Introduce themselves to people.
- Get others interested in an issue.
- Interview a person over the phone for a survey.
- Plan a budget.

When the middle school students were asked what they liked about PA, many of them offered responses that reflected feelings of empowerment and community involvement: "It's cool that kids have a say in our community." "Most people think that teens are just lazy, but not in this program; we are getting things done." "We can actually change the world into a better place." "It proves that kids are as important as anybody else is and that we can make a difference."

The students' progress is not lost on their coaches. "At our second to last meeting, I sat down and had a talk with the group about what members learned. They were using words like freedom, improvement, influence, community, and power. I found this incredible."

EDUCATING TOMORROW'S SOCIAL STUDIES TEACHERS

Public Achievement is also an experiment in teacher training since most of our coaches are studying to be social studies teachers. They develop a more sophisticated, yet practical understanding of democracy and become better prepared to be active democratic citizens. One coach wrote in her journal, "I think that this class has made me a better citizen because now I am more willing to get involved in politics to try to better the community." They also become aware of the developmental abilities of teenagers and learn how to motivate students. They inevitably compare the active, student-centered, and democratic pedagogy of PA with a more standard approach. One university student wrote,

> I will be student teaching in the fall, and this was a great opportunity to experiment
> and experience dealing with students on my own. I now feel I can design a class-
> room and teach a curriculum which will help students gain the skills essential to
> become socially responsible.

In the next section, we explore the nature of the collaboration, focusing on the relationships among educators and between middle school and university students. Finally, we give some examples of the actions and projects undertaken by PA teams.

THE PUBLIC ACHIEVEMENT SCHOOL YEAR

Middle school students apply for PA in the spring, about the same time university students are registering for the class. By September, we need to adjust the middle school enrollment to match the expected number of coaches. We aim for an average team size of around six or seven. In recent years, we have involved approximately 180 middle school students and twenty-six to thirty university student coaches. The university citizenship class begins with about eight hours of orientation and preparation. University students spend a couple of hours with middle school staff and students on a site visit to learn about the policies, expectations, and layout of the school and to discuss the developmental stage of this age group. In September, we hold a one-day orientation to familiarize them with PA and give them some coaching tips.

When the Dakota Meadows school year starts, we spend three Thursdays getting ready to form the issue teams. The challenge is to get students to think seriously about social and political issues and to consider the feasibility of studying and acting on the various choices. We begin by putting each university student with a random group of middle school students to share expectations and brainstorm issue ideas. The second week, coaches and teachers lead everyone (even students not in PA) in the homerooms in exercises to suggest ideas for PA teams. The third week, at a schoolwide Issues Assembly, middle school students stand and nominate issues or problems for teams. Later in homeroom, PA participants vote on their choices of issues for the entire year. The site coordinator, professor, and teachers confer in selecting the team membership. Most students get their first choice of team. In their university seminar, coaches choose teams, a fateful decision because they will coach the same team for nine months. Each team has one coach and four to nine middle school students.

Teams meet every Thursday for forty minutes. For the first few weeks, coaches follow an agenda suggested in our coach manual.[7] Coaches are encouraged to follow suggested PA activities such as writing an agenda, building team spirit, rotating leadership, and discussing democratic concepts and the problems, projects, and issues that motivated them to join. Teams write mission statements and adopt rules. The coach models the role of facilitator and introduces other leadership activities that students should take turns performing in the future. Teams research their issues through field trips, phone calls, surveys, and library and/or electronic research. We have found that the teams that interact early on with the outside world, through speakers, interviews, or field trips are more likely to develop a realistic action plan. Without these experiences, some teams get stuck between utopian dreams and feelings of powerlessness. Teams that accomplish some action or project usually learned early on how to bite off a small chunk of the big problem with which they started.

As the weeks roll by, there are ups and downs. In the spring, teams become aware that time is running out. Some kick into high gear, cramming to "get something accomplished." Others work steadily to implement clear plans. Some, having been unsuccessful with "Plan A," try to develop a "Plan B." Others do not. As the year ends, the coaches help the teams evaluate not only what they "accomplished" but also what they learned and how they have changed.

Educator-to-Educator Collaboration

This teamwork between undergraduate students and middle school students is nourished by an institutional collaboration between the middle school and the university. Departments of political science do not normally collaborate with K-12 schools. As the political science professor, I (J.K.) visit the middle school weekly with my coaches. I get to know the principal, the teachers, the counselors, and the support staff at the middle school. The principal helps me and my students build relationships with teachers and staff. A former coach now works as a site coordinator (sometimes part time as school staff, sometimes as a volunteer) to manage program details and build relationships. An Americorps (national service) member assists her.

Table 1. **Outcomes for Public Achievement Teams, 1999-2000**

COACHES REPORTED HOW MANY SEVENTH AND EIGHTH GRADERS DID THE FOLLOWING AT LEAST ONCE.

INTERNAL SKILLS AND ACTIVITIES	TOTAL	%
Served as a meeting facilitator	80	62
Helped adopt a mission statement for a group	126	97
Helped adopt rules for a group	121	93
Discussed and resolved a difference of opinion within a group	108	83
Helped shape a meeting agenda and used that agenda in a group	85	65
Voluntarily completed task/homework showing responsibility	96	74
Negotiated, bargained, and compromised within their group	103	79

EXTERNAL POLITICAL AND PROFESSIONAL SKILLS		
Interviewed/visited with adult authority	76	58
Did library or Internet research on group issue	60	46
Helped design a survey and analyze the results	51	39
Helped write a petition and get signatures	33	25
Wrote a letter to a public official or other decision maker	44	34
Negotiated, bargained, and compromised with people outside of group	74	57
Spoke in public	79	61
Wrote a grant	55	42

CONCEPTS AND IDEAS		
Discussed meanings of citizenship, their role in a democracy	108	83

The collaboration grew out of a conversation between Jane Schuck, the principal of Dakota Meadows, and myself (J.K.). The social studies faculty and other teachers gave their approval before launching the program in 1997. Initially, we offered the program only in the seventh grade. At the end of that first year, teachers petitioned the principal asking that PA be expanded to include the eighth grade as well. In the second year, we accommodated all interested students, which resulted in teams that were too large. We currently cap enrollment at about 180. The student excitement also puts pressure on other middle school electives scheduled at the same time. The teachers and principal creatively adjusted the school schedule to resolve these problems.

As a teacher at the middle school, I [J.M.] saw how Principal Jane Schuck's enthusiastic response to the philosophy of PA helped catapult our school and the university into a new relationship. Our staff was brought into the planning of how PA would become part of the school. Dakota Meadows has always been a community-based school, hosting many groups and organizations and providing meeting places. An early challenge of PA was for the school to provide space. With one-third of the school in PA, several teachers agreed to consolidate study halls, thus freeing some classrooms for PA. Still, not every PA team gets a classroom; some meet in the lunchroom, the library, or at tables in hallways.

We are gradually strengthening the university/middle school relationship. Teachers meet with the professor and site coordinator during the summer to compare schedules, discuss challenges, and agree on innovations. The site coordinator works in the school and helps grow a network of supportive and enthusiastic teachers. Teachers have assisted in coach training, issue brainstorming, team formation, and discipline issues.

PA-generated student action can disrupt the status quo in the school. For example, students want to administer surveys, make phone calls, meet during class time, put up posters, and discuss policies. Teachers have suggested policies to manage any disruption from such activity. Several teachers have attended national PA conferences. We would like to see a mentoring aspect added to the program, whereby several college coaches would be linked with a seasoned teacher who would offer her or his expertise. This year, several teachers will serve as the first Public Achievement Liaisons (PALS; i.e., teachers who observe teams and coaches each week, join in coach debriefing meetings, and bring ideas and concerns of other faculty to the PA leadership). PA teams will also set the agenda for some homeroom sessions, and coaches will try to reinforce vocabulary and other content from classes.

We have seen the positive impact of PA on the school and vice versa. There are inevitable challenges and disruptions. But problems create change, and change is the perfect atmosphere for learning, not only for middle school students and college students but for teachers and university professors as well.

Undergraduate Student-to-Student Collaboration

There is something special about putting middle school students and university students together. For the middle school students, it is a chance to interact with young adults who look like they jumped out of a Mountain Dew ad, teachers, but not quite teachers. To the middle school students, their coaches are far enough removed from their own age to be respected, but close enough to be "cool." One university student described the relationship in an advisory letter to future coaches. "You have the luxury of existing somewhere in between teacher and student. You may not get the respect of a teacher all the time, but you will get the benefit of being seen as a friend and somebody that can be trusted."

Our university students learn how to be effective leaders and cooperate with youth in community action. They understand the developmental abilities of middle school youth, and get to know well the young people with whom they work. By getting off the college campus, they learn about the lives of the youth and the power structure of a local community that may be new to them.

Our university students say that PA is one of the most important experiences they have had in their preparation to teach social studies. Their citizenship course helps them experience democracy, not just as a governmental system but also as a principle of life, and as both a purpose and methodology of education. They see how democratic experience changes the participants. At the end of the year, one university student shared the following:

> I can honestly say that my life has changed as a result of this class. It is hard to explain all that I have learned because some of it has touched me in ways that I don't even understand yet. I cannot imagine another experience that could have taught me more than I have learned about democracy, citizenship, and politics in this class. For me, mixing the readings with the active learning that Public Achievement provided was an intense, frustrating, challenging, and exciting learning experience; an experience I will certainly carry with me forever. (PA coach, 1999)

Examples of PA Team Actions and Projects

The most tangible outcome of the project is the public work of the civic action teams. We mention a few examples here. Our web site tells a fuller history of each team (krypton.mankato.msus.edu /~jak3/pa). Teens for the Environment organized a school-recycling program and cut lunch waste by 20 percent. The Tobacco Hackers published a list of nonsmoking restaurants, met with business owners, and awarded certificates. Rage Against Poverty sponsored a benefit music show and raised $500 for Food Not Bombs, a local charity. The Pet Patrol published a brochure on responsible pet ownership and organized a supply drive for the Humane Society. Teen Trouble Solvers researched, published, and distributed a brochure on teen suicide and depression. The Cuddly Counselors worked with the school counselors to ensure more privacy for students seeking help. Teen pregnancy teams produced a web site, a radio public service announcement, and an informational packet.

Let's look in a little more depth at one team. During our second year, five boys and one girl, all eighth graders, formed a team interested in transportation issues in general and bicycling in particular. They called themselves the Biker Likers. Their coach was a young woman who is now a social studies teacher. She set high expectations, helped them see options, and let them run their own meetings and make their own decisions. Together they paid careful attention to acting democratically in the group and respectfully in public. They observed that people their age relied heavily on bicycles for independence and transportation. Their mission statement committed them to encourage bicycling. They designed, conducted, and analyzed a survey of their classmates to identify needs and priorities, then focused on increasing the number of bicycle racks around town. Based on the survey, they identified particular businesses, patronized by their peers, where there were no bike racks. They developed an action plan, divided chores, and began to phone and visit businesses to assess interest in installing new racks. As the year came to an end, the only business willing to talk about cost sharing was a small Dairy Queen ice cream store. Several team members met with the owner, who was serious and challenging but agreeable. The team then researched bike rack styles and costs, and applied for and won one of our in-house PA mini-grants. Team members then negotiated the store owner's contribution with him. Although the school year ended, this team persevered and ordered a bike rack. When the rack came in June, team members assembled it with the owner's help. With the adult leaders, the team organized a "Grand Opening" of the bike rack and invited their coach back to town. This ribbon cutting event netted both TV and newspaper coverage.

Teachers Talk to Teachers
HEATHER BAKKE

As a new staff member at Dakota Meadows Middle School, I was not involved with the development and implementation of PA. Initially, the only thing I knew about the group was that college students were working with seventh and eighth graders. When I asked my students what they did in PA, they told me they worked on projects that interested them. As a social studies teacher, I soon warmed up to the idea of students having an active role in the community. I asked my advisees to keep me informed throughout the year about their PA teams. But the power of PA didn't really hit home until my advisee, Susan, asked for some help with a project.

Susan and three teammates needed a teacher supervisor so they could do some phoning after school. I invited them into my classroom and continued to grade papers. This group proceeded to call every social hall in Mankato, looking for a venue to hold a concert to raise money for the homeless. I was struck by their professional phone skills. They asked very pertinent questions about cost, insurance, and availability. I couldn't believe that I was watching a group of eighth grade girls.

It was after this incident that I began to notice that PA members had a "tool kit" of useful skills: phone calling, decision making, conducting surveys, petitioning, and collaborating. Students were learning firsthand the skills that we all need to be effective participants in our community. No class in middle school provides these experiences and skills.

Does the experience gained in PA generalize to any social studies class? Initially, I thought that there would not be a connection between Human Heritage, a survey course of ancient cultures, and PA. After all, what could ancient civilizations have to do with the Biker Likers or Rage Against Poverty? For many students, the development of civilizations was a non-issue: civilization had always existed, and they didn't question when or why it happened. When I asked my classes why civilizations developed, typical answers were, "It just happened" or "People were forced to by kings."

In discussions, however, I was surprised to find some students who used words like "community" and "ownership." They talked about how life was better when people worked together. They pointed out that the people living in Mesopotamia had some common challenges and resources. They had to figure out a way to grow food, and although they lived near two rivers, they needed to make this water useful. These common needs and resources, and how people responded to them, led to civilization.

Later in the year, when we were talking about the Greeks and democracy, a cluster of students surfaced who could talk about the positive aspects of democracy and how democracy differed from other forms of government. They could clearly differentiate the Greek form of democracy from our own. Curious, I finally asked these students why they knew so much about government, and many of them replied, "Public Achievement."

JASON MILLER

The hands-on activities offered by PA are perfect for the energetic middle school student. The earlier we can show students how they can make a difference in their community, the better off our society will become. Middle school students are famous for their inconsistency, but they are able to commit to a project that means something to them personally. When the topic is meaningful, there are no limits on learning.

Howard Gardner defines understanding as having "a sufficient grasp of concepts, principles, or skills so that one can bring them to bear on new problems and situations, deciding in which ways one's present competencies can suffice and in which ways one may require new skills or knowledge.8 PA gives this opportunity to students. Whether it is making phone calls to local agencies or organizing a school assembly focused on their issue, students have real learning experiences through which they develop skills and put them into authentic practice. The skills learned through PA are skills that will carry over into other areas of their lives, and will stay with them in the future.

PA fits perfectly with Gardner's belief that education for understanding comes when students work in environments that challenge them:

> To adopt the roles that are ultimately occupied by skilled adult practitioners, and to engage in the kind of self-assessment that allows one ultimately to take responsibility for one's own learning. Involvement in significant projects and regular discourse with one's peers increase the possibility that one's own stereotypes and misconceptions will be challenged and that a more realistic and comprehensive perspective will begin to emerge.[9]

Professors Talk to Professors

JOSEPH KUNKEL

A professor considering getting involved with PA must realize that there is no template or program to follow. Flexibility and an experimental attitude are essential. PA, like democracy, requires attention to many relationships between diverse actors. I often feel that we are experiencing a set of contradictory demands or dilemmas. Doing the best we can and trying to find the right balance is the challenge of continuous improvement.

There are many logistical challenges. Scheduling is an initial problem, since PA teams need to meet all year and university classes run for only a fifteen-week semester. When our students get permission to register in the fall, they are told that they must agree to register for the spring semester also. They earn two credits each semester. I put more time and work into this class than any other. I can do it because it is a labor of love. A small "alternative assignment" (teaching eleven credit hours per semester rather than the normal twelve) helps a little.

Because PA aims for democratic initiative, it is hard to know how much to intervene in the work of the teens. I think of this as the trade-off between "let it be" and "make it so." This dilemma can be seen in three aspects. First, coaches must permit their teams to find their own way, but they must also help teams see that democracy is self-rule, not anarchy. Disruptive students cannot be allowed to destroy the group, but coaches cannot act as dictators. Second, the choice of issues for teams is critical, but we adults cannot impose our ideas, even though we think we know what might be the more feasible among various proposals. Finally, those of us who "coach the coaches" wonder how much and when we should intervene to advise or correct coaches (or teams). Coaches need a lot of discretion if they are to experiment. But we cannot simply cut them loose and not give them help, advice, and direction.

I also feel a strong tension between my own emphasis on concepts and democratic theory and the university students' need for practical suggestions related to coaching. Both theory and practice are needed, but there seems to be a trade-off. Students want help with the "how" of PA coaching. I want them to learn the "what" and "why" of democracy. We wrestle with the dialectical opposites described in David Kolb's model of experiential learning.[10] Our goals are learning and empowerment. But to learn and become effective, we must find ways to connect concrete experiences, reflective observation, abstract conceptualization, and practical experimentation.

There is also the dilemma of the democratic classroom. I am used to being the expert, but if we are to learn democracy, our class must act democratically. In the Tuesday seminar, students are challenged to shape the agenda, lead discussions, and evaluate the learning activities. This takes them out of the comfort zone they are used to in more typical classes. But I cannot abdicate my responsibility to set high standards and set the direction. Public Achievement forces me to experiment with active learning and democratic discussion. It causes me to evaluate my teaching style and approaches to all my classes.

CLARK JOHNSON

Our students must complete a set of education courses and a host of required content courses in the social sciences. We added a required class on citizenship to the social studies major because we wanted more attention given to citizen participation. Because Joe decided to embrace an active learning model, we got a whole lot more than more political science content in the major. The citizenship class gave a surprising bonus because both the content and the method emphasize participation by empowering learners. Rarely do university courses so integrally link theory and practice.

Although the faculty in professional education could guide such a project, we think it is especially advantageous that citizenship is offered in political science. After all, a better grounding in content areas is often cited as a critical need for tomorrow's teachers. Concepts such as citizenship, power, democracy, interest, and community find their disciplinary home in political science, not education. Civic education is still addressed in our social studies methods course, but now our students enter this class with a nine-month experience of guiding young people in team building and civic action. As a result of this common experience, I noticed that students in my methods class could articulate a vision of secondary social studies infused with democracy, citizenship, and student initiative. These are the same kinds of changes that Heather and Jason see in their students.

Joe sees these changes in his students, but also in himself. Joe has also become much more involved in our Social Studies Council (which governs the program.) Previously, Joe had limited experience with secondary social studies like many of his colleagues. Now because of PA, he better understands middle school youth, what they can do, and possibilities for citizenship education at the secondary level of schooling.

Institutional Collaborators

We recognize that the realities of political life will always present us with limited resources, and we need to do our best within those limits. Some of what we have learned about available resources may be applicable to other locations and is summarized below.

The key resources that allowed us to establish Mankato Public Achievement were a committed university professor and a welcoming middle school administration and staff. We believe that a partnership between a university or college and a K-12 school is the best model for a successful PA program. But it is not the only model. Youth groups or clubs are sometimes the "sites," while parents or volunteers are the coaches. But the higher education/K-12 collaboration is well suited to emphasize both real-world experience and learning within a culture that values collaborative experimentation and continuous improvement.

COACH MENTORS

At the end of each year, we have been fortunate to have three to five coaches who want to continue the learning experience. Sometimes they register for independent study credit, sometimes they work as Americorps members, and sometimes they simply volunteer. Whatever the case, they serve as coach mentors to twenty-five to thirty coaches. These veterans give input on course planning, help with coach training, try to mentor the new coaches, and occasionally serve as substitute coaches. They visit a cluster of teams and help keep the professor informed.

COACHES

The basic reason we prefer the model of a partnership between a university and a K-12 school is that university students make great coaches. As part of a university class, they can be prepared on both the practical and conceptual levels. The experience is so different from their other classes that once they understand PA, almost all are enthusiastic and eager to join the experiment. Students in many majors could be successful, but our social studies majors are especially well suited for PA because it matches their personal career preparation.

FUNDING

It does not take a lot of money to launch PA. Our first year we had virtually no outside funding. Our second and third years we operated on budgets of $3,000 to $6,000. We provide transportation to get university students to and from the middle school and participants to national PA events. We also offer about $2,000 to the PA teams for their expenses, but require them to apply for shares of this money as competitive mini-grants. We provide T-shirts at the end of the program and food at celebrations.

Most of our funding is from the Mankato Area Healthy Youth program.[11] MAHY's mission is to nurture our community's youth in accordance with the national and local research of the Search Institute. MAHY administers grants from the Minnesota Department of Children, Families, and Learning to agencies such as Mankato PA who are committed to building youth assets. Mankato PA commits to building specific assets identified by the Search Institute as important for the healthy development of youth. Communities in many states may have organizations with missions similar to Mankato Area Healthy Youth. We expect you will find funding agencies that may be willing to fund PA and its combination of democratic idealism, real-world practicality, fun, and intergenerational mentoring that is central to Public Achievement.

AMERICORPS NATIONAL SERVICE PROGRAM

Another key partner for us has been the Americorps program.[12] For three years, we have been accepted as an Americorps site through which we can recruit a coordinator who contributes thirty-eight hours each week. In our case, the coordinator works at Dakota Meadows Middle School as part of our site coordination effort. Three of our coaches have been Americorps coordinators at our PA site as their first job after graduation. They have coached teams, done clerical work, and helped with PA events outside of school. They have been extremely valuable additions to our team. The service mission of Americorps is a reason that PA sites throughout the nation have been accepted as community partner sites and invited to hire members with the Americorps Service Program.

Conclusion

Public Achievement has not only increased a sense of empowerment and responsibility in the coaches (university students) and members (middle school students). We, as teachers and professors, are more optimistic than ever about the potential of young citizens to influence public events. In building our school/university collaboration, we have had to use many of the democratic skills and strategies taught in PA. Our understanding of concepts such as citizenship, power, democracy, diversity, and personal interest is much richer. We are more willing and able to cooperate to improve our communities, our nation, and our world.

NOTES

1. B. Erlanson and R. Hildreth, *Building Worlds, Transforming Lives, Making History: A Coaches Guide to Public Achievement* (Minneapolis, Minn.: The Center for Democracy and Citizenship, 1997); The Center for Democracy and Citizenship, 130 Humphrey Institute, University of Minnesota, 301 19th Avenue, S., Minneapolis, MN 55455; 612-625-0142 (phone) or publicachievement.org (web).
2. The National Commission on Civic Renewal, *A Nation of Spectators: How Civic Disengagement Weakens America and What We Can Do About It* (College Park: University of Maryland, 1998).
3. Harry C. Boyte and James Farr, "The Work of Citizenship and the Problem of Service-Learning," in *Experiencing Citizenship: Concepts and Methods for Service-Learning in Political Science*, eds. R. M. Battistoni and W. E. Hudson (Washington, D.C.: American Association for Higher Education, 1997).
4. *Ibid.*; Harry C. Boyte and N. N. Kari, *Building America: The Democratic Promise of Public Work* (Philadelphia, Pa.: Temple University Press, 1996).
5. National Council for the Social Studies, "A Vision of Powerful Teaching and Learning in the Social Studies: Building Social Understanding and Civic Efficacy," in *Expectations of Excellence: Curriculum Standards for Social Studies* (Washington, D.C.: Author, 1994), 157.
6. Sandra Schnitzer, "Designing an Authentic Assessment," *Educational Leadership* 50 (April 1993): 32-35.
7. For a copy of the manual, see the Mankato Public Achievement web site, krypton.mankato.msus.edu/~jak3/pa.
8. Howard Gardner, *The Unschooled Mind: How Children Think and How Schools Should Teach* (New York: Basic Books, 1991), 18.
9. *Ibid.*, 224
10. David A. Kolb, *Experiential Learning: Experience as the Source of Learning and Development* (Englewood Cliffs, N.J.: Prentice-Hall, 1984).
11. Mankato Area Healthy Youth, P.O. Box 3367, Mankato, MN 56002-3367; 507-387-5643, 800-450-5643, or rndc.org/mahy; Search Institute, 1998, 700 S. Third Street, Suite 210, Minneapolis, MN 55415; 800-888-7828 or search-institute.org.
12. Corporation for National Service, 1201 New York Avenue, NW, Washington, D.C. 20525; 202-606-5000 or americorps.org.

Integrating the Curriculum and Examining Social Issues in the Sixth Grade

Andrew J. Milson
Laurie Elish-Piper
Portia Downey
James Nordstrom

The Scene (J.N.)

As an elementary school principal, there are times I tell myself, "You're not doing the job if you don't get some criticism now and then." This was one of those times. There were several parents waiting in my office. These were not the parents whom I expect to see in my office with occasional complaints. They were the ones that I have been accustomed to seeing at the Parent Teacher Organization meetings. They were usually cordial, helpful, and supportive, but the school secretary had already warned me that something else was brewing.

The night before had been parent orientation night. Amidst the discussion of classroom rules, expectations, and instructional goals, their children's teacher had said something that the parents found quite unsettling. The teachers were working with university professors to implement an integrated unit; no social studies text, English text, or basic reading text would be coming home for the next eight weeks. Instead, a novel and an occasional resource book would show up.

After a brief description of their concerns, the parents hurled a flurry of questions at me. "Did you know that this was going on?" "How will this prepare my child for seventh grade?" "Where is my child going to learn about world governments, grammar, climates, customs, and sentence structure?" "Is this some kind of university experiment?" "Yes, I want my child to enjoy reading and enjoy school, but don't we need to prepare him for the state competency tests?" "Doesn't the novel that students will read, *The Giver*, deal with controversial issues?"

I asked myself, "Where do I start?" Do I tell the parents that sixth graders would find the basic reading textbook boring and the social studies text even worse? Do I explain that much of our social studies text is too abstract and unrelated to the concerns of their children? Will they accept that preparing their children for active citizenship requires examining social issues? We talked about engaged learning. We talked about meaningful concepts in meaningful contexts. We talked about integrated learning. We talked about issues and values. We talked about uniting the theoretical and the practical. We talked about their children's future.

Current Issues

Teachers are often encouraged to examine persistent social issues and value dilemmas with students as a means of developing the knowledge, skills, and values important for citizenship in a democracy.[1] Social studies provides an opportunity for students to wrestle with many of the issues and dilemmas they will face as citizens in a democratic society: individual liberty versus majority rule, cultural variety versus cultural assimilation, national security versus individual freedom, national versus state versus local community control, worker security versus employer rights, and global business competition versus the national interest.[2] Studying such issues provides an opportunity for children to "work with others, learn how to handle conflict, solve problems, develop concern for others, and interact with the value issues that they encounter daily in their environment."[3]

This sounds reasonable enough in theory, but putting an issues-centered curriculum into practice may pose problems for elementary teachers.[4] Some parents may be uncomfortable with the idea of their children engaging in discussion of value-laden issues. Indeed, many elementary teachers and school administrators are hesitant to venture into topics that may result in debate. Furthermore, the issues-based approach is time consuming. Elementary teachers facing the time constraints associated with teaching reading, math, and writing may find it difficult to spend the time necessary for in-depth examination of social problems.

Interdisciplinary Study

Elementary teachers are often advised to seek opportunities to integrate the curriculum.[5] Indeed, the definition of social studies offered by National Council for the Social Studies (NCSS) states, "Social studies is the *integrated* study of the social sciences and humanities to promote civic competence" [emphasis added].[6] Curriculum integration is typically proposed as a way of accomplishing multiple subject matter, skills, and values-related goals in a more holistic, meaningful, and time-efficient manner.

The benefit of time efficiency is perhaps one of the greatest practical advantages related to curriculum integration. As Lindquist noted:

> The most precious gift we can give our students is time to read from many books, time to research questions, time to wrestle with conflicting interpretations, time to wander through divergent paths of social studies, and time to revisit previous questions in a new context. Yet in today's overcrowded classrooms, time is one of the least available commodities we have. Integrating skills is one way I gain time in my classroom.[7]

Theoretically, curriculum integration is a key ingredient within a social studies program. Social studies has been described as naturally integrative because it "provides opportunities for students to read and study text materials, appreciate art and literature, communicate orally and in writing, observe and take measurements, develop and display data, and in various other ways to conduct inquiry and synthesize findings using knowledge and skills taught in all school subjects."[8]

Although it offers both practical and theoretical advantages, integration is among the proposals for curricular reform that suffers from an apparent theory to practice gap. Although integrated curriculum is typically advocated in the literature and in teacher education courses, the practice has not been consistently implemented in elementary schools.[9] As a result, preservice teachers have experienced a great deal of cognitive dissonance as they learn about one approach in their university courses and see an entirely different approach in practice.[10] Moreover, if implemented inappropriately, integration can actually undermine curricular goals. As Alleman and Brophy noted:

> Too often, activities described as ways to integrate social studies with other subjects either lacked educational value in any subject or promoted progress toward significant goals in other subjects but not in social studies. Rather than expanding the scope and enhancing the meaning and importance of the social education curriculum, these so-called integration activities disrupt its coherence. In effect, they amount to intrusion of language arts or other skills practice exercises into social studies time, and, thus, are better described as invasion of social studies than integration with social studies.[11]

Bridging the Gap between Theory and Practice

The partnership between the Harlem Consolidated School District (north of Rockford, Illinois) and Northern Illinois University (hereafter referred to as the "partnership") began in 1995. The partnership currently involves twenty-eight elementary teachers (mentor teachers) in the Harlem District, twenty-eight elementary education majors (interns) at Northern Illinois University (NIU), six clinical faculty members in Harlem, and five NIU faculty members. Harlem teachers serve as mentor teachers for NIU interns during their clinical experience, which occurs during interns' last semester. The clinical field experience consists of one day a week for ten weeks culminating in full-time, onsite work for three weeks. The clinical experience incorporates special presentations by Harlem teachers on topics such as classroom management, math manipulatives, and team teaching. Additionally, interns complete a Teaching Inquiry Project (action research) on a classroom challenge and present their findings at the Harlem-NIU Partnership Conference at the end of the semester. The interns also benefit from collaboration among NIU methods instructors who prepare some joint assignments and engage in occasional team teaching during Integrated Curriculum Experience (ICE) sessions.

The partnership focuses on five key goals: (1) developing and implementing integrated curriculum, (2) promoting reflective practice, (3) using technology effectively in the classroom, (4) connecting university methods courses and clinical experiences to Harlem classrooms, and (5) providing ongoing professional development opportunities for Harlem teachers. The mentor teachers and NIU professors (partnership team) have attempted to accomplish these goals through the development of integrated, thematic resource units of study (hereafter referred to as "units") for each grade. Although not entirely intentional, the units have all used social studies as the context for integration. The expanding horizons curriculum sequence, common in elementary social studies programs, is evident in six goals, stated as thematic questions, upon which the units are based:

1. How can we promote a healthy life-style for ourselves and our families?
2. How and why do animals establish and live in communities?
3. How and why do people establish and live in communities?
4. What can we do to promote water quality now and in the future?
5. How do the various perspectives on the American Revolutionary War affect our understanding of war?
6. How are the members of communities interdependent, and how do these interdependencies affect communities and their members?

The units are intended to serve as exemplars of curriculum integration that incorporate best practices and address national standards, state goals, and district outcomes in the major subject areas. Each unit includes a variety of authentic assessment techniques and technology applications. These units are used for demonstration and engagement purposes in the university methods courses. Methods instructors provide opportunities for interns to experience activities during the course. During the clinical experience, the mentor teachers and interns team teach lessons from the units and reflect on the lessons as models showing how to connect theory and practice.

Developing the Integrated Units

Units have been developed collaboratively over the past five years, but they are not static, and the development processes have changed significantly. Each summer, a group of approximately thirty mentor teachers in the Harlem District participate in a one-week professional development seminar during which five university professors representing different content fields discuss concepts and approaches that will be taught in methods courses. Teams of mentor teachers and university professors then work together to prepare lessons to be included in the units. Each year the units are modified as mentor teachers make suggestions for new lessons or lesson revisions. Once the academic year begins, the interns also play a role in updating the units. Several activities and assessments developed by interns have been incorporated into units at various grade levels.

During the first year of the partnership, clear-cut roles were established wherein the mentor teachers wrote the unit materials and the university professors critiqued them. A total of sixteen educators crowded around the table on a weekly basis, and debate and gridlock typically followed. Perhaps the old proverb "Too many cooks spoil the broth" is the best way to explain this situation. With sixteen educators around the table, the process felt intimidating. One teacher never uttered a word during any of these meetings. Moreover, the theory-to-practice gap between university and school perspectives became magnified.

The units initially focused on the Science-Technology-Society (STS) theme[12] and used the Taba curriculum design model.[13] Although the STS model worked well for the intermediate grades, it was challenging to implement in the primary grades. In addition, although the Taba model provided a clear framework for developing units, many of the teachers and some of the university faculty found it cumbersome and constricting. Clearly, these initial efforts did not create a true partnership, as the hierarchical structure between professors and teachers caused tension, frustration, and hostility to develop between the two groups.

As the partnership has matured, the process of developing the units has become more collaborative and flexible, as will be described below. Although each unit contains strengths and weaknesses, we have chosen to focus on the development of the sixth grade unit. This unit exemplifies the strength of the partnership and the changes that have occurred since the first years. Compared to the units developed early in the partnership, the sixth grade unit is more practical and includes more specific activities than the university professors teach in the methods classes. It is not a copy of a unit model drawn directly from the literature. Rather, it reflects the participants, their priorities, preferences, and wisdom. The sixth grade unit has revealed an unfortunate problem with using social issues as a basis for curriculum development, which raises provocative issues about including controversial issues in social studies instruction.

Creating the Sixth Grade Unit

The sixth grade unit grew out of conversations among team members as they sought to find a context that would be meaningful for students. They discussed the characteristics, needs, and abilities of sixth grade students. They reviewed the district curriculum guide and read and reviewed a variety of children's and adolescent literature. All of the conversations and reviews seemed to lead back to issues of how these students fit into their families, schools, communities, and world. Issues of interdependence, roles, responsibilities, and individuality continued to surface.

Based on these discussions, we selected the book *The Giver*[14] as the core novel for the unit. The team felt this novel would provide many opportunities for students to become meaningfully engaged as they considered roles in their families, schools, communities, and world. *The Giver* examines life from the perspective of a young boy in a utopian society, without conflict, fear, pain, or personal pleasure, that has chosen utilitarian security over individual liberty. Each child in this community is observed by a Committee of Elders to determine what function he or she will serve. Once a child reaches the age of twelve, he or she is assigned a role such as laborer, child care specialist, doctor, or engineer based on his or her personality and apparent talents. The main character, Jonas, is selected to serve in the honorable position of "Receiver of Memory." Jonas's training consists of meeting with an Elder known as "The Giver" who transmits "memories." Jonas gradually becomes aware of the "Truth" as he "receives" memories of pain and pleasure and is forced to understand social concepts such as love, justice, and freedom that are unknown in his community. The partnership team felt that the social issues examined in *The Giver*, such as freedom, justice, human rights, power and authority, and euthanasia, would help the sixth grade students examine their own beliefs, think critically, and develop decision-making skills.

In some years, Goals 2000 grant monies were available to support curriculum development to pay mentor teachers and professors to develop the units. The sixth grade unit, however, was created during a year when no external funding was provided for the unit development. Because of the lack of funding, partnership coordinators, Laurie Elish-Piper (a professor) and Portia Downey (a teacher), accepted the bulk of the responsibility for developing the unit. They sat side by side at Portia's kitchen table with two computers, stacks of resource books, the district curriculum guide, textbooks, literature, and university methods texts. They started each session with a burst of brainstorming, and then moved to the computers to write drafts of lessons they shared promptly with each other. They determined how to balance the desires of the university faculty (more cooperative learning, technology, hands-on activities, social issues) with practical concerns voiced by the teachers (explicit vocabulary instruction, use of textbooks, rubrics for assessment). Without a long-standing relationship and mutual respect, they would have had difficulty processing, filtering, and balancing these requests. The unit development process, however, actually seemed to strengthen their relationship as they realized that they were more often in agreement than on opposing sides. This clearly was a major shift from earlier attempts at developing units in which the larger group was somewhat paralyzed by its size and perceived hierarchy. The larger team still helped develop the unit theme, select literature, and suggest activities.

While the team has had success implementing the sixth grade unit in almost two dozen classrooms, problems have arisen. As the opening scene of our chapter illustrates, a small group of parents expressed concerns regarding the unconventional nature of the unit and the controversial social issues raised in *The Giver*. For example, one element of *The Giver* that a few parents found objectionable was the discussion in the story of "stirrings" that developed in young adolescents. In the story, medication is promptly prescribed that eliminates these pubescent developments in the children. The team struggled greatly with these few, but vocal, objections to the unit. We asked ourselves, "How do we balance the expectations of the local community and parents with conceptions of powerful social studies and meaningful instruction as defined by teachers and university professors?" "Do we cave into the demands of a small group of parents?" "Do we risk the public relations problems that could arise if the partnership is associated with controversy?" "Is it fair to put administrators in the unpleasant position of responding to parental complaints each year?"

An Ongoing Dialogue

We have had many opportunities to discuss the benefits and drawbacks associated with this type of collaboration. We each view the partnership from somewhat different perspectives because of our different experiences and roles within this endeavor. Jim Nordstrom is the principal at Machesney Elementary School in Machesney Park, Illinois. He has been with the district for twenty-four years and has been an active supporter of the partnership since its inception. Portia Downey, the district coordinator for the partnership, is a sixth grade teacher at Machesney Elementary with fifteen years of teaching experience. Laurie Elish-Piper, the university coordinator for the partnership, is an associate professor at NIU with a specialty in literacy education. Andy Milson is an assistant professor at NIU with a specialty in social studies education and recently became involved in the partnership. The following conversation is about the insights that we have gained through this work and the advice that we would give to others who might be considering such collaboration.

Portia: In the beginning, it seemed that the university was very theory oriented and the teachers were very practical. We teachers weren't interested in writing goals or objectives, but when we did the first units, we spent weeks and weeks going through state goals, national standards, and district outcomes, and we had to write down every one. And we could hardly stand it. I had to come part way and realize that I do need to know what goals and standards I am addressing in these units. So it made me stop and look at everything I do. I started to see the importance of writing all of these interdisciplinary units based on goals.

Jim: From an administrator's viewpoint, I am thinking to myself, this is what we need. We need to make sure that teachers are goal oriented and outcome based. It's not okay just to have fancy lesson plans or interesting activities, but they have to have some kind of goal and specific objectives in mind. I sometimes battle with teachers about this. You might have a wonderful lesson, the kids were very active and involved and enthusiastic about it, but what did they learn from it? What are they going to learn long-term from that activity?

Laurie: Initially, so much emphasis was put on goals and standards, and we were so wedded to the Taba model that the balance was thrown off. I'd say we spent months and months doing all that front matter so that it got to the point that the lessons and the activities were lost. We needed to readjust things.

Portia: It did take time for us to all get to know each other and respect the knowledge each of us had. When we really started to make progress was when we felt a mutual respect. I needed to learn a lot from the university, and the university needed to learn a lot from us. When we combined our knowledge, we accomplished a lot, but we did not have that in the beginning. We had to gain each other's respect.

Jim: I think that the conflict really was stretching people and was a good form of professional development. You hear of people who are in conflict having to defend their ideas, promote certain ways of teaching and certain subject matter, and being challenged by other people, and I think all of that stretches a person. There is no partnership that works or lasts very long when only one side has something to bring to the table. Both sides have to have something to bring to the table and, hopefully, they understand that and respect that. And that's what took time to develop.

Laurie: If we wouldn't have had all of the conflict in the beginning, maybe things wouldn't have progressed to the good point where they are now. If people just agreed to do something even if they didn't believe in it, I think it would have caused the partnership either not to grow or to have people bow out. I think it is important to accept that if there is conflict, it's okay. Things aren't going to fall apart if we don't agree on everything, but we can work through it. I think that has really strengthened us.

Andy: It's certainly easy to give up on something that doesn't seem to work out at first. One of the best aspects of this collaboration is the message that it sends to the interns. They see all of us working together and struggling together to make difficult but worthwhile things happen. I think they start to see that integration and teaching in general isn't simple. It's something that you have to stick with if you want it to work.

Portia: One of the big barriers in our educational system is the isolation of the teachers. There are a large majority of teachers who go into their classrooms, shut the door, teach by themselves, and don't share their ideas. They don't get out there and see what is going on, and they teach the same thing over and over again. Through this partnership, we have gotten a lot of teachers out of that cycle. We have this group of mentor teachers that are all doing the same unit at the same time all around the district. They really learn a lot from each other. I think working at the summer workshop where everyone's ideas are welcome and we try to improve and update the units has helped solve the problem of isolation. We're showing the interns that right from the beginning, you should work together with other teachers. You don't have to have your own little interdisciplinary unit that's only used in your classroom, but it's a good idea to get other people's input.

Jim: Even when you are teaching a less integrated lesson, you are still making connections between subject areas because that becomes your philosophy. You know that social studies is not something that's just taught from 2:00 to 2:50 in the afternoon, but it's something that we relate to all day long. So I think that that's maybe a much more subtle indication that this work on integrated units has made a big difference. Even though teachers aren't sitting down every day and trying to write integrated units, integration is occurring. It becomes a new mindset.

Portia: Teachers also start to understand the need to make connections to the students' real lives. They now feel comfortable with interdisciplinary curriculum and making connections between the subject areas, but the big tie-in is when they finally understand the need to make a connection to students' lives. That's where I have seen a big difference.

Andy: I definitely noticed a difference between the two sections of the elementary social studies methods course that I taught last fall. In the Harlem partnership section, I knew which mentor teachers the students would be working with and what they would be teaching. It made it much easier to make connections between the methods course and the field experience. Whereas in the other section, the students didn't know the teachers at another school, they didn't know what topics they would be teaching, they didn't know whether the teachers had computers in their rooms or not. Many of these interns went into less than ideal situations. They came back saying, "My teacher just reads out of the social studies book and that's it." This made it very difficult for the students to try out new methods in the field, and they didn't always see models of quality social studies teaching.

Laurie: The interns are often left to sink or swim. In the partnership, we give them life jackets by providing layers of support. It's really not appropriate to expect them to be able to go out there and implement wonderful, meaningful lessons so early in their development. On the flip side, though, sometimes there is so much support for them that they feel incredibly empowered. They form this collective identity and begin saying, "I need this" and "You should change that." We really want them to become meaningfully engaged, to be active learners, to take control and responsibility for their learning, and to become reflective, motivated teachers, but sometimes it's a little intimidating.

Andy: All of the support and collaboration do have their drawbacks. I noticed that students in the partnership section sometimes reject new ideas in the methods course more quickly than those who have had less experience in the field. I have students read a very practical book by Tarry Lindquist[15] on integrating the curriculum. It seemed that many of the students in the partnership section were so aware of the challenges associated with teaching that they were quick to dismiss some ideas as too difficult or controversial or time consuming. The students in the other class tended to be more open-minded. I guess naive would be another way to put it, too.

Portia: Being open-minded is important, but teachers also have to be realistic about the communities where they teach. Having gone through the controversy with *The Giver*, I am very much aware that you need to be very careful. It has made me a little apprehensive because I don't want to go through all this work and then have the parents cause a problem and then have a negative effect on the partnership. It's a struggle because it is such a great unit and *The Giver* is the kids' favorite book. It's just a couple of parents who object to it.

Jim: And that's the thing to focus on: it is just a couple of parents. Some are not even totally against *The Giver*; they just want to ask, "Why can't we do something nice, sweet, and old-fashioned with our kids?" To some extent, the answer is "The kids won't buy it." I see why the students are enthusiastic about *The Giver*. They are emerging adolescents and are dealing with the issues raised by the book—being controlled and required to do certain things versus having individual freedoms—the value of life, the value of freedom.

Portia: That's exactly why they like it—because they like talking about those kinds of issues. It made them feel like we were giving them permission to have real feelings about it. We were treating them like they were old enough to handle it and have their own ideas and to take a stand on the right thing to do. They don't go "yuck" when you get out the book.

Andy: Which is probably the absolute opposite of how they feel when they get out their social studies textbook.

Laurie: The interns pick up on the fact that the kids are more motivated and engaged with the interdisciplinary unit. They also realize how important it is to have high goals and expectations for their students. When I observed one of the interns leading a discussion of *The Giver*, I complimented her on the quality of the discussion and the high level of engagement among the students. She responded that she was really surprised by how the kids reacted to the book. She said, "When I first saw this unit, I was thinking 'there's no way I can get kids to do this,' but now I really see how capable kids can be when they are motivated."

Portia: Yeah, it has to be high interest. I think the kids really valued the social issues in *The Giver*. It seems that when teachers are looking for ways to make social studies more interesting, they don't even think of social issues as social studies. They think of social studies as geography and learning about the countries of the world and about the people and their customs, but not really their own beliefs or their own issues.

Andy: So this unit development has made teachers start to think about subjects like social studies a little differently? I'm sure that is not always easy and probably requires a real investment from the teachers.

Portia: I have to be honest; this type of partnership and change does take a lot of time, but I think it needs to be part of a teacher's philosophy not just to improve instruction in their classroom but also to improve instruction for all teachers in the future.

Jim: From a practical level, I'm always asking myself, "How do I convince people to get involved in this?" I think you need to have practical, concrete incentives out there for people to get involved in the first place. For our teachers, offering things like staff development credits, university credit, paid workshops, classroom materials, lunch, release time, and so on helped to provide the extrinsic rewards to get people started. Of course, the intrinsic payoff comes later. Time and money I think are two practical issues.

Laurie: The willingness to stay with it through the rocky periods is important, too. It is a lot easier to just say, "Forget it." It's a lot of extra time and effort, and having that commitment and staying on is really critical. Time and money make that a little easier. Another constraint from the university perspective is that it took several years to get to the point where we were given permission, so to speak, to change some things. At first I heard, "You can't do that, because we have always done it this way." That's a real challenge especially at a large university where there are many layers of bureaucracy. It was also very difficult, at first, as a tenure-track, new faculty member to feel comfortable enough to debate with tenured, senior-level faculty who had been at the university for fifteen to twenty years and who could realistically be sitting on my promotion and tenure committee.

Andy: I can certainly relate to the somewhat precarious position of a tenure-track faculty member. Laurie called me before I had even moved here and I was very excited about becoming involved in the partnership, but as I got further into the semester, I started realizing what a time commitment it is. I started to wonder how valued my participation in the partnership would be when I go up for tenure and promotion. Fortunately, I am finding ways to connect the partnership work to other goals that are valuable, such as research and writing. It's definitely a balancing act.

Portia: You always can find time to do what you really believe in. I started out small with the project and it has grown. Sometimes I get under a real time crunch, but it has become such a passion of mine because I believe that this is the way to improve future teachers. But I think, too, that your administration has to be supportive. Jim is very good about understanding that I might have to take a phone call or need half a day to go do this or that. So you have to have administrative support from the superintendent to your principal.

Jim: The timing was really good, because the Harlem School District happened to be very ripe for this kind of program. There would be a lot of resistance in a lot of school districts to doing things differently, but we happened to have a superintendent who was really promoting the idea of risk-taking and "thinking outside of the box." So the big challenge is going to be finding the school district that is right or, at least finding the right support and time in your school district, to do experiments like this.

The state is now helping us out with professional development. Teachers are required to be involved in professional development, so we're providing something that they need and that they'll benefit from. So it's even more of an incentive because they have to do something and this looks appealing.

Andy: It seems that you have a lot of planets aligning. You have the state offering the incentives to the teacher. You have a superintendent who is supportive and willing to change. You have an energetic principal who is willing to support it and a dedicated teacher who's going to coordinate it. You have faculty who are willing to spend time, have their theories challenged, and be informed about what's happening in schools. And you have to have support from the university administration to change things or at least not to complain when you try to do something a little bit different.

Conclusion

Developing and teaching an integrated social studies curriculum in a meaningful context, while examining value-based issues, is not a simple goal to be accomplished quickly and easily. Such an effort requires time, dedication, flexibility, and, most importantly, collaboration. Although the partnership described in this chapter has been in place for five years, the challenges associated with bridging the institutional differences linked to school/university collaboration are continually present. As we seek to improve the preparation of elementary teachers by using integrated units based on social studies themes, we will continue to ask questions such as, "How do we negotiate the sometimes competing needs and demands of parents, elementary students, teachers, university professors, preservice teachers, and administrators?" "How do we balance the concerns of some parents about limiting children's exposure to certain kinds of information with our belief that students need opportunities to examine social issues in school?" "How do we compromise without sacrificing either important theoretical principles or daily practical concerns?" There are clearly no simple solutions to such questions, but through collaboration, we are better able to understand the perspectives of all involved. Such an understanding would seem to be a critical first step toward improving social studies teaching and learning.

NOTES
1. Shirley H. Engle and Anna S. Ochoa, *Education for Democratic Citizenship: Decision Making in the Social Studies* (New York: Teachers College Press, 1988); Carole L. Hahn, "Controversial Issues in Social Studies," in *Handbook of Research on Social Studies Teaching and Learning*, ed. James P. Shaver (Washington, D.C.: National Council for the Social Studies, 1991): 470-480; Byron Massialas and C. Benjamin Cox, *Inquiry in Social Studies* (New York: McGraw Hill, 1966); Jack L. Nelson, "The Historical Imperative for Issues-Centered Education," in *Handbook on Teaching Social Issues*, eds. Ronald W. Evans and David Warren Saxe (Washington, D.C.: National Council for the Social Studies, 1996): 14-24; Fred M. Newmann and Donald W. Oliver, *Clarifying Public Controversy: An Approach to Social Studies* (Boston, Mass.: Little Brown, 1970); Donald W. Oliver and James P. Shaver, *Teaching Public Issues in the High School* (Boston, Mass.: Houghton Mifflin, 1966).
2. National Council for the Social Studies, *Expectations of Excellence: Curriculum Standards for Social Studies* (Washington, D.C.: Author, 1994).
3. Dorothy Skeel, "An Issues-Centered Elementary Curriculum," in *Handbook on Teaching Social Issues*, eds. Ronald W. Evans and David Warren Saxe (Washington, D.C.: National Council for the Social Studies, 1996), 231.
4. Richard E. Gross, "Reasons for the Limited Acceptance of the Problems Approach," *The Social Studies* 80 (1989): 185-186.
5. Tarry Lindquist, *Seeing the Whole Through Social Studies* (Portsmouth, N.H.: Heinemann, 1995); Tarry Lindquist, *Ways that Work: Putting Social Studies Standards into Practice* (Portsmouth, N.H.: Heinemann, 1997); Tarry Lindquist and Douglas Selwyn, *Social Studies at the Center* (Portsmouth, N.H.: Heinemann, 2000); Margit McGuire, James F. Marran, Silvia Alvarez, Susan Austin, Jere Brophy, George Mehaffy, Pat Nickell, Linda Preston, and Michael Young, "A Vision of Powerful Teaching and Learning in the Social Studies: Building Social Understanding and Civic Efficacy," *Social Education* 57 (1993): 213-223; National Council for the Social Studies, *Expectations of Excellence*.
6. National Council for the Social Studies, *Expectations of Excellence*, 3.
7. Lindquist, *Ways that Work*, xv-xvi.
8. McGuire, Marran, Alvarez, Austin, Brophy, Mehaffy, Nickell, Preston, and Young, "A Vision of Powerful Teaching and Learning," 217.
9. Timothy Shanahan, "Reading-Writing Relationships, Thematic Units, Inquiry Learning . . . In Pursuit of Effective Integrated Literacy Instruction," *The Reading Teacher* 51 (1997): 12-19.
10. J. Gary Knowles, Andra L. Cole, and Colleen S. Presswood, *Through Preservice Teachers' Eyes: Exploring Field Experiences Through Narrative and Inquiry* (New York: Merrill, 1994).
11. Janet Alleman and Jere E. Brophy, "Is Curriculum Integration a Boon or a Threat to Social Studies?" *Social Education* 57 (1993): 287.
12. James R. Giese, Lynn Parisi, and Rodger W. Bybee, "The Science-Technology-Society (STS) Theme and Social Studies Education," in *Handbook of Research on Social Studies Teaching and Learning*, ed. James P. Shaver (Washington, D.C.: National Council for the Social Studies, 1991): 559-566; John J. Patrick and Richard C. Remy, *Connecting Science, Technology and Society in the Education of Citizens* (Boulder, Colo.: Social Science Education Consortium, 1985).
13. Hilda Taba, *Curriculum Development: Theory and Practice* (New York: Harcourt, Brace, & World, 1962).
14. Lois Lowry, *The Giver* (New York: Bantam, 1993).
15. Lindquist, *Seeing the Whole Through Social Studies*.

Appendix A: Sample Lessons from Resource Unit on Interdependence (Grade 6)

Sample Initiating Activities

A: ROLES IN OUR LIVES

This activity requires students to think about the roles they and other members of their classroom, school, and family communities play. This activity will introduce students to the important concepts of roles and interdependence. First, ask students to brainstorm the roles played by people in the school. Encourage them to think of the multiple roles that each person plays in making the school function smoothly. Use the students' ideas to create a semantic map or web to show how the many roles are connected together. Next, discuss what would happen at the school if a specific role were not fulfilled. Guide the students to discover that all members play important roles in making the community operate successfully. Extend the activity by asking students to consider roles played in their families and community.

B: RULES

This activity will help students think about the importance of rules in their lives. By connecting to students' lives in their classroom and school, they will be able to think about the practical impact of rules in real life. Discuss the classroom rules that were developed at the beginning of the year and/or the school rules. Why is each rule necessary to keep the classroom running smoothly? Are there any rules that need to be added? Which rule is broken most frequently and why? If you were going to change a rule, which one would it be and how would you change it to improve the classroom/school community? Ask students to develop a list of ten rules that they feel would help them make positive contributions to their community.

Sample Developmental Activities

A: LOVE

Background from *The Giver:* Jonas learns about the concept of love after The Giver's favorite memory transmission of a warm and loving family celebration. But Jonas becomes confused after he asks his parents if they love him and his mother responds, "You have used a very generalized word, so meaningless that it's become obsolete." Jonas realizes that humans must experience all types of emotions and feelings, both good and bad, in order to "know" love. Discuss the following questions with students: What does love mean? How would Jonas's community be different if the people understood the meaning of love? What would be better/worse? How do both good things and bad things help us to understand the meaning of love?

B: EUTHANASIA

In *The Giver*, people are "released" when they are judged to be too old, a rule-breaker, a "difficult" baby, or otherwise inadequate or "uncertain." Using a strategy such as "Pro-Con" cooperative groups,* consider the issue of euthanasia using examples from modern society (e.g., Dr. Jack Kevorkian and assisted suicide).

Sample Culminating Activities

There are many potential activities and products that would allow students to demonstrate their understanding of the concept of interdependence. The following are two possibilities.

1. Groups of students create a newspaper from the community described in *The Giver* including editorials on key issues such as euthanasia.
2. Hold a mock trial of a community leader from the book on charges of destroying the community by supporting policies detrimental to interdependence.

---

* See David W. Johnson and Roger T. Johnson, "The Pro-Con Cooperative Group Strategy: Structuring Academic Controversy Within the Social Studies Classroom," in *Cooperative Learning in Social Studies: A Handbook for Teachers,* ed. Robert J. Stahl (New York: Addison-Wesley, 1994): 306-331.

High School

School Schedules: A Key to Time and Team Teaching in the Eleven American Social History Project

DAVID GERWIN
VASSILIOS MANOLIOS

The Scene (D.G.)

It is early May. Spring is here, but there are still a few more weeks of school before the kids can smell summer. The teachers talk about the New York State Regents exams, anxious to finish covering the last units before they halt instruction and begin to review for the test.

Bill Manolios, in his third year of teaching English at Bryant High School in New York City, is teaching a ten-minute lesson on "Ways of Organizing Notes." He is focused and earnest, knowing exactly what he needs to do in a short time. He demonstrates the difference between sorting notes by importance and sorting them chronologically, giving examples from one student group that is writing about gangs. He shows them how they can break notes into description (definition, background, importance), causes (social, economic, and political), and then effects and solutions. Again, drawing on the work of the students researching gangs, he makes suggestions about moving from an article, to notes, to their own papers. The students are mostly attentive, though some of them are impatiently flipping through their own notes or articles, and some are making lists of information they need from the library, or specific books or articles they need fetched. A few are looking out the window, but that ends when the time comes to break into groups. With thirty minutes left, they get into their research groups, except for the students designated by each team to go with me, the professor from Queens College, to the school library. As we walk up the stairs, we pass Lia Papodopoulos, the social studies teacher on our team, who is coming down from her classroom to work with several of the groups.

Gus, Kasha, Sharifa, and May are studying alcoholism; Teodora, Chris, Sulanz, and Luis have chosen "women's unequal condition"; Delai Paula Dina and Elizabeth prepare to discuss prostitution over the past century; Besma, Lelja, and Oscar have poured more thought and hard work into their study of education than we imagined; other teams are writing about child labor, immigration, child abuse, and housing (including homelessness). Despite overcrowding that forces Bryant High School to run on two shifts (the morning shift starts at 7:15 a.m., and the afternoon shift ends after 5:00 p.m.) and a crumbling outdoor track and field, the school has a library that makes research possible. Microfilm files and working printers make a large variety of news articles easily available. The library has hard copies of recent statistical and reference works. A section on New York has the recent one-volume *Encyclopedia of New York City* edited by Kenneth T. Jackson.[1] And the library has spent money on recent and relevant books. The group working on education can find old and new volumes by Diane Ravitch on education in the nation and New York, as well as Jonathan Kozol's *Savage Inequalities*.[2] A history section has books on child labor written for junior high, high school, and college students. Books on alcoholism, prostitution, and homelessness give current information and some references, although many do not include much historical perspective. When the bell rings, the students do not have to rush downstairs to the next class. Instead, they continue working. They have arranged a copying schedule among themselves so that they are taking turns at the one copy machine. I help people with topics that are not well represented in the library collection, while a librarian works with students using the microfilm. I glance at my watch and tell the students to wrap it up.

With twenty minutes to go, we return to Lia's classroom, where the groups are still hard at work. My students scatter to their individual teams to draw up lists of items to find in the public libraries. I listen to one group as its members make plans to interview the principal (about current educational issues) and a 30-year veteran teacher at Bryant (about the past). With about ten minutes left in the period, Lia reviews the due dates for drafts and presentations. Afterwards she distributes a handout on New Deal legislation and reminds students that they have homework in the textbook about several of the big agencies Roosevelt created and about some ways the Great Society extended the work. She takes a few questions, and then reminds them that they will begin looking at twentieth century foreign policy next week. The bell rings and everyone leaves. After a few words with Lia, I leave, too, trying to remember where in the neighborhood I parked my car, and beginning to think about my afternoon classes at Queens College.

What Team Teaching Means to Us

The goals of the American Social History Project's "Making Connections" program are straightforward:

▶ To shift the focus of history from the traditional "presidents and politics" approach to a multicultural, "bottom-up" narrative of what average people were experiencing
▶ To promote an American studies/humanities approach combining literature and history
▶ To emphasize writing across the curriculum
▶ To have students take an active, more independent role in their work

This last goal includes student-centered "active learning" that emphasizes constructing interpretations of primary sources and fiction in history and in English.

This chapter focuses on one aspect of the program, the team teaching of a high school social studies teacher, a high school English teacher, and a City University of New York faculty partner.[3] Although many limited definitions of teaming exist, over the course of a semester, we arrived at a highly collaborative, interdependent practice that nearly erased the distinctions between English and social studies and among the three faculty. Strictly focusing on the content would have led to an article on an "American studies" approach to the classroom. Interested readers can find such a description of our work in a lesson plan published in the *Magazine of History*.[4] Here, particularly in thinking about university/high school collaborations, we reflect on the centrality of time to classroom practice. A marvelous article by Joseph Cambone, "Time for Teachers in School Restructuring,"[5] distinguishes between many types of time in school life, from administrative time to daily and annual time cycles. Frequently, teachers involved in restructuring or collaborative processes make difficult choices between instructional time and planning time. In particular, we describe how, through our collaboration, we poured extraordinary amounts of time into the class, but also made time for ourselves and for our students.

The daily school schedule structures all our efforts. From the beginning, the Bryant High School administration made everything else possible through scheduling. The scheduling gave no extra time to the teachers, just locked in a particular schedule. This was a condition of their participation in the project, but many schools do not live up to the commitment. This scheduling difficulty is one of the growing pains involved in moving from a start-up to an institutional program. The American Social History Project began as an attempt by Dr. Herbert Gutman at the City University of New York (CUNY) to write a U.S. history textbook that centered its narrative on the social history research of the sixties and seventies. *Who Built America?*[6] was the result; it was followed by a CD-ROM, then a series of videos and supporting materials for classroom use. The education program began as an offshoot of this publishing project and received initial funding from the Aaron Diamond Foundation. As a self-funded project, it could force schools to reschedule as part of the application process. The seed money established Making Connections as a successful teacher development program. It is now funded directly through contracts with the New York City Board of Education. Working on contract for the public schools gives the program less leverage in dictating terms, and schools do not always follow the model-scheduling pattern described below.

The American Social History Project (ASHP) is a collaboration between a social studies teacher and an English teacher. The model we followed is a common prep (preparation) period, followed by English and social studies classes that are scheduled back-to-back, leaving one flexible period for each teacher (which

Figure 1: Team's Block Schedule

Teacher	Period 3	Period 4	Period 5
Lia Papodopoulos Social Studies	Prep Period	Prep Period	Social Studies
Joint Function	Joint Planning Time	Can join/teach ▼	Can join/teach ▲
Bill Manlios English	Prep Period	English	Prep Period

could be used as a solitary prep period or as a team-teaching period). The students were block scheduled into both classes for the entire year, instead of having different groups for English and for social studies that changed with each semester (see Figure 1).

Scheduling Accommodations (V.M.)

Ideally, we should get these conditions met. The only drawback for the administration is that the students must be programmed into the class far in advance, and cannot be capriciously removed. Supervisors, however, have more demands to worry about when scheduling teachers. It is important to point out that we did not have any more preparation time than any other teacher. Each of us in the school, by contract, has three preparation periods a day. All the school did was agree to program those preparation periods strategically so that we could meet to plan and team teach. We agreed to dedicate two of our preparation periods to the program and relinquish our right to use those periods in other ways. We gave up the time we needed to grade papers and plan lessons for our other classes, and had to make up this time after school. Therefore, the sacrifice we made was much greater, in my mind, than that made by the administration.

It is also important to point out that when these scheduling requests were not granted, we had far less success than when we did. For example, one year we did not get a common prep period and were forced to meet after school. This made it more difficult for us to meet. Another semester we were given a common prep period right before the class met, but we were not given a prep period when the other teacher was teaching. Thus, we could not team teach. Both times there was a noticeable decline in the quality of the program. I've come to realize through these unfortunate experiences the importance of the scheduling requests made by ASHP.

Other scheduling matters include allowing teachers to sit down at the end of the year and select the students who will be in the ASHP class for the next year. Ideally, we would look for students with a high attendance rate and an average between 65 and 90. The class that we describe in this article was not, however, chosen using this method. Students were just programmed into it by the programming office. The benefit of choosing the students yourself is being able to create a multicultural and mixed-ability student body whose members are consistently present. A multicultural class helps reinforce our emphasis on point of view by bringing out various differing perspectives, making for more lively conversations. The mixed-ability grouping makes it easier for us to participate in real cooperative work, in which students are actually helping each other to learn. And the consistent attendance record guarantees that we can sustain long-term group work. Having these structures in place is essential for the success of the program.

Forming the Collaboration

To complete our team, the City University of New York (CUNY) provided the money for a course release that allowed a CUNY faculty member (D.G.) to participate in the program by joining a team in Bill and Lia's school for all three periods two or three times a week. CUNY is the largest urban university in the nation. The American Social History Project is affiliated with the CUNY Graduate Center. The central administration of CUNY has made funding available that pays for faculty at other CUNY colleges to be released from some of their teaching assignments in order to work with ASHP. Thus, administrative funds paid Queens College, CUNY to release David from one course and assign him to the ASHP team at Bryant High School.

The school also paid Bill and Lia per-session money for their participation in the monthly ASHP workshops that alternated between full-day Saturday sessions and three-hour meetings on Thursday afternoons. These sessions included planning time for all the teams at the fifty schools in the program.

Control Over Our Day: Time and Team Teaching (D.G.)

Tight class schedules do not allow for the rhythms of personal life (no knocking off early on a Friday and staying late on a Monday) or for making adjustments for professional tasks. One cannot flip third and fourth period to mark papers before you meet the class. The need to meet classes and provide quality instructional time within inflexible blocks of time often prevents teachers from participating wholeheartedly in restructuring efforts.[7] Nevertheless, we poured time into the class. We met before class during the prep period. We met at ASHP sessions. We met during vacation at Lia's apartment. I met Billy at Queens College on Thursdays, where he was a participant in another workshop, this one on teaching global humanities. The investment of that planning time paid off for us in an incredible change in the way we handled the classroom.

In our case, between the structure put in place by the school and the time we invested in planning, team teaching in two periods actually gave us some control over time. Imagine the flexibility gained when someone else could take your class for the day and give you a double period another day.

We also made time. Within any given class you have only forty minutes of instructor time. A team doubles that (taking some students to the library) or triples it (sometimes all three of us met with student groups for both periods). More student work gets reviewed, many more revisions are possible, fewer students flounder, and that means projects get completed on schedule. Three people (two teachers and a professor) grading student essays makes getting them back faster and more manageable. We "made" more classroom time.

As a university partner, I also made time outside of the classroom. When I met Bill at Queens, I usually handed him stacks of documents I dug up at the college library, or lesson plan drafts, or student papers I had graded. Sometimes I gave him handouts that we copied at Queens College because we had a faster turn around there than at school. As our partnership developed and our vision of a good class came to emphasize work with original documents, student research, and student judgments, the ability to have access to outside materials in a timely and classroom-ready fashion became crucial.[8]

As we move back toward the narrative of the collaboration, bear in mind that the thoughts about time and team teaching you have just read are the conception of team teaching that emerged from our collaboration. We began our partnership in a much more tentative fashion and expanded it slowly over time.

Our Process and Some Tangible Outcomes

Bill: During my third year of teaching English at Bryant High School, I was presented with an opportunity to participate in ASHP. I had only taught literature and was intrigued with the idea of integrating literature and history. Lia Papadopoulos, also a new and enthusiastic teacher, would be my history partner, and together we would teach a one-year course on American history and literature to a group of about thirty-four juniors. We decided to combine a thematic and chronological approach, a method that gave us the structure when needed and the flexibility when desired. We would explore the theme of conflict the first semester and the theme of progress the second.

During the first semester, we studied the conflicts between Native Americans and Europeans and visited the Museum of American Indians. We studied the conflict between the colonists and the British, published a class newspaper on the American Revolution, studied government and law, and held a mock trial. Considering it was our first semester in the project, we were quite successful, but only felt that we were truly connecting with one another at the end of each unit when we collaborated on projects. It wasn't until David joined in the spring term that a more integrated, interdisciplinary approach emerged.

David: The schedule of joint preps and back-to-back classes provided the structural conditions for a deep collaboration. In practice, for the first semester that Bill and Lia worked together without a university partner, the potential was only partially fulfilled. Most days they did not meet during their common prep period; there were simply too many other claims upon their time.

Bill: In retrospect, many crucial things occurred early on in our collaboration that ensured our later success. Before David's involvement, Lia and I did not meet regularly during our common preparation period, resulting in haphazard planning. With five classes and more than 150 students to teach per day, some obstacle to planning would always creep up: running off or picking up copies, conferring with students or parents, and marking papers. David's decision to be with us twice a week forced us to meet and plan during our prep period.

David: On my first day at Bryant High School, February 4, 1998, I met briefly with Suzanne Valenza, the ASHP Queen College seminar leader, and Bill and Lia. I had been detained at the front desk, where no one could find a pass admitting me into the building. Bill rescued me, and when I arrived at the faculty lounge, there was time for only a short introduction, a quick look at the books and topics for the semester, and a discussion of when I would come (Tuesday-Thursday). Bill and Lia apologized that their classes were not currently linked, but said they hoped to bring the classes together. Suzanne and I rushed with Bill to the English class, while Lia returned to the social studies office.

Suzanne and I sat in the back left corner of a traditional classroom, the desks all in rows and the teacher up front. Bill did not leave the area of his desk during the entire period. The English class was in the middle of a unit on Civil War short stories, to be followed by one on Civil War poetry. For that day, Bill had assigned Ambrose Bierce's "Incident at Owl Creek Bridge." The students had a homework sheet on which they had answered questions about the story, some interpretive, others factual. According to the "Aim" for the lesson on the board, Bill was teaching about characterization. But what I heard that day were a lot of questions about the plot. After it became clear that no one had read the whole story (which has a surprise ending), he gave the students a summary. Instead of close readings or supporting their reactions from something specific in the text, he led them in a discussion of the plot he had summarized. Since he seldom referred directly to the text itself, and just discussed the meaning of the story generally, I wondered why he had asked the students to read the story in the first place.

Upstairs, Lia's class had already begun its study of Reconstruction. In my notes, I recorded astonishment that she led a general discussion about Reconstruction for which the students had no information. They were not memorizing facts, and they were not engaging in a brainstorming session about the options facing the nation at the beginning of Reconstruction. They were discussing, at a surface level, what sorts of things might have gone on during Reconstruction, while Lia put up an array of organizations and terms as board notes. None of this was the innovative pedagogy I had been expecting from ASHP teachers after half a year in the program.

Afterwards, Suzanne and I went out to Dunkin Donuts. Over coffee (my field notes record a medium, black, no sugar), she told me what ASHP expected of me as the CUNY partner in this classroom. Sit in the back. Relax. Help Lia and Bill plan a way to bring the classes together. Co-teach a little as Bill and Lia become comfortable with my presence. Model having the desks in a circle. Read documents more creatively. Suzanne talked about the mock trial Lia and Bill had team taught for a week at the end of December, how hard the teachers and students had worked, how they were "poised for take-off." She was clear about my role, and told me to take time to form partnerships with the faculty, talk through the curriculum, and change slowly, incrementally, as they want to or as they become comfortable with me.

As I came regularly, we had meetings during the prep period and exchanged comments during class. They focused, at first, on the need for a plan to bring the classes together. Bill said he would start the class reading the *Song of Solomon* by Toni Morrison[9] on February 23 and end it on March 13. He had his coverage of the book planned. The question was, Where would social studies meet him, and would the students do any project for both teachers? We talked about the possibility of doing something thematic so that the courses would tie together, and decided to arrange the social studies class to present the African American experience from 1877-1963, the years covered by the book. Lia felt that she knew this material far better than she knew Reconstruction and she could carry it off, and I pledged to get some materials together and help her. During group work on Civil War poetry, I suggested to Bill that I could teach part of the English class, perhaps something on Milkman's class position, and the range of social mobility in African American Detroit in the thirties and forties. I accused Bill of having all the fun, and he said, "Yeah, you can stand up here for a few classes." We talked about the possibility of doing another trial to repeat the success of last semester. The next day I came with some trial material of my own, when Bill announced that he did not have time for a trial in his class, and neither did Lia. They would never get through the book/time periods if they did. We settled instead on focusing in on the development of segregation, and got some material together on immigrants as well as blacks, in preparation for the book *Maggie* by Stephen Crane.[10]

Bill: The extent of David's participation in class came up early, and David made it clear that he was there to support us, not to lead us. His role in the classroom and the extent of his involvement, he said, would be left entirely to our discretion. Intentionally or not, David elected to make his involvement in the classroom gradual rather than immediate. By doing so, he reinforced the idea that it was our classroom. More importantly, it permitted David and the students to get to know one another, and it likewise allowed us to learn more about each other, both personally and professionally. We realized, for example, that although we taught on different grade levels, we shared many common goals. We were all deeply committed to our students, to our profession as educators, and to our families.

After he taught a short lesson on Toni Morrison's *Song of Solomon,*[11] David became an integral part of the classroom as we explored ways to integrate history and literature in meaningful ways. With each new ambitious project, we learned valuable lessons about making an integrated classroom work. Once, for example, we combined both periods to discuss the different ways people deal with racism. We began with a debate on whether or not violence is justified. Then David led the class in a close reading in which students chose significant passages from the text and reacted to them as they examined the main characters' opposing viewpoints on the subject. Finally, we had students read the views of Martin Luther King, Jr., and Malcolm X and relate them to those of the characters. We learned that we don't need to wait until the end of a unit to make connections. By locating a few central sections in the literature that could be tied into the history, we could collaborate more frequently and even strategically prepare students for the more extensive end-of-unit projects.

David: The class on Martin Luther King, Jr., and Malcolm X was, for me, a turning point in our collaboration. Up until then, when I taught part of a lesson, it was just me up at the front of the room instead of Bill or Lia. It was not jointly planned, and it did not change anything fundamental about the teaching. But that class was different. In *Song of Solomon*, the main character, Milkman, has a confrontation with his best friend and accuses him of sounding like Malcolm X. The scene is set in Detroit in 1963 at the very moment when Malcolm X delivered his famous "Speech to the Grassroots." I got a copy of the speech, showed Bill and Lia the similarities between the chapter and the speech, and proposed a lesson. In the prep period, we marked the passages we thought were most significant. I asked if we could have the students run their own discussion based on the passages that spoke to them, while sitting in a full circle. Bill and Lia agreed. During the English period, we gave the students part of the speech to read and told them to mark the passages that seemed important to them, and to compare them with the chapter we were reading in *Song of Solomon*. When we switched to the history room, Lia had already set up the large circle, and the students took their seats. With all three of us present, I introduced the discussion, asking them to raise their hands; after each person finished, that person called on the next speaker. They discussed most of the passages we had found important, their arguments persuaded us that the other lines were significant too, and they really saw the larger political points that connected Malcolm X's speech and Toni Morrison's fiction. The selection from King was a short response to both viewpoints that touched off a heated debate. By the end of the double period, students had a strong sense of the debate over nonviolence that was starting to divide the civil rights community.

Bill: Another turning point came after completing *Song of Solomon*. While reading the novel, I noticed that the author alluded to many myths, fairy tales, and folk tales. I made copies of these stories and gave them to the students. They were to read them all, but were assigned to write about how one of those stories related to *Song of Solomon*. I then placed them in groups according to their assigned story, and they prepared a presentation for the class. Finally, I introduced the test, which was to write their own fairy tale or myth that would relate to *Song of Solomon*. Together we worked out a rubric for grading their stories. They wrote, critiqued, and revised them. When they submitted their final drafts, we were shocked to see that some students wrote stories up to fifteen pages long. Throughout this alternative assessment activity, Lia and David were patient with me. The activity didn't exactly tie in very well with American history, but rather than dissuade me from carrying it out, they encouraged and supported me. In fact, we abstracted some of the principles and applied them to future collaborations. We realized, for instance, that giving students a structure and clear expectations was important, but helping them acquire a sense of ownership over their work by offering them the freedom to choose what to write about was just as important if we wanted anything of substance.

David: While Bill worked to complete the fiction writing, Lia and I extended the thematic approach to African American history to include looks at the women's movement, environmentalism, and the gay rights movement. These were fairly standard classes, remarkable only insofar as we were talking about the 1980s and it was only the beginning of March. We went back to the 1880s to look at the rise of cities, industrialization, and immigration, but all the while we were grading and suggesting revisions to the English papers.

When we started working on the new unit, we proceeded largely from documents. We used selections from *Plunkitt of Tammany Hall*[12] to give the political machine view of city politics and *Twenty Years At Hull-House*[13] to give one reform perspective. *How The Other Half Lives*[14] provided us with Jacob Riis's description of life in the tenements, and the mixture of compassion and loathing he felt toward the immigrants and their children. Selections from *A Bintel Brief*[15] and *The Life Stories of Undistinguished Americans as Told by Themselves*,[16] though somewhat doctored by their publishers, allowed some of the new Americans to speak for themselves. Some of these sources came from my bookshelf, Bill pulled some things off the web, and Lia brought some sheets from the social studies department resource shelf. All of these sources threatened to confuse our students completely, drown them in materials, and throw off the course. We had to work hard to get them to go beyond reading the documents and accepting them as true. We had to help them understand how to work with different views of the same situation, and this was equally true as we started the next book in English class.

Bill: While reading our next book, Stephen Crane's *Maggie: A Girl of the Streets*,[17] we learned one other important lesson. David had given the students an assignment after reading the book in which he asked students to rewrite an aspect of Maggie's story from a divergent viewpoint. We were disappointed with the results. Students either made general statements without supporting them, or merely repeated the plot without altering it much. We identified the problem: students were not familiar with the concept of point of view and had difficulties understanding what to do and how to do it. To help them, we prepared a talk show using both the literary characters in *Maggie* and the historical figures of the Progressive Era.

David: The show's topic was "People Who Feel Their Problems Are Beyond Solving," and it featured Maggie, her mother, brother, and lover. Historical guests included Jane Addams, George Washington Plunkitt, and Jacob Riis. The double period allowed us to have students write prepared statements (including audience opinions) during "English" and then stage the show during the "social studies" period. All three of us were in the classroom the entire time. Bill hosted the talk show while Lia taped it.

Bill: The show was a success, and we used it as a springboard to discuss with the class the concept of point of view and to help them improve their rewriting of *Maggie*. This experience taught us that we could indeed teach students difficult concepts if we discovered ways to relate the concepts to more familiar elements of their own experience. More importantly, we began to feel that our collaboration went beyond simply making connections between English and history to making connections between the subjects and the lives of our students.

David: In teaching point of view, we also tried to articulate ideas about interpretation. We used a standard school worksheet on President Teddy Roosevelt to look for "facts" versus "interpretations" and say aloud that calling him an "active" president or "good" president is an act of interpretation, and that students could reach different conclusions from the relatively few facts the worksheet provided.

Bill: Toward the end of the term, we met at Lia's apartment during Spring Recess to plan for the remainder of the year. We wanted our students to integrate and further the knowledge they had gained about New York City and the problems people encountered living in it. After four to five hours, we had outlined a three-part project that we introduced to the class as the end-of-term project. The first part was a collaborative research paper in which students were to describe a social problem in New York City from the 1880s to the present, analyze its causes and effects, and offer viable solutions. The second part asked students to conduct an oral history interview that would shed more light on their topic. Finally, each group was to prepare a presentation through which group members would synthesize what they had learned and present their knowledge to the class in a creative fashion. We did not consciously attempt it, but the end-of-term project incorporated all the lessons we had learned about successful interdisciplinary teaching.

By having students work on social problems, students were able to benefit from the work we had already done on the topic. By focusing on New York City, students were motivated to learn more about their topics and felt more comfortable evaluating what they read. The pressure of learning to write an academic research paper was mitigated by the use of group work and interesting subjects that were somewhat familiar to the students. More importantly, we offered students many choices that gave them a sense of ownership over their projects. For example, we began the project by brainstorming some of the problems that existed in New York City during the time in which *Maggie* took place, the late 1800s. Students mentioned problems such as alcohol abuse, child abuse, racism, inequality, prostitution, housing, and many more. We then asked students to consider which problems still exist today, and students were surprised to notice how many problems Maggie faced that still exist today. At that point, we asked the students to come to the board and print their names under the topic they were interested in studying further. Students had further choices. For instance, we informed students that their presentations could take any form, and we suggested the following: role playing, exhibit, news broadcast, documentary, radio or television show, panel discussion, debate, or some type of video presentation.

David: This project represents the most dramatic curriculum change that came out of our team teaching. Rather than read another book, or teach a series of lessons on twentieth century America, we assigned and worked on this long-term research project. To help give the students a context, and to help with the standardized New York State Regents Examination, I used two periods to give a lecture (with handouts) on major New Deal and Great Society legislation, and discuss how it changed domestic conditions. But the time that would have been spent in classes on domestic politics from 1920 to the present was given over to trips to the library, writing, interviews, and revision. During those weeks, Lia scaled back her history teaching, and concentrated only on U.S. foreign policy. Both Lia and Bill said at the time that by working so closely with me, they had started to think more about the next step, college and work, and less about the curriculum as its own end. From this perspective, having students conduct and present their own research project was more important then covering more events or another book. It was also still aligned with state and city learning standards. In the end, these students scored about ten percent higher on the Regents exam than the department average. We decided they must have covered enough material after all.

Bill: The most important insights for interdisciplinary teaching came from this project. I learned that the best teaching comes not when you teach students what you think they must know, but when you teach them those things about which they want to know. The developmental lessons gave way to mini-lessons and more one-to-one and group conferences. We helped students learn the skills they would need to write the research paper successfully. They learned how to read sources critically by distinguishing between and evaluating opinions and facts, and by recognizing the relationship between general and specific statements. They learned how to take effective notes in order to organize them and prevent plagiarism. We had not planned to have students cite their works, but after discussing the idea, we decided that we would try it. Students were introduced to many of the skills they would need in order to do all of these things. They learned about organizing note cards, the importance of and relationship between the works cited page and the parenthetical citations in the text, and about different methods of incorporating notes into the final paper. We also wanted students to conduct their own research. We told students that while we were willing to supply each group with sources from the 1880s, we would expect them to find their own sources for the present. We arranged for a visit to the library, and students were introduced to the resources that they would need to conduct their research.

For the next few days, students continued reading their sources and sharing their research with one another. Finally, when the first draft was due, students compiled the different sections and created their bibliography. We closely scrutinized each paper, made many recommendations in writing, returned the papers, and gave another deadline for a revision.

We then introduced the oral history interview in greater detail. We compared the journalistic interview and the historical interview we were asking them to do.[18] A journalist goes after a specific story, often interrupting answers and avoiding digressions. An oral historian listens and asks clarifying questions, but allows the interviewee to tell the story in an extended fashion. Oral history interviews are most successful when they alternate comments about the big picture (how people in general felt about some-thing) with specific and detailed examples from the interviewee's own life. We explained that we didn't want a transcript of the interview. We wanted them to write an integrated essay that (1) had a clear thesis, but that also described what happened; (2) related some interesting stories; (3) explained what new learning transpired; (4) placed the interview in the context of the research that had already been conducted; and (5) reflected on the experience and process of doing the interview. Although students complained about all the work that they had to do, once they began to work on the interviews, they started to realize how exciting the assignment actually was.

There were many moments when we, too, shared in our students' joy. I remember when Michelle came to see me early one morning to tell me that she had contacted one of the authors she had cited in her report and he agreed to a personal interview. Besma, Lejla, and Oscar, who were working on the topic of education, came to see me right before going to interview the principal of our school. They later confided that the project was meaningful for them because they not only learned about their topic, but they also met the principal of their school.

Finally, students were told about the presentations in greater detail. We explained that the purpose of the presentations was for each group to share its findings with the rest of the class, but to do so in a creative fashion. We thus forbade any direct presentation of any of their findings. Students decided to debate the use of child labor, to videotape interviews with students and teachers from local high schools about the problems in public school education, and to do many other creative presentations.

A Teacher Talks to Teachers (V.M.)

In hindsight, our collaboration worked because we took time to get to know each other and to establish an understanding early on. We felt that David was there to support us and that he was a member of the team. He was not there merely to observe, criticize, or suggest ways to improve. Collaboration can fail for many reasons: personality conflicts, inconsistent goals, lack of planning, low self-esteem, and a hostile administration. For us, the benefits of collaborating outweigh any of the dangers that might be associated with it. Indeed, one of the ways to make teaching more satisfying and professional is to expand opportunities to meet new people and form partnerships that will combat the isolationism many teachers feel, partnerships that might even turn into life-long friendships.

A Professor Talks to Professors (D.G.)

Here is a gross generalization: The greatest gift a classroom teacher can give is an open door. Most people who pass through that door are inspectors/evaluators who are neutral at best and hostile at worst. I realize this is not always the case, but I was always aware that Bill and Lia were taking an enormous risk in openly welcoming me into their daily teaching lives. Much of the magical transformation that came about in those classrooms had more to do with the side effects of my presence and very little to do with my own specialized knowledge of American history or social studies education. In sitting down to plan with me and explain their courses, Bill and Lia were also meeting regularly to plan with each other. In walking in from outside the school, my presence, not my expertise, also reminded them of the demands of the college and outside world. This consciousness changed what they valued in the classroom and led to the research project. The suggestions I made, for the Malcolm X lesson, or the oral history project, came later on and were not the crucial reasons why we formed a team and transformed our classroom practice. The most important ingredient was the willingness that Bill and Lia showed to let me into their classes, my appreciation of that extraordinary action, and our combined comfort with letting the collaboration take its own time. And it is not over. Lia has moved out of New York City but we are still loosely in touch, while Bill and I are still writing about that semester and looking forward to future collaborations.

NOTES

1. Kenneth T. Jackson, ed., *Encyclopedia of New York City* (New York: New York Historical Society, 1995).
2. Jonathon Kozol, *Savage Inequalities: Children in America's Schools* (New York: Crown Publishers, 1991).
3. For more information on the program, see www.ashp.cuny.edu/mc.html.
4. David Gerwin and Vassilios Manolios, with Lia Papadopoulos, "Using Stephen Crane's *Maggie* to teach the Progressive Era," *OAH Magazine of History* 13 (1999): 33-35.
5. Joseph Cambone, "Time for Teachers in School Restructuring," *Teachers College Record* 96 (1995): 512-544.
6. American Social History Project, *Who Built America?* Vol. 2 (New York: Pantheon, 1992).
7. Andy Hargreaves, *Changing Teachers, Changing Times* (New York: Teachers College Press, 1994), 104-140.
8. Steven Zemelman, Harvey Daniels, and Arthur Hyde, *Best Practice: New Standards for Teaching and Learning in America's Schools* (Portsmouth, N.H.: Heineman, 1998), 115-134.
9. Toni Morrison, *Song of Solomon* (New York: Signet/New American Library, 1977).
10. Stephen Crane, *Maggie: A Girl of the Streets* (New York: Norton, 1979).
11. Morrison, *Song of Solomon.*
12. William Riordan, ed., *Plunkitt of Tammany Hall* (Boston, Mass.: Bedford Books, 1994 [1905]).
13. Jane Addams, *Twenty Years at Hull House* (New York: Macmillan, 1938 [1910]).
14. Jacob Riis, *How the Other Half Lives* (Boston, Mass.: Bedford Books, 1996 [1890]).
15. Isaac Metzker, ed., *A Bintel Brief: Sixty Years of Letters from the Lower East Side to The Jewish Daily Forward* (New York: Ballantine Books, 1971).
16. Hamilton Holt, ed., *The Life Stories of Undistinguished Americans as Told by Themselves*, 2d ed. (New York: Routledge, 1990).
17. Crane, *Maggie.*
18. Donald Ritchie, *Doing Oral History* (New York: Simon and Schuster, 1994).

Dual Agendas of Reform and Research: Implementing the Reforms of the Coalition of Essential Schools through "World Connections"

Twelve

MERRY M. MERRYFIELD
STEVE SHAPIRO

The Scene

It is January 8, 1992. Cold gray skies threaten snow as we hurry past construction on the new wing, one of the more tangible signs of growth at Reynoldsburg High School in Reynoldsburg, Ohio. But we have more profound changes on our minds as we settle down around the table in the principal's conference room to discuss what is being learned from Merry's documentation of our team's implementation of Coalition of Essential Schools (CES) reforms. For four months, Merry has been spending one day a week working with the World Connections team as we plan and teach ninety-two tenth graders through personalization, backwards-building curriculum, performance-based assessment, and interdisciplinary teaming (discussed in more depth later in this chapter). Present today are Dan Hoffman (principal), Cheri Dunlap (assistant principal), Merry Merryfield (professor from Ohio State University [OSU]), and the team members, Steve Shapiro (social studies), Barb Levak (English), Debbie Calhoun (math), and Bob Wilson (biology).

Dan: Thanks, Merry, for giving us in advance the copies of your write-up of the World Connections team meetings and classroom observations. We appreciate your time with the team and welcome this opportunity to discuss what everyone is learning about teaching through Coalition of Essential Schools principles. In reading the transcripts of the team meetings, I was particularly struck by the way each person plays specific roles and how unique his or her contributions are. The team seems to work well because of the obligations members feel to each other. They don't want to let each other down. You have captured how much they care about each other.

Bob: This is true, but it also means we feel a lot of pressure to "maintain" the team.

Barb: When I read back over the transcripts of the team meetings, I can really see the stress we are under. Implementing the Coalition of Essential Schools reforms for the first time is redefining the role of the teacher as well as the students.

Steve: I see how we often have more questions than answers. Making decisions over the curriculum is continuous, and our ideas are constantly emerging, changing, being debated, and revised. At least now after four months of struggling with these decisions, we are becoming used to the ambiguity and flexibility. This information reads as though social studies and English drive the themes. Merry, maybe you need to spend more time with Debbie and Bob since there may be a social studies bias at work.

Debbie: It isn't necessarily bias. You are trying to document what is happening and as the initial sentence states, English and social studies are where the real connections are.

Cheri: The transcripts of the classes are useful since the teachers and administrators rarely get to see each other teach. This description of how teachers actually integrate content areas is important when the team or school is called upon to describe the process. But CES principles are not just content integration.

Merry: And there are very few data on student thinking about the exhibitions, teaming, the block scheduling, or personalization. Should I try to address those information needs? What's not in here that I can help with?

Bob: How about student attitudes toward active involvement in the classroom? We want to introduce student portfolios and start reflective writing next month.

The meeting continues with discussion of themes in the documentation and ends with decisions to use portfolio assessment and interviews to learn about student thinking.

Our Conceptualization of Improving Social Studies

In the 1990s, educational reformer Phil Schlecty prefaced his ideas on school reform by imagining what a group of Martians would think about our system of education if the group happened upon a typical American high school. He speculated that the Martians, after spending a day observing in a school, would probably report back to their leader, "We have landed in a place where the younger generation goes to watch the older generation work." This observation also holds true for many social studies classrooms and illustrates two great ironies of social studies education. We are trying to prepare students to be active citizens in a democracy by requiring them to be passive learners in the classroom. Second, our content area is often identified as the most boring subject by peer-obsessed adolescents, yet it has the word "social" in the title!

In this chapter, we discuss how we have worked together to apply the principles of Coalition of Essential Schools reforms so that students are actively involved in content that is meaningful to them. The CES principles grew out of the work of Ted Sizer, a researcher at Brown University, who undertook a major project in the late 1980s to understand the American high school. For a year, Sizer followed the schedules of randomly drawn students in high schools across the country. He learned about high schools through the eyes of students as he observed schools and talked extensively with students about their concerns and issues.[1] From his research, Sizer identified problems with the deep structure of American high schools and formulated a network for whole school reform that came to be called the Coalition of Essential Schools. He recognized that the high school's structure of six to eight forty-five- to fifty-minute classes and a teaching load of 120 to 180 students a day kept teachers from giving students sufficient personal attention, and prohibited their assigning work that is complex and requires extensive time to grade. Teachers rarely worked together across disciplines, and, consequently, students did not see relationships between the literature they read in English and the cultures studied in geography or their work in art, music, foreign languages, or science despite obvious connections in the real world around them. He noted that the survey-style of most curricula (such as all of world history in 180 days) places an emphasis on coverage and memorization of superficial data, not depth of understanding of important issues, thinking skills, or application of knowledge. In studying school district organization, he came to realize how the people closest to students had the least control over the curriculum, resources, or the organization of the school day. The principles of the Coalition of Essential Schools address these problems and others.

When we first met, Reynoldsburg High School was beginning to implement the CES principles. Our World Connections team was focusing on these four: (1) personalization, (2) student as worker, teacher as coach, (3) performance-based assessment, and (4) backwards-building curriculum. We believe these reforms strengthen social studies instruction.

Personalization

When we created our first interdisciplinary teams in the spring of 1990, teaming across social studies, language arts, science, math, and art rarely happened in American high schools. It has grown more popular as teachers have recognized teaming as one way to address the lack of personal attention that individual students receive in most large high schools. Many students feel alienated by their school and lack a sense of belonging. Many parents of high school students have no contact with any of their children's teachers throughout the school year. Our team's goal was to create a more personalized school experience for the ninety students our team of five teachers shared. The teachers on our team met daily to talk about student issues, their learning styles, their problems, and their successes. The result was that we understood each student more fully than we would have without the team discussions. We conducted team conferences with students and parents and collaborated on interdisciplinary planning so that we understood what students were learning in their other core classes and could coordinate skills, content, and assignments across our content. We created a newsletter to keep parents informed about what their children were doing in school. Formalizing advisory arrangements, we made sure that each of our students had one teacher who worked with him or her on special issues ranging from career planning to administrative tasks. The team collaboration led to our knowing our students and their parents better than we ever had before and the students working more closely with us.

Student as Worker, Teacher as Coach

The second goal we addressed was the CES principle of student as worker, teacher as coach. We thought about Schlecty's Martian scenario and envisioned a classroom in which students were actively involved in their own learning through collaboration and engagement similar to an adult work environment. Creating this environment involves extensive teacher planning, and maintaining it requires intense coaching of students throughout the learning and assessment process.

Although there is certainly a place for direct instruction, many social studies teachers rely exclusively on students passively receiving information from lecture, videos, and the authority of the textbook, and giving it back on worksheets and tests. If we are preparing young people to make decisions as citizens in a democracy, however, they need practice in finding new knowledge in history and the social sciences, evaluating conflicting information from many sources, and analyzing issues facing their communities, nation, and world.

Backwards-Building Curriculum and Performance-Based Assessment

Backwards-building curriculum rests on the CES assumptions that (1) students should master a limited number of essential skills and knowledge and (2) schools should help students use their minds well. Every history teacher is familiar with the problem of finishing a school year somewhere around the topic of World War II. Being unable to complete a course of study often results when teachers try to teach everything and run out of time before getting to some essential knowledge. Sizer would argue that social studies teachers must make tough decisions about what is most important in the curriculum rather than let the school calendar make those decisions for them. Thus, the backwards-building process begins with teachers making very difficult decisions about what knowledge and skills are truly essential for a particular course. If we try to teach students everything that has ever happened, we will not only run out of time, but we will have to give superficial treatment to all topics so we can "cover" content and move on. An overview of topics is clearly not the best way to help students use their minds well.

There are several important elements in backwards building. First is the process of identifying essential knowledge and skills to be learned in a unit. Next, the teacher develops essential questions that students will be expected to answer by the end of the unit. The assessments are then developed to examine how the students can use essential knowledge and skills to answer the essential questions. Finally comes the process of planning daily lessons that prepare students with the skills and knowledge needed to complete the unit assessments successfully.

In developing the unit assessments, our team members looked to our essentials and asked ourselves, "What can our students do to demonstrate that they have mastered the essential knowledge and skills?" Notice the implication of activity in the question: What can our students do? Frequently, social studies educators rely on multiple-choice, fill-in-the-blank, or matching questions as our main form of assessment. Reliance solely on these traditional assessment practices raises some important questions for social studies teachers. Do traditional tests show that students have mastered and can use knowledge and skills? Do traditional tests require students to use higher-level thinking? Will students ever complete a traditional test after their school years? If knowledge is useful for something beyond school testing, why not assess students on their ability to use the knowledge in ways that we expect them to use it in their adult lives? Our second goal, performance-based assessment, is an attempt to deal with these challenging questions.[2]

Assessment is the primary means by which we communicate to our students what we believe is important. No matter how much we pontificate about the importance of learning the lessons of history or about the importance of active citizenship, our students continue to ask the same question: Is this going to be on the test? We must ask ourselves the difficult question, "Why is it important for students to study social studies?" Then we must make sure that our assessments engage students in those processes. Performance-based assessment is needed to evaluate students' ability to demonstrate citizenship.

An Illustration of Beginning the Backwards-Building Process through Essential Knowledge, Skills, and Questions

To illustrate how one begins backwards building, we are drawing from a unit plan that we wrote about in 1995. We briefly outline how the World Connections team selected the essential knowledge and skills and developed the essential questions. For an in-depth look at the backwards-building process and a detailed description of the construction of the authentic assessments, see the actual unit plan.[3]

STEP 1: SELECTING THE ESSENTIAL CONTENT

Our World Connections team identifies themes for the year by using the curriculum mapping strategy developed by Heidi Hayes-Jacobs at Columbia University.[4] The unit discussed here was developed after our team's curriculum mapping identified the existence of international conflict and the desire to resolve it as part of the curricula for our biology, English, and global studies courses. The global nature of our program goals shaped our approach in choosing content because we wanted the conflicts studied to have global implications and be characterized by global dynamics that have an impact across national borders and involve different types of world actors.

With the unit theme identified as international conflict resolution (the management or resolution of conflicts that affect people in more than one part of the world), we began making decisions on the specific content (knowledge and skills) for global studies. We looked for possible connections with the curriculum guide for global studies by creating a list of topics in the course that would lend themselves to the study of conflict resolution. The list contained several historical as well as contemporary conflicts. We narrowed our choice of content to the racial conflict in South Africa or the Arab-Israeli conflict in the Middle East. Both topics met the interdisciplinary criteria of involving global dynamics, many types of world actors, and local-global connections. Both topics appeared in the news almost daily, and we had extensive instructional materials and resources in the school and community about each conflict. The Arab-Israeli theme could easily tie in historically to the English course readings.

In the end, however, we chose racial conflict in South Africa because of considerations about our students. Racial prejudice, "differences" between so-called "White" and "Black" Americans, and related discrimination are significant issues in our students' daily lives. They hear about and deal with racial conflicts in the school, the community, our nation, and the world. As social studies teachers, we believe that we must prepare our students to overcome racism, particularly the "Black/White" issues that are so much a part of American and world history and contemporary life here and in many other countries. We also recognized that our students, like most Americans, know little about Africa, African peoples, and nations beyond the stereotypes of films or the war and starvation stories that characterize most print and television coverage of the continent. We also knew that the larger interdisciplinary unit would give students the opportunity to make connections with other international conflicts, such as those in the Middle East and elsewhere, as part of their final assessment.

Racial conflict in South Africa also demonstrates how conflicts within a country spill out to affect economic choices (e.g., foreign investment and marketing, roles of multinational corporations), political relationships (bilateral decisions to boycott, ban imports, or restrict movement of people, "pariah" status in the world community), and cultural matters (ban on entertainers going to South Africa, ban on participation in the Olympics) around the world. Because racial conflict is a global issue, the study of South Africa can provide insights into the management of racial conflict in other parts of the world.

Essential content is the body of knowledge and skills essential to a working understanding and application of the topic or theme. In identifying essential content, we ask ourselves, "If we were to see one of these students in a couple of years and strike up a conversation about South Africa, what would we expect that he or she would still know about the topic?" We use this question because we have found it is important not to get so bogged down in the details that students fail to understand the vital concepts or generalizations. It is important to remember that when we give a traditional test, a student who doesn't know 15 percent of the information on test day receives a very respectable grade. The same student, a week later, will certainly remember less about the topic than he or she did the day of the test. It is a sobering experience to consider how that student would do on the exact same test if it were taken a year or two or a decade later. It is our opinion that in an effort to "cover" everything, we have buried students under a blanket of trivia and denied them an internalized, meaningful understanding of the "big picture."

Our list of essential knowledge emerged from brainstorming, debate, and careful consideration of what the students needed to know in order to apply the South Africa conflict to other international conflicts and peacemaking. The process of reflecting and prioritizing is important (see Figure 1). We also began to think about which skills would be most appropriate for the unit. We outlined essential skills during the early planning process and revised and updated them as we planned the assessment and developed the lessons. See Figure 1 for the essential skills.

STEP 2: DEVELOPING THE ESSENTIAL QUESTIONS

Just as Socrates was able to teach important lessons to his students by asking them thoughtful, fundamental questions, we as teachers use questioning to develop reflection and higher-level thought processes. It is extremely valuable for teachers to think about and identify fundamental questions that get to the core of the complex issues related to a unit's significance. The CES researchers and practitioners refer to these as essential questions. Our entire team works together to develop essential questions for our interdisciplinary units; a teacher in a self-contained classroom can follow the same process.

There are several characteristics of essential questions. First, they are broad, open-ended questions that bring about serious discussion, debate, and critical thought. Second, essential questions do not have a "correct" answer. Rather they have many possible answers, each of which can be defended with ideas and evidence. Third, essential questions go to the heart of content. Through the study and debate of essential questions, students take apart, examine, apply, and learn the unit's most important knowledge and skills. The real test of essential questions is, Must the students master the essential knowledge and skills in order to answer the essential questions? The questions are revised until we are confident that there is this congruence between the essential knowledge and skills, and essential questions.

Although our team generates a single set of essential questions for an interdisciplinary unit, an individual teacher can do the same for a self-contained classroom. While there is no magic formula, our team tends to use four to six questions for a given unit. We also attempt to sequence the questions from most basic to most complex. Our team began the process of developing essential questions on international conflict resolution by considering the nature of these questions, the content of the unit, and the characteristics of our students. As we brainstormed ideas, we wrote them on the board for consideration. Questions were rejected if they did not meet the criteria of essential questions (see above), fit the demands of interdisciplinary connections to biology, English, and global studies, or meet the needs of our students. Our initial list read as follows:

1. What causes international conflict?
2. What makes a conflict "global?"
3. In what ways can international conflict be resolved?
4. Is it necessary that international conflict be resolved?
5. What causes conflict resolution to be long lasting?
6. What are hurdles to conflict resolution?

Figure 1: Webbing Methods and Resources for Essential Knowledge, Skills, and Questions

lecture, readings, newsclips, text
primary sources—speeches, documents

timeline of race relations
and conflicts

atlases, maps,
gov't statistics

Essential Knowledge

1. Major historical and contemporary steps in the South African evolution of racial conflict...

Biko's *I Write What I Like*, *Mine Boy*, *Kaffir Boy* Mandela's *No Easy Walk to Freedom*

2. The relative size, geography, economic and political power of different racial and ethnic groups...

Inkatha

3. Multiple perspectives (of South Africans and others)

bankers and divestment DeBeers and diamonds

4. The role of economics in the racial conflict...

Simulation for multiple perspectives—Starpower? Red Green? Ba Fa Ba Fa?

5. The role of political forces struggling for power...

6. The use of the military, violence, negotiation...

World Bank data

UN peacekeepers

Gandhi, M.L. King

ANC Freedom Charter

filmstrip *Mosiac of Progress* video *South Africa Belongs to Us* or *Cry Freedom*

writing the proposal

Essential Skills

work in English

1. Abilities to conceptualize, write work in English, present and defend a proposal...

2. Abilities to analyze, evaluate and predict the effects (dynamics)...

3. The ability to work collaboratively with peers...

decision-trees

group process and presentations

dynamics webbing

The Essential Questions

Link to essential knowledge (above)

1. When is a conflict global?

link to 1, 4, 6

2. What causes conflict to be global?

link to 6

3. What are the ramifications of global conflict and its management or resolution?

link to 1, 3, 5, 6

4. Why is conflict resolution difficult to achieve?

5. How can we determine most effective resolution to conflict?

link to 2 and 6

7. What are the ramifications of conflict?
8. Why do we need to think globally?
9. How can we determine the most effective resolution to a conflict?
10. How do global conflicts affect you?
11. Why is conflict resolution so difficult to achieve?
12. How does a global perspective affect the way you understand conflict?

In looking back over the suggestions, question 8 was quickly eliminated as unnecessary (the students had been studying global perspectives all year) and too broad for the theme. Question 3 was eliminated because it does not require sufficient critical thought, and can be answered by listing approaches to conflict resolution. Question 5 was eliminated because we felt that it required study that would not be included in sufficient depth in this unit. Instead, we could include this issue by revising question 7 to read, "What are the ramifications of global conflict *and its management or resolution?*" We felt that question 12 was redundant and could be eliminated because it would be answered through the revised number 7. Although question 4 was closed-ended, it struck us as provocative. However, we decided it would emerge anyway when students pondered alternative approaches to conflict resolution.

After much debate and a few days to reflect on connections with our subject units, we chose the essential questions you see in Figure 1 as these require that students use all the essential knowledge and skills. Our next step was to develop the final assessment in which students had to answer the essential questions. (See the case study by Shapiro and Merryfield for the planning and rubrics of the final assessment.[5] Sections on writing lesson plans for the unit follow the assessment section.)

The CES principles offer a compelling vision for what American schools can be. Their application in the social studies classroom produces an educational environment that is truly aligned with our core beliefs as social studies educators.[6]

Our Process of Collaboration and Some Tangible Outcomes

Our collaboration was initiated in the spring of 1991 as Reynoldsburg High School began to implement the CES reforms. At that time, Steve was in his second year of teaching high school social studies, and Merry was in her third year of teaching social studies and global education at OSU. We first met when Reynoldsburg's district administrators invited OSU faculty to come and discuss possibilities for collaboration. There were many tensions in that first meeting as teachers sat on one side of a large table, professors on the other, and administrators explained what they saw as the potential for our work together. Steve wondered what these OSU faculty were supposed to do when they didn't seem to have much expertise on Coalition of Essential Schools reforms. Merry was concerned that the reform appeared to be top-down, and collaboration was being forced since Reynoldsburg and OSU administrators ran the meeting.

Later, however, when we met by ourselves, it became evident that there were ways in which our interests overlapped, and we could benefit by working together. Steve and his four colleagues on the World Connections team were constructing an interdisciplinary global education course for tenth graders. Although each teacher had expertise in his or her subject matter, none had experience in conceptualizing global education across several disciplines, applying CES reforms, or planning instruction every day with such a large team. The team saw in Merry a resource person who could provide expertise and resources in global education and a researcher who could document the team's process of working together to implement CES reforms. Merry would also provide an outsider's perspective within the team meetings, and her notes and writing could be used to help others understand the complexities of backwards-building curriculum, performance-based assessments, and team-teaching interdisciplinary units developed around global themes and issues.

At that time, Merry was engaged in a research project with elementary, middle, and high school teachers who were considered the best among global educators in Columbus, Ohio. When Steve explained the dynamic curriculum of World Connections and the plans that the team had for integrating content from math, science, art, language arts, and social studies around global themes and issues, Merry saw a wonderful opportunity to expand her own research in global education and learn about CES reforms firsthand. Although Merry had read Sizer's *Horace's Compromise*, she had no firsthand knowledge of how teachers apply CES reforms in their practice. Thus, our weekly collaboration began in September 1991, with separate but overlapping goals.

Steve's primary goal was to work with his team to develop and teach interdisciplinary "World Connections" through the CES framework. Merry's goal in collaborating was to learn about the team's process of instructional decision making in global education and see Coalition of Essential Schools reforms in action. From September 1991 to June 1992, Merry participated in the team's 7:30 a.m. planning meetings once a week, shared resources and expertise on global education, interviewed teachers and students, and observed the connections' block being taught. Merry also collected and analyzed documents each week that ranged from drafts of rubrics and teacher-constructed instructional materials to invitations to parents and exhibition notices. Once a month, Merry, Steve, and the other team members met for breakfast at Bob Evans or after school at Chi Chi's so they could take time to get beyond daily decisions and reflect on the profound changes that they were going through as teachers.

Every ten weeks, Merry provided a copy of her notes to each team member so that members could read and reflect on the transcripts of the planning meetings, the classroom observations, interviews, and the themes and issues emerging from their work together. Before these data were shared with the administrators in January (described briefly in the scene at the beginning of the chapter), the team members had edited Merry's work by adding in some explanations or notes and deleting a few sentences and conversations that were considered too sensitive to share with anyone beyond the team. Over the 1991-92 school year, Merry's documentation also included transcripts of interviews with students, administrators, and other Reynoldsburg teachers who were not directly involved in Coalition of Essential Schools reforms. By spring, the weekly meetings, observations, and occasional debriefing sessions also led to our decision to share what we were learning through presentations at some state and national conferences and through writing an article for *Educational Leadership*.[7]

That first year was an intense and unforgettable learning experience for us. Our work together changed in the second year. Merry met with the World Connections team much less frequently as her support wasn't really needed and other collaborative work in teaching and writing developed. Interested in learning more about global perspectives, Steve entered OSU's graduate program in social studies and global education and began his own study of global education. We worked together with several other teachers to apply what we were learning about teaming, personalization, authentic assessment, and "teacher as coach, student as worker" to initiate OSU's Professional Development School (PDS) Network in Social Studies and Global Education.

We first team taught our field-based ten-credit-hour social studies methods course at Reynoldsburg and other schools in the PDS network in 1992. Other courses followed to meet the needs of both OSU students and Reynoldsburg teachers. Merry and Dan Hoffman, the principal of Reynoldsburg High School, team taught a graduate course on Coalition of Essential Schools reforms for OSU students. The following year, Merry came back to the high school to teach a three-credit-hour global education seminar for twenty-five Reynoldsburg teachers.

Since 1991, there have been many tangible outcomes of our ongoing collaboration, including a dozen conference presentations and several journal articles and chapters.[8] Desperate for detailed instructional materials on how to develop backwards-building curriculum units, we wrote our opus, an eighty-two-page chapter that social studies teachers still use as a step-by-step guide in learning how to develop essential questions, plan rubrics for performance-based assessments, and integrate social studies content with language arts, art, and science.

As we write this in March of 2000, we are team teaching social studies methods and require our preservice teachers to develop skills in personalization, interdisciplinary instruction, authentic assessment, and backwards-building curriculum. CES reforms have spread throughout our PDS Network to other middle and high schools.

There are also several significant yet intangible outcomes from our collaboration. Because of our work together, we each have new knowledge of educational reforms, extensive cross-cultural experiences within each other's institutions, and, above all, friendship based on trust and collegiality. We have learned how to use social studies content as scaffolding to construct interdisciplinary units, and we can teach others to do so. We can structure exhibitions where students demonstrate their abilities to use their skills in research and higher-level thinking and their knowledge of history and the social sciences to address authentic issues within the local community and the world. We have a tacit understanding of the "honeymoon" period of educational reforms and recognize the difficulties that come with sustaining innovations over time. We also have come to understand ourselves as educators better and are aware that both of us enjoy the creativity of developing innovations and the dynamics of new challenges much more than we do the institutionalization and maintenance of educational reform.

A Teacher Speaks to Teachers (S.S.)

The decision to work with a university professor on a collaborative project should not be made lightly. There are many potential pitfalls that I discuss in this section. First, however, I want to outline some of the benefits that such collaboration can offer a practicing teacher.

CONSIDER THE VALUE OF AN OUTSIDER

The most obvious benefit of this type of school/university collaboration is having an outside observer who can give you feedback on your work. Although all good teachers try to reflect on their work, the pace of schools is such that we often fail to find adequate time to capture the lessons from our daily work. Further-more, we are often so close to the work that we have trouble viewing it with any objectivity. Merry's presence throughout our first year of teaming provided us with an invaluable source of outside feedback. In many cases, Merry's feedback came in the form of questions that led us to draw our own conclusions. At times, she provided research or theoretical knowledge to complement our practical experience. When our stress levels were so high that we approached the brink of emotional collapse, Merry was able to place our discomfort within the contexts of others' experiences in education reform. In a profession marked by isolation, this collaboration provided invaluable community.

Just as an "authentic" audience helps our students achieve greater success, Merry served as an authentic audience for our work as teachers. Although each team member was professional and conscientious, the presence of a university professor in our meetings and in our classrooms pushed us to be at our very best. That Merry chose to research our team gave us a sense that what we were doing was important. We did not want to disappoint her or our students and colleagues. Knowing that our work was being observed and written about led us to rise to the occasion and achieve our goals.

Merry's presence also had a positive effect on our students as they dealt with the changes of CES reforms. Of course, our students were aware of this outside presence (and her laptop!) in their classrooms. Who is she? Why is she here? Why did she choose to come to Reynoldsburg? Why our classes? As we attempted to answer these questions (and occasionally Merry addressed them directly), our students gained a sense of pride in their school and themselves. They began to believe that they were receiving a high-quality education—a conclusion we would have had trouble convincing students of on our own. When Merry interviewed students, they felt empowered and important as they were explaining their learning to a university professor. I am convinced that our students learned more during that school year because a university professor's presence caused them to reflect on their learning. They also enjoyed seeing research in action and wanted to do their best to impress her.

Know the Score

When Merry and I began to discuss her research, I was entering my third year of teaching and was still finding my way in the profession. I am certain, looking back, that I had no idea what I was getting into when I agreed to work with her that year. Despite my ignorance, the collaboration was a great success. In hindsight, however, there are several pieces of advice that I would offer to a teacher considering entering into a similar collaboration.

The most fundamental advice I can offer is to enter into collaboration only with a university professor with whom you have a strong, trust-based relationship. Allowing someone into your classroom is a leap of faith. There are hundreds of decisions that a teacher makes every class period, and a critical viewer can draw harsh judgment on even the best of teachers. You must believe that the university professor is a partner and supporter of your work. You need to have the confidence that he or she will be able to help you improve in a constructive manner. Finally, you need to see the collaboration as mutually beneficial. Beware of being "used" for research on a professor's pet project. The project should be one that offers professional benefit to you, not just publishing opportunities to the professor.

Second, I encourage you to establish clear ground rules before the collaboration begins. What are the limitations of the professor's role? What kinds of feedback do you want? What role do you expect to have in the review of observation notes and publication materials? If you know the rules up front, you will greatly reduce the likelihood of hurt feelings or miscommunication later.

Have the Courage to Learn

Once the collaboration begins, it is crucial that you don't turn the work into a "dog and pony show." Let the researcher see everything, even that which you know is not pretty. If we begin to perform for the researcher, the integrity of the collaboration is destroyed. If a strong trust relationship exists, you can allow the reality of the classroom to show, warts and all. If the professor cannot see the whole picture, the collaboration becomes a public relations project, not a process of professional inquiry. Finally, be open to constructive comments and questions. Defensiveness is the great enemy of growth. Although a teacher may not agree with every observation the professor offers, he or she needs to make a concerted effort to honestly seek to understand the feedback he or she receives. So often, as teachers, we get defensive before we have even heard the end of a critical sentence. Listen. Think and reflect. Allow some time to pass. Continually remind yourself that the purpose of your involvement is to grow as a professional, not to prove you are right. An open mind is a necessary condition for successful school/university collaboration.

There are tremendous benefits to be gained from participating in research studies with university professors. When Merry and I began to work together, I saw myself as a high school teacher. As a result of my participation in this project and the series of events that followed, I have experienced an exponential expansion of my professional world. My work with Merry ultimately led me to the following: a master's degree, multiple published writings, presentations at an array of professional conferences, collaborative teaching of preservice teachers at the university level, and overseas involvement in a civic education project in Poland. School/university collaboration can open doors to your growth as a teacher and the expansion of your professional world.

A Professor Speaks to Professors (M.M.)

My work with Steve and Reynoldsburg High School has transformed my thinking about school reform and, in many ways, shaped my teaching and research. Why? First, working with teachers over a year as they talked about and implemented complex reforms provided an environment for learning within a community where any and all of us could raise questions, identify issues, or suggest alternatives. Second, Steve is an extraordinary teacher from whom I had much to learn. And third, he has been willing to go beyond the usual roles of a classroom teacher and work with me in developing a course, team teaching, presenting at conferences, writing for publication, and working with OSU on international projects.

The cumulative effect of working across cultures and tasks created a place for us to rethink our assumptions about educational reform. Although I have learned much from him within the contexts of his school, the other collaborative work has given us precious time to put our heads together to create, reflect, and learn together. Based on my experiences, here is some advice for other professors:

SEEK OUT OVERLAPPING AGENDAS AND BENEFITS FOR TEACHERS AND SCHOOLS

Research and publications are integral to our work as professors. Many of us are interested in questions that take us into schools and provide us with opportunities for interaction with students and teachers. Often, professors enter schools with research proposals in hand and work through the district's bureaucracy to find schools and classrooms where we are allowed to collect data. Teachers may be asked to accept into their classrooms a researcher who gives out questionnaires to students or a professor who sits in the back of the room observing instruction, with no benefit to the teacher at all.

What I've learned over the last decade is that my research and writing (and my learning) improve when teachers and I both benefit professionally from working together. This does not mean teachers have to become co-researchers or take on any of my responsibilities. It does mean that both parties need to work out what the collaboration means day to day and how each participant will benefit. Just as Steve has enjoyed contributing in many ways to work that led to my promotions from assistant to associate to full professor, I have been delighted to contribute in small ways to his work with state, national, and international audiences and the awards he has won for his expertise and creativity in authentic assessment, curriculum development, and educational leadership.

LEARN HOW TO CROSS SCHOOL AND UNIVERSITY CULTURES

Part of school/university collaboration involves learning to interact within another institution's culture. It is critical to keep in mind that it is not just the university professor learning how to navigate the school culture but also the teacher learning to interact with university people. It can be quite a shock to see one's colleagues through the eyes of teachers. I've often been amazed at university and professional meetings when professors talk about teachers as though they are the "other" or make assumptions that teaching teachers is some sort of one-way street (what, professors learn from teachers?). It is much worse, however, when they express these ideas in front of teachers.

Some years ago, I was invited to be on a panel at a College and University Faculty Assembly (CUFA) conference because of some work I was doing in teacher education reform, and I asked if some of the teachers who were responsible for the reform could present with me. After we made our fifteen-minute presentation on what we had learned through four years of collaboration in developing and team teaching a ten-credit-hour, field-based, and authentically assessed methods course, the next presenter got up and told the audience that "such collaboration is impossible" and standards would fall if teachers got involved in teacher education. I can remember turning to look at Steve and the other teachers as it registered that we, and our work, had just been put down in a most humiliating way. In leaving the session, we struggled to cope with the audience's lack of interest in our work or support for school/university collaboration to improve teacher education.

LISTEN TO AND LEARN FROM TEACHERS, THEIR LIVED EXPERIENCES AND SCHOOL CONTEXTS

Professors need to learn to listen to teachers. We need to accept that we do not have practicing teachers' expert knowledge. If we want to understand today's classrooms, we must listen to teachers, value their experiences and expertise, and let them teach us. I've learned much about social studies and global education by listening to teachers talk about their students, their travels, and ways they select content and methods to meet the needs of the school community. Without an understanding of the contexts for teaching and learning, our "theories" are not grounded. It is through work with teachers that we can develop authentic learning for both university and schools.

NOTES

1. Theodore Sizer, *Horace's Compromise: The Dilemma of the American High School* (Boston, Mass.: Houghton Mifflin, 1985).
2. Bil Johnson, *The Performance Assessment Handbook: (Volume 2) Performances & Exhibitions* (Princeton, N.J.: Eye on Education, 1996).
3. Steve Shapiro and Merry M. Merryfield, "A Case Study of Unit Planning," in *Teaching About International Conflict and Peace*, eds. Merry M. Merryfield and Richard C. Remy (Albany: State University of New York Press, 1995).
4. Heidi Jacobs, *Interdisciplinary Curriculum: Design and Implementation* (Alexandria, Va.: Association for Supervision and Curriculum Development, 1989).
5. Steve Shapiro and Merry M. Merryfield, "A Case Study of Unit Planning," 62-90.
6. The following are back issues of the Coalition of Essential Schools journal, *Horace*, that we have found especially helpful: "Asking the Essential Questions: Curriculum Development," *Horace* 5 (1989); "Performance and Exhibitions: The Demonstration of Mastery," *Horace* 6 (1990); "What's Essential? Integrating the Curriculum in Essential Schools," *Horace* 9 (1993); "Developing Curriculum in Essential Schools, *Horace* 12 (1996); "Demonstrating Student Performance in Essential Schools," *Horace* 14 (1997); see also the CES web site www.essentialschools.org.
7. Barbara Levak, Merry M. Merryfield, and Robert Wilson, "Global Connections," *Educational Leadership* 51 (September 1993): 73-75.
8. See Merry M. Merryfield, Elaine Jarchow, and Sarah Pickert, eds., *Preparing Teachers to Teach Global Perspectives: A Handbook for Teacher Educators* (Thousand Oaks, Calif.: Corwin Press, 1970); Merry M. Merryfield and Connie S. White, "Issue-Centered Global Education," in *Handbook on Teaching Social Issues*, NCSS Bulletin 93, eds. Ronald W. Evans and David Warren Saxe (Washington, D.C.: National Council for the Social Studies, 1996).

Collaborating on High School Economics

Nancy Mallory
Steven L. Miller

The Scene in a Classroom

At the end of a microeconomics unit, eleventh grade students are presenting their group's proposed solution on the national debate about the minimum wage.

Ms. Mallory: O.K., class, our first student group is ready to present.

Ben: What is Dr. Miller's group hearing?

Ms. Mallory: They are listening to a group talk about the Grand Canyon pollution issue. Are you ready to begin?

Cherise: Yes. We didn't compile a fancy computer project, but we wrote a paper that includes our ideas about what should be done in the minimum wage case study.

Jill: First you might ask, "What is the minimum wage and why do we need it?"

Josh: Well, the minimum wage is a price floor that is imposed by the federal government on the labor market.

Jill: Prices, therefore, cannot fall below the floor. So, if the minimum wage is $5.75, by law, no one can get paid below that level.

Josh: When we thought about the minimum wage case, therefore, our options were to leave the current wage rate alone, raise it, lower it, or eliminate it altogether. As a group, we believe that it should be raised.

Cherise: There are several reasons that we believe this is the best solution. First, the country is experiencing low unemployment now, so the current rate of $5.15 must be below the market equilibrium point.

Jill: Secondly, raising the minimum wage will get rid of wage inequality. Workers will believe they are being treated more fairly. For example, those workers who manufacture CDs like *Hotel California* will work harder if they get a raise because they will feel valued.

Josh: Yes, these issues were important, but the biggest reason we decided to raise the minimum wage is because of the inelasticity of the demand for labor.

Cherise: Let's show them the graph before you get into inelasticity.

Our Vision of Improving Economics Instruction

Our project was a five-week microeconomics unit taught collaboratively in three classes of high school juniors and was based on our interest in improving instruction in economics. We were interested in examining whether economic issues that are a focus of public policy can enhance the learning of economics by students. Also, we were interested in the efficacy of backwards-planning combined with authentic assessment as a general approach to planning, executing, and assessing social studies instruction.

THE TRADITIONAL ECONOMICS CURRICULUM

To better understand what is different in our collaborative project, we might begin by describing the traditional high school economics curriculum. Economics instruction typically emphasizes student learning of particular concepts. The concepts build upon each other to develop still more concepts, and are ultimately combined to form generalizations, which are the constructs that have significant power to explain real-world events and inform policy.

Let's unpack the concepts in one such generalization, the *law of demand*. Obviously, one concept is *demand*, the quantity of some good or service that people wish to purchase at some price. For students to understand this concept they must also learn the concepts called *quantity*, *good*, *service*, and *price*. When a graph is made of the different quantities demanded at different prices, the result is a *demand curve*, which shows the inverse relationship between price and quantity demanded (i.e., the curve slopes down to the right when using the conventional method of placing price on the vertical axis). The demand curve is expected to have a negative slope because of the *income effect*, the *substitution effect*, and *diminishing marginal utility*. Note that all of these concepts are necessary for the attainment of a full understanding of one of the simplest, albeit most fundamental, economic generalizations—the law of demand, which means that people generally want to buy less of something at higher prices than at lower ones.

We hope this illustrates that economics, like other social studies disciplines, is packed with concepts. Thus, it is not surprising that the teaching of high school economics emphasizes the student acquisition of concepts. Many teachers think of it as learning the basic building blocks or constructing the fundamental foundation of the discipline. It is utterly necessary to do so in order to understand ever more sophisticated concepts and, ultimately, some of the powerful generalizations in the field.

Another aspect of the traditional approach is that it is typically organized around the structure of the discipline. Most high school textbooks are arranged this way, and in a sense resemble simplified versions of college textbooks. As such, this reinforces the emphasis on teaching concepts according to a predetermined pattern modeled on the way in which they are traditionally presented.

NANCY'S CONCERNS

This project was really born from Nancy's dissatisfaction with the economics portion of her American government/economics course. She traced much of her disquiet to the traditional approach's almost exclusive concentration on student acquisition of concepts and generalizations, instead of the use of these generalizations to understand the real world. She was also unhappy with the way concepts and their applications are linked in the traditional approach. For example, to the extent that her textbook contains applications, these are often not the major focus. Instead, the applications seem to be designed more as illustrations of the concepts rather than demonstrations of the usefulness of economics. Nancy wanted much more of an emphasis on economics in the real world.

Another of her concerns resulted from the aforementioned pyramid structure of the discipline. A student's lack of understanding can compound if the teacher moves the class on to new concepts before the students fully understand what has already been taught. She felt that the traditional approach was driving her through the concepts before she had adequately checked student progress. Paradoxically, this concern meant that her evaluation of student work was also confined to the level of student concept acquisition. She really wanted more.

Nancy felt that this concentration on concepts in both instruction and evaluation was stifling opportunities for students to work at the highest thinking levels. Nancy wanted to move beyond the application level (to use Bloom's well known taxonomy) to deep analysis and evaluation. She reasoned that this was consistent with her desire to center her instruction on economics in the real world. Indeed, she had the feeling that she and her students were missing the real promise of economics.

DIFFERENCES IN THIS APPROACH

In our collaboration we sought to address Nancy's concerns with an alternative approach to planning, instruction, and assessment. We began by deciding to place authentic tasks at the center of a unit of instruction. Thus, we decided to employ the backwards-building planning model described by Shapiro and Merryfield[1] and Sizer.[2] In this approach, the teacher begins with a vision of the authentic tasks students are to accomplish and plans backwards to identify essential skills and knowledge students must acquire to complete the task successfully. Note that the content is determined by the task rather than selected from the textbook or the teaching of traditional units. Thus, the emphasis of the unit shifts automatically from "concept acquisition" to "solving the problem."

We selected three real problems students were to solve. Each problem involved a current economic issue that we hoped would be relevant to students' lives and about which there is ample information. We picked the following:[3]

▶ Minimum Wage Issue: Should the minimum wage be raised? If so, by how much?
▶ Microsoft Issue: Should Microsoft be broken up into several smaller companies?
▶ Grand Canyon Pollution Issue: What should be done about the problem of pollution haze in the Grand Canyon, if anything?

We determined that we wanted students to work in cooperative teams. Each team would address one of the problems. Moreover, since we wanted students to be able to propose and defend their solution to all of the three problems, they were told that the final unit test would include questions on all three of the issues. We planned for this by assigning at least one group to each problem in each of the three classes. The authentic task of each group was to create a presentation in which they would "teach" their classmates their analysis and solution of their issue. Students were allowed to select the format of the presentation from among: a website, *Astound* (similar to *PowerPoint*), or traditional "white paper." The solutions to problems had to include at least these three elements:

1. The economic theory related to the issue;
2. Facts and data related to the issue; and
3. Expert opinion about the issue.

In the backwards-building approach, it is important for the teacher to identify and help students learn the content relevant to solving the problem posed by the authentic task. In our project, this was the economic theory mentioned above. Note that all three of the issues require students to learn much of the typical content in microeconomics, such as supply and demand, and all three require a decision about government action. To analyze the national debate about the minimum wage, students must learn about the effects of price ceilings and floors. The Microsoft and Grand Canyon pollution cases involve students in learning about the category of problems known as "market failures."

After we identified the necessary content, we established a plan that included classroom activities to teach the content, a series of short evaluation exercises (quizzes and worksheets) to check for student understanding, and some class periods for students to conduct Internet research in the computer lab and work in their groups on their projects. So that students could use their time in the lab productively, we provided some leads on Internet locations that had expert opinion and data.

Our Process of Collaboration and Some Tangible Outcomes

Few aspects of teaching are as difficult and rewarding as working with another person to achieve a common goal. Our collaboration, which involved planning and then team teaching a five-week economics unit to high school students, proved comfortable enough for us to work closely together and dynamic enough to allow us to grow over time. We had worked together previously in our Professional Development School Network (PDSN), and were ready to begin work on this unit in the winter of 1998. During our time together, we moved among three stages of collaboration—conversation, experimentation, and dialogue—and we attribute the success of our project to this process.

We began just by talking. We thought about our individual goals. Steve wanted to reestablish a connection with high school students, and Nancy wanted to improve her economics teaching, in particular her assessment techniques. We talked about teaching a unit together at the high school level and what it might look like. During these early conversations, we shared our perceptions of the problems with traditional economics teaching. We dreamt of other possibilities; if we could work together in Nancy's high school classroom, what could we accomplish? What opportunities could we give the students? We asked each other questions, defined terms, stated preferences, and established a common language. This conversation led to a basic understanding of each other's beliefs, which proved essential later during the actual unit.

Once we secured all of the administrative approval needed for our project, we continued our conversations, but added the experimentation component. During our casual meetings at Steve's house, we thought of new ways to approach the teaching of the same content, and then we experimented with the students. For example, using real-world cases as the focus of instruction was a new technique for Nancy, and talking about how it would work helped her prepare for working with the students. We also learned many hard lessons from day-to-day experimentation. Most activities that we presented to the students took longer than we hoped, and we had to adjust many of our lessons. We were genuinely trying to view our collaboration as an experiment, and these adjustments as problem solving. This type of intellectual and emotional partnership enabled our collaboration to flourish even when a particular lesson did not work as well as we had hoped. Although we based our experiments on our understanding of solid educational theory and our experiences, we pushed ourselves beyond our traditional comfort level.

As we taught each day together, adjusting our planning by phone and email at night, our collaboration evolved in two special ways. First, we developed team-teaching "telepathy." After teaching for approximately two weeks, we had talked about issues deeply, had tuned into each other's concerns, and had begun to "read" each other's minds. We also read each other's nonverbal language and teaching style. Because this telepathy helped us connect about content, methodology, and student needs, it made us a more potent team.

The second way in which our collaboration changed as we taught is that we reached the third stage: dialogue. During the dialogue phase, we questioned and challenged one another's assumptions, always digging deeper to understand each other's ideas. We sensed that "dialogue" was not the same as "conversation." For example, we were now talking about real issues that had emerged during the day's teaching, rather than hypothetical plans about what we might do one day. Thus, the dialogue felt more focused, intense, and urgent than our previous conversations. The conversation and dialogue phases are not, however, mutually exclusive. We used both types of talking as parts of an ongoing process.

One of the amazing phenomena that we discovered is that as we worked together, our dialogue grew deeper and more meaningful for several reasons. First, as we taught together on a daily basis we faced several practical pedagogical questions. Some of these questions arose simply because we were team teaching and linking two teachers' styles, and some arose because of our experimentation with backwards-building planning. Secondly, in order to reflect constructively and solve problems, we discussed both theoretical and practical issues. We found ourselves working hard to match our pedagogical and cognitive beliefs to our behavior with the students.

Lastly, our dialogue deepened over time because our collaboration heightened our level of personal investment in the process and in our own growth. Our inward struggles with the collaboration led to deeper dialogue because we trusted one another. We invite you to listen in on one of our conversations.

Scenario: Hanging out at Steve's House after School to Debrief

In this scenario, we are discussing how to deal with an unexpectedly low set of quiz grades. This was of concern because we were using periodic quizzes as a means of insuring that the students were understanding the concepts they would need to address in their project.

Nancy: I don't know what happened, Steve. They did so well on the demand quiz that I never thought they'd do so poorly on the supply quiz. What should we do?

Steve: My greatest concern is that they won't have the concepts they need to analyze their case studies for the final assessment. There is clearly a sizable group that does not understand key concepts like "what is the role of marginal cost in supplier decision making?"

Nancy: Yes, I agree they need these concepts, but you can only stay until April 30th. I don't think that we can add another mini-unit now.

Steve: No, we can't do that, and the way we have designed our calendar only allows us to move the project forward by one day.

Nancy: What are our options? We can't change the project.

Steve: We really have two paths to follow. We can forge ahead and ask them to continue working without re-teaching, or we can take a day, go over the quiz, and re-teach the concepts.

Nancy: I like the idea of re-teaching, but if they are too focused on their quiz grade, will they understand those concepts that confused them?

Steve: You know your students. How do you think they'll respond?

Nancy: They will want to know why they got such bad grades. Some will focus on the concepts, but many will lose sight of the learning.

Steve: Can we do anything special to set the tone before we re-teach?

Nancy: I guess I can go over the key and ask them to table discussions of fairness until we finish class. It's certainly worth a shot.

Steve: Maybe if we re-explain the connection of the concepts to the projects, it will be an easier sell.

Nancy: I'm game.

Collaboration: a Teacher Talks to Other Teachers (N.M.)

After this collaboration, my teaching improved in several tangible ways. I experienced changes in myself as well as in my teaching. Although I majored in economics in college, I had not felt very confident about teaching some of the most difficult concepts. During our time together, I asked many questions, particularly about economics, that I probably would not have asked in a workshop setting because I felt more comfortable asking Steve. The ongoing dialogue with Steve made me a better and more confident teacher.

After working with Steve, I understood many of the economics concepts better, and felt more comfortable asking informed questions when I did not understand. By watching Steve and trying new methods myself, I can more astutely match the best method to the content I am trying to teach. Additionally, I used several new resources and learned how to better access resources on the World Wide Web.

My increased confidence and these new resources enabled me to develop a unit on hyperinflation that I am currently teaching; it employs the backwards-building method, the case study approach, and the use of technology. In addition to using these methods in my economics units, I have applied them to the other class I teach. Last fall, I taught a unit on culture hearths in my World History class. I planned the unit backwards from the final assessment, which was creating a museum of cultural artifacts. While the unit can certainly be improved, the methods made very old cultures come to life for the students, and I believed they learned more actively than they had in the past.

INSIGHTS

At first when Steve offered to collaborate with me I felt selfish. I figured that it wasn't fair or right for me to have another whole adult in the classroom helping me. As I worked with him, however, I realized that my extra time spent reading, questioning, and thinking made me a better teacher on many levels. As I gained confidence I better challenged my students to think more critically; previously I never would have thought of this connection between my attitude toward the material and theirs.

As my students struggled with their solutions to their case studies, I watched them and listened to their conversations and questions. I was truly amazed by two different patterns of behavior. One was the greater extent to which many of the students thought critically when presented with a real world case. The other reaction that puzzled me was the resistance of a number of students to these more challenging tasks. Some students appeared much more at home with a traditional approach based on reading the textbook and memorizing its main points. I still wrestle with this resistance to engaging the challenges posed by case studies, and am considering what might be the most effective way of orienting these students to a case study approach.

One of the most impressive overall results of our collaboration was that most students became much more self-confident about demonstrating their analytical skills as they discussed complex topics. On the whole, students were more willing to speak up and, with the practice they obtained, became more able to articulate arguments and counter-arguments.

To assess the students' learning, I assigned them a longer essay test than I usually do. I felt comfortable about assigning them a more difficult task because of the development of their analytical capabilities and thinking skills that I observed in the classroom during our collaboration. On average, the results were good, suggesting that students had reached a new level of understanding of economics.

ADVICE

If you launch this type of collaboration, you need to tolerate your own ambiguity. Team teaching requires extra patience when you are unclear about what the other person is saying or thinking and when you are trying something new. This uncertainty can be very discomfiting when, as a teacher, you are used to being "in charge." Be patient with yourself and with the process, and know that you will surrender some control in your classroom.

You will also be the teacher to whom students look when there is a problem. Be prepared to field lots of questions about why the collaboration is happening, especially if new techniques accompany it. Students, like teachers, are creatures of habit and will need some time and sensitivity to adjust. I found that by listening to their concerns and accepting full responsibility for grading, I was able to help them through this adjustment period.

The other piece of advice is to really connect with your partner teacher. Choose someone whose company you enjoy, talk as much as you need to, and laugh together at your mistakes and struggles. Humor and friendship helped our teaching immensely, and the students benefited from our camaraderie because we modeled the type of learning community we wanted them to develop.

Collaboration: A University Professor Talks to Other Professors (S.L.M.)

INSIGHTS

It was rewarding and fun to get back into the classroom after too long an absence. One gets the chance to reconnect with high school students and gain some new experiences, as well as refresh old skills. It is amazing what one forgets after being away from high school teaching for a few years, especially some little ideas that are helpful in working with pre-service teachers in the licensure program.

For example, there was the tension between making sure that all of the students were on top of what we had taught and moving the class along. Economics concepts pyramid on top of one another. If a student misses some fundamental point early in the lesson, she or he is unlikely to understand some other concept or generalization later in the lesson, or perhaps in the next lesson, or a lesson taught next week. So, one wants to make sure that all students thoroughly understand what has been taught before moving on to the next concept.

And yet, the diversity of ability in the classroom virtually ensures that several students will not "get it" on the first pass. I learned anew that for some of our "visual learners," all those graphs in economics are helpful; but to others, they proved to be an additional obstacle for them to overcome. Did we provide enough "plain language" explanation for them? I hope so. There were some native Russian-speaking students, a few of whom I was sure hadn't been in the United States long enough to really keep up with the technical language. I was impressed with how hard they tried and feel I might have done more to help them. In one section, a particular student (Bless him!) was insistent on asking for a re-explanation, sometimes several re-explanations, whenever he didn't understand the concept after the activity was completed. This seemed to happen every day! In another section, a few bright students delighted in challenging assumptions or posing counterexamples, leading to lengthy side excursions. In both cases, our schedule was becoming imperiled, and other students were tuning out as these instances threatened to become small conversations involving just a few of us.

Now, all teachers know this, and we give advice to our preservice teachers on how to handle it. It is, however, different to confront it every day, every period . . . always having to make a split decision on whether to deflect a question, or invite a student to come in later for a detailed response. I tried to take my cues from Nancy on this, especially early on as she intervened with a "Maybe we can talk about that later," or a "Can you come in fifth period so we can go over it some more?"

This leads me to the most important insight in making a collaborative effort such as this work: trust your partner. I found Nancy's judgments to be virtually infallible when it came to "reading" her classes. This began before I ever stepped in the room. She characterized each class (e.g., "this group needs mothering") as we discussed our overall plan, and she was dead on. This extended to reading the level of our success day-to-day, and to understanding what made individual students tick. This was indispensable for me, since I was only in the classroom for a bit more than five weeks.

ADVICE

For teaching collaboration of this kind, consistency and duration are key factors. For university faculty, it is difficult to clear one's entire morning calendar every day for five weeks. Nonetheless, this was my commitment to my partner and her students, and it paid off. Soon, the students began to see me as a regular fixture of the classroom, not as a "special guest"—there for a day and gone the next. I really got to know the students, which is rewarding in itself, but also important for successful teaching. Our collaboration was enhanced by my deeper understanding of her students, our ability to compare "reads" on the day's efforts, and an improved sense of the rhythm of the classes. I am sure that had the project been substantially shorter, or had I not been present every day, both my teaching and our collaboration would have suffered.

Nancy and I might have been clearer with each other at the outset on classroom management, or (if you prefer) discipline. In the beginning, we were so focused on the project, the activities, the calendar, and so on, that we just didn't think about it. And, at first, there was no reason to discuss it. I entered the class with a mystical aura of university professor and the students were perfect angels when I was conducting an activity or presenting some information. Inevitably, however, the time comes when the aura evaporates. I suppose you know you are accepted when the students treat you just like another teacher. Initially, Nancy handled the routine disruptions. But, eventually I perceived a need to establish my own authority. I had observed Nancy closely when she was teaching and tried to mimic her style, but occasionally I let the "real me" come out. During one of our post-class dialogues, I confessed to Nancy that I felt I had mishandled a reprimand of one student. I was relieved when she assured me I had acted appropriately, but I clearly had been more assertive than she would have been.

Finally, I learned again the need for flexibility in the face of the demands to "cover the material." We were determined to provide real depth in this microeconomics unit, even if it meant omitting some material Nancy had usually covered. We planned carefully, gathered engaging activities, and built in some extra time for re-teaching. Our initial schedule didn't survive the first week! Eventually, as the dialogue above shows, we were running up against the hard deadline of my departure. University faculty know that teachers confront this problem all the time. It is, nonetheless, different to face it so directly and good to be prepared for it when it happens.

NOTES

1. Steve Shapiro and Merry Merryfield, "A Case Study in Unit Planning," in *Teaching About International Conflict and Peace*, eds., Merry Merryfield and Richard Remy (Albany, NY: State University of New York Press, 1995).
2. T. R. Sizer, *Horace's School: Redesigning the American High School* (Boston, Houghton Mifflin Company, 1992).
3. These were all burning issues in the spring of 1999 when we were co-teaching. For example, the judge had not yet rendered his "finding of fact" in the Microsoft case.

Collaboration on Campus: Teaching Rural High School Students through College Methods Classes

SANDRA BRENNEMAN OLDENDORF
M. REISZ RINEY
JACK HUTCHISON

The Scene

I (S.B.O.) stood in the doorway of my college classroom watching Ro, an African American college student and football player, talk about life in Los Angeles. Tim and Mark, two preservice teachers from my social studies methods class, had invited Ro to speak on the topic of culture to twenty high school freshmen. The students had been bussed to the campus from their school forty miles away. The goal was to help the high school students understand that all cultures should be understood and respected, and that differences are okay and should be celebrated. When it was time for questions, the students asked about gangs and rap music. What followed was a lively exchange.

> *Romi (freshman):* Do you actually like rap music?
> *Ro:* Rap music represents many things about my culture: poverty, street life, police, and drugs. It is like country music for many of you.
> *Romi (freshman):* Then how about country music?

When Ro admits he does not like country music, the freshmen try to convince him that country music is good stuff and rap is not. Ro tells them that he can't relate to country music, cowboys, and rural life in general. Julie, the high school teacher, tells me she is excited about the dynamic verbal exchange about the merits of rap versus country. She explains later that her students have few opportunities to talk with someone with a different background in such a candid way. She notes that in the county where these students live, jokes about people from other cultures are common. When the class ends, many of the freshmen crowd around Ro, as if he himself were a rap star, to ask more questions.

Improving Social Studies Education in Rural America

In this chapter, Sandra Brenneman Oldendorf, a college social studies methods teacher, Mark Reisz Riney, a college English methods instructor, and Jack Hutchinson, a high school social studies and English teacher, describe a collaborative project between two rural high schools and a small college in Montana. Over three years (1996-99), students from the high schools came to the college for a full day, once a week for six consecutive weeks. Preservice teachers taught lessons prepared in conjunction with the college methods courses (called micro-teaching). The project involved 170 high school students, 15 teachers (three of whom were social studies teachers), 160 preservice teachers (60 in social studies methods), and 9 college methods instructors. Although this project involved all subject areas, our focus was on the social studies teachers, social studies methods students, and social studies and English methods instructors. Many of the lessons in social studies were integrated with literature, speaking, and writing.

At the beginning, the goals of this collaborative project were the following:

1. To provide preservice teachers with hands-on experience with high school students in small groups in which management would be less of a concern
2. To provide a supportive environment where preservice teachers could try innovative ideas and teaching practices that put greater emphasis on student understanding and active learning

3. To enrich the curriculum and provide access to technology for high school students in rural schools
4. To provide public school teachers with an opportunity to contribute to preservice education

The conceptual framework underlying these goals is grounded in three main ideas: (1) that preservice teachers need a safe environment to try the ideas promoted by their college teachers and the research on best practice; (2) that high school students, preservice teachers, classroom teachers, and college methods instructors can come together and construct new knowledge about teaching and learning; and (3) that a rural setting offers unique opportunities for school/college collaboration.

The first belief in the conceptual framework, that preservice teachers need a safe place to test actual lessons based on the theories they are learning, is advocated in *The Right to Learn* by Linda Darling-Hammond.[1] She stresses a hands-on approach when she states that:

> Teachers learn just as their students do; by studying, doing, and reflecting; by collaborating with other teachers; by looking closely at students and their work; and by sharing what they see.

In this project, Sandra and Mark asked their methods students to develop lessons or a unit that incorporated primary sources, writing, small-group discussions, and multiple perspectives in examining history and literature. Many of these are elements of the history workshop approach,[2] which was presented in one of the texts used in the social studies methods class. These requirements for their lessons also supported the constructivist theory as taught in their other teacher preparation classes.

Robert, a preservice teacher, developed a lesson on the Holocaust in which theory and practice came together. He used primary sources, videotape, and guided lecture to explain the persecution of gypsies, intellectuals, people with disabilities, and Jews. The goal was to tell a more complete story of discrimination and persecution. When Robert asked for feedback, a high school student responded, "I learned that it wasn't only Jews who were killed, but it was all races and religions that were killed."

The freshmen in Jack's classes were studying European history, so Jack asked the preservice teachers working with these students to choose a country or region in Europe for their lessons. Ross and Jim, the preservice teachers, chose France. Ross and Jim made French history come alive for the high school freshmen. Their decision to show a French film from a ranching town was one example of such risk taking. The students were not immediately excited about watching a film with subtitles. Some of them questioned whether a French film would have any connection with their lives.

Another team of preservice teachers, Glenn, Ryan, and Nick, used two strategies to help sophomores understand the Russian Revolution and issues facing Russia today. First, they combined art and social studies to try to help students studying Russian history understand the opulence of the Romanovs. The goal was to set the scene for students to understand that the riches of the ruling family, in contrast with poverty among the masses, helped contribute to a revolution. They had the sophomores paint wooden eggs gold and decorate them in the style befitting the bejeweled Fabergé eggs. Painting the eggs was a way for students to make a symbolic but concrete connection to the Romanovs. Jill, a social studies and art teacher who was observing, was excited about the lesson and said she might use the idea in her classes.

The second strategy they used was to invite a guest speaker. After much encouragement from Sandra, Glenn called Tanya, an educator from Russia, who had recently moved to Montana. She agreed to speak to the high school students. By the time she came to campus, Glenn, Ryan, and Nick had decided to invite the other students and professors to hear Tanya. The result was an audience of about fifty college students, college professors, high school teachers, and high school students listening and talking with Tanya about life in Russia and her political views. Although these activities might have taken place in other settings, the college campus proved to be an ideal forum.

The second part of our conceptual framework was the belief that having high school teachers, students, preservice teachers, and college instructors work together reflects the spirit of constructivism.[3] This was demonstrated when preservice teachers collaborated with one another in planning lessons, when professors and classroom teachers negotiated lesson content that would fit the goals of each group, and when high school students learned in different settings and with different teachers. For example, Dean, a high school history teacher, wanted the freshmen to learn about culture. At his school there were only three social science classes offered—World History, U.S. History, and U.S. government—and none of them emphasized culture. After several discussions, Sandra, Mark, and Sarah, the arts methods instructor, and their teacher counterparts agreed to focus on Native American culture in the West. The social studies methods students had been reading James Welch's *Killing Custer*[4] so they had a background on this battle and the cultural conflict between white society and Native American cultures.

As noted earlier, teaching from a constructivist perspective is the Piagetian notion that new information is used to challenge previously held beliefs in order to reshape what the learner previously believed.[5] This occurred when the preservice teachers invited Jeanne, a Dakota Sioux, to be a guest speaker. As part of her presentation, Jeanne talked about Indian spiritual beliefs and the resentment that many Indians felt when Christian missionaries came to "save" them. Some of the high school students raised questions about why the speaker rejected Christianity. It was definitely a moment of cognitive dissonance for both the preservice teachers and the high school students.

A third part of the conceptual framework is the idea that "small is better." In this case, small means rural. Developing this project in a very rural part of America offered many benefits and unique insights. Wendell Berry argues it well: "My feeling is that if improvement is going to begin anywhere, it will have to begin out in the country and in the country towns."[6] Taking Berry's idea a step farther, it is our belief that the rural setting offers unique perspectives to be gained about good teaching and good teacher education.

The Process of Collaboration: Negotiations and Assessment

Getting this project started involved sensitive negotiations. New superintendents in our two high school districts in the mid-1990s asked the college for assistance in providing a stronger curriculum for their students. One of the high schools had no art classes. Neither school had access to more than a few computers and there was no access to the Internet. Lab equipment and library resources in both schools were limited. Methods instructors from the college attended school board meetings in both communities to propose that the high school students be sent to the college once a week for six weeks, with one hour each visit devoted to each subject area. The curriculum would be developed collaboratively with the high school teachers, the college methods instructors, and the preservice teachers. The high school students would be taught lessons by preservice teachers and be given access to the college technology and library.

The school boards were composed of conservative, independent-minded individuals who asked many tough questions about cost, which students should come, and whether the experience on campus would be as good as having classes with their own teachers. Although cost was a major topic, many mitigating points were suggested. Some board members realized that having the students go to the college for experience in technology, for example, would be more cost-effective than providing the same level of technology at the school. Another pointed out the importance of meeting state standards and said that coming to the college would help to meet standards in technology and art.

When deciding which students should visit the campus, one school board initially wanted to send only the best students as a reward for their high achievement and good behavior. The college instructors convinced this board that the preservice teachers needed to work with the full range of students. The biggest issue with school board members was a defensive stance about the teachers they had hired. More than one member said, "We trust the teachers we hired to know what's best for our students." Some members felt that the college instructors were suggesting that the schools and teachers were deficient, and, therefore, the high school students needed to come to the college. A turning point was reached at one board meeting when some of the teachers present said they wanted the high school students to go to the campus. They thought that the project might benefit them because they would be observing new teaching methods, and they liked the opportunity to provide feedback to preservice teachers.

In the other community, parent enthusiasm carried the day with the school board. After several meetings, both school boards voted to support the micro-teaching concept and continued to do so over three years. Each year the program was re-negotiated.

The college methods instructors met with the teachers and administrators at their respective school sites to discuss concerns about instruction related to different cultures and the politics of school/university collaboration. Logistics, accountability, scheduling, and expenses were the top items on the agenda. The logistics were made more challenging because there was no outside funding for the project. In the end, the schools agreed to provide student lunches and transportation; the college would provide paper and notebooks for the high school students.

Negotiations with the teachers focused on mutual benefits. First, they wanted rural students to have access to a much larger library, computer technology, lab equipment, a broader curriculum, and exposure to people from other cultures. The methods instructors, on the other hand, emphasized that they needed help from the teachers in order to create realistic direct teaching experiences for preservice teachers. In addition, the methods faculty agreed to conduct free in-service days for the teachers either at the school site or on campus.

Curriculum

The curriculum was determined each semester by negotiations among the methods instructors, the classroom teachers, and the preservice teachers. The teachers wanted the material to reflect the topics being covered in the regular classrooms, and they usually suggested a broad topic such as European geography and let the preservice teachers pick the specific country or region. In addition to the examples of the interdisciplinary unit on Native Americans and the unit on culture, other social studies units featured the Holocaust, Montana government, China, Japan, Eastern Europe, geography, Russia, and the Westward Movement. Almost all units featured guest speakers, primary sources, Internet activities, writing and speaking, and library research.

Accountability and Assessment

Many teachers raised concerns about accountability and assessment. Typical questions included, "How would the student work be evaluated?" "Would the preservice teachers give grades?" "Will students work if grades aren't given?" Some teachers from both schools were emphatic that grades should be assigned because they believed their students would not take the work seriously without this form of accountability. In their methods classes, the preservice teachers reviewed research indicating that not all students are motivated by grades and that students can be motivated to learn by other extrinsic and intrinsic factors. Mark, Sandra, and other methods instructors suggested that the high school students keep notebooks instead of grades. The preservice teachers would evaluate effort, level of participation, and evidence of achievement. Then the teachers could use these evaluations in whatever way they wanted in determining the students' grades. We agreed that the student work would be assembled into notebooks and sent to teachers and parents at the end of the six weeks.

In the following discussion, we look at the project through the eyes of Jack, a social studies and English teacher in a high school of forty students. Then Sandra and Mark reflect on and analyze what they have learned.

Jack's Perspective (J.H.)

You are now about to participate in a role-playing exercise. Each of you will be playing the part of a prisoner in a Prisoner of War Camp run by the Nazis. You are about to undergo an intense interrogation. Be very careful about how you answer the questions. Your answers may very well determine if you live or if you die.

This is the introduction to a unit on the Holocaust that I observed. As the class continued, each student was given the chance to save his/her life by giving the interrogator the answers that he or she wanted to hear. If the wrong answer was given, a punishment such as being confined to a space under a table was inflicted. If the correct answer was given, a reward was attained.

The lesson was highly successful. The teaching approach included a great deal of creativity and drama. It involved an extensive amount of interactivity, and, above all else, it was meaningful for the students. The preservice teacher had a successful hour teaching this group of students. The teacher was Jake, a senior in history education. I am the regular social studies and English teacher, but in this setting, I was an observer.

Underlying this experiment is the question of whether small rural school districts should use local college campuses to enhance their curriculum. More specifically, should a regular classroom teacher consider this teaching approach a viable option for his/her classroom?

One consideration is whether there is actually more being taught in this environment than the specific lesson. Is there exposure and acculturation that is taking place in the college setting that students would not receive in their regular classroom?

In another classroom across the campus, a group of students was taught a lesson on Mainland China. Rick, the preservice teacher, invited Paul, a college student from China, to talk about his childhood. The students asked many questions. Paul eagerly answered them. I noticed the rapport that was evident between my students and this preservice student from a different culture. Such sharing is difficult to create using the traditional textbook or video. Having class on the college campus provided resources that are richer than reading about other cultures in a textbook.

Another important part of my curriculum is Montana government, which is required for graduation. In my classroom we have a government textbook, a copy of the state constitution, and a daily newspaper subscription, but very limited Internet access. What do I gain by loading my students onto a school bus at 8:30 in the morning and riding fifty miles to the local college campus? One reason is the opportunity to spend an hour or two in the college's technology center to make use of the largest world library, the World Wide Web.

Instead of twelve students and me sitting around two computers at the high school, each student is able to work at a computer in the computer lab and receive special instructions from the student teachers. The subject for one day was the state legislative process. The college students divided the high school students into four different groups, and each group focused on a different piece of legislation. The groups researched the legislation presented in Helena during the daily session, reviewed the background of that legislation, and focused on the sponsors of the legislation. Through this process, they formulated their own ideas about the legislation and legislative process. This was truly hands-on learning that is not available at our high school.

In another classroom, the college student teachers used resources from campus that were not available in our rural classroom. Foreign language teachers are rare in small rural schools. In this college classroom, a group of freshmen high school students got an introduction to the French language. It was not a formal French language class. It was a world history class taught by Jim and Ross whose objective was to show the similarities and contrasts between French and American cultures. To do this, they decided to show a foreign language film, *The Return of Martin Guerre*.

They were surprised that these high school freshmen had never seen a foreign language film with subtitles. The students' assignment was to pay close attention to the relationships that developed between the various characters. Jim and Ross were especially hopeful that the students would notice the role of women in this society. The students were asked to focus on the culture of this particular period of French history and to make comparisons to early periods of American history.

Each day the students watched the film for twenty minutes and then discussed it. I was not surprised that my students were at first very reticent to participate, but I noticed that the dynamic style of one of the student teachers slowly began to draw them into the discussion. To my surprise, I noticed that the student who responded the most to this new interactive approach was the most introverted girl in my regular classroom.

By the second meeting, this girl not only "came out of her shell," but most of the rest of the class had followed her lead. A good class discussion resulted. By the end of the period, the student teachers had had success with most of the students. They told the students that this foreign film was remade in the United States as a popular Western. Jim asked, "Did it seem familiar to anyone?" Only one boy knew the film, but this boy appeared to be bored throughout the lesson. The cadet teachers realized that they now had a way to involve this student actively. The boy became the resident student expert on the American film. As he was questioned in the ensuing lessons about the comparisons between the two films, his status as a member of the class grew dramatically.

By the end of the unit, I felt that the preservice teachers' experiment with foreign films had been successful. Not only had they shown me the value of such a method, but they also had success reaching two students who had been underachievers in my history classroom. This experience convinced me that the use of film in teaching history is invaluable with today's high school students. Since that first experience, we have watched *Sommersby*, the American version of the film, and have spent many more hours using film with other topics I teach in history.

Not all situations that took place in this experiment, however, were positive. Some of our students felt that the trips to Western Montana College were days off from school. Sometimes, we had to make sure that these students made it to their appointed classes. At first, this was hard to do with only a few teachers chaperoning, but the Western teacher education faculty responded by providing "guides" to help make sure that students who left one classroom arrived across campus at another classroom on time.

Another major problem was accountability. Our students questioned whether they had to do the work assigned by the Western teachers. They did not receive a grade for this work, so how important was it that they do it? This attitude not only affected their performance on assigned work but also on their attentiveness in the classroom. I think that to make the experiment accountable, some type of grade must be given.

In my classroom, I have had a number of fine student teachers, but I also have had student teachers who I have prayed would choose another profession. This leads to a third major problem with the experiment, the quality of teaching that takes place. The teaching cadets who are organized and prepared are usually outstanding. However, I have suffered watching those students who are just trying to pass the course. The question that my school board continues to ask is whether the experiment is more beneficial than holding regular classes at our high school.

Sandra and Mark's Perspectives

We designed several specific instruments and methods to evaluate this collaboration including (1) questionnaires, (2) selected oral and videotaped interviews with participating teachers and preservice teachers, (3) debriefing sessions with all participants, (4) observational and anecdotal evidence, and (5) journals kept by preservice teachers. Using these sources of data, we reflect on the dynamics of what happened, what we learned, and what it might mean for future collaborative endeavors.

What We Learned from the Teachers

Based on the results from teachers who returned surveys and the teachers who were interviewed, most supported returning to the college in future semesters. They cited the following as strengths of the project: observation of new teaching strategies, positive impressions of interdisciplinary lessons, use of technology, and the interactions with guest speakers. Concerns were raised about preservice teachers' limited background knowledge and what the high school students were missing from their regular lessons at their school.

The preservice teachers also learned from the teachers. Learning worked both ways. One preservice teacher mentioned Dean, a high school social studies teacher:

> He is so patient, and I respect his insights. He tells us what we have done well . . .
> and how much we have improved and he gives us good ideas. He even said that he
> has thought of some new ideas from us . . . and I think that he really means it.

Dean also noted that it was important for the high school students to "get different perspectives than mine . . . on issues in social studies."

Jack's reflections from his teacher's point of view have been especially valuable. He let us know what was working and what wasn't. He made specific suggestions to the preservice teachers to help them in planning their next lessons. He was very supportive in letting our methods students try ideas such as French movies with subtitles. Not every teacher would agree to this degree of experimentation with his or her class. However, most of the teachers who came to campus and observed the lessons supported experimentation. They wanted to see ideas that they might take back to their own classrooms, and they wanted the students to experience different teachers.

What We Learned from the High School Students

During the three years of the project, the high school students often gave social studies high marks. According to one student, "Social studies is not boring because of the teachers." Another student said, "The coolest part was learning stuff about another culture [Los Angeles] from someone who lived there."

One thing we learned from the students is that having a guest speaker from another culture gave the preservice teachers, and us, a chance to see how the students were constructing knowledge. The information they were given was not always the information that they wanted. A group of four preservice teachers invited Eva, an art professor, to talk about what it means to be Jewish and to lose family members to the Holocaust. But when it came time for questions, the high school freshmen wanted to know if she had children, if they celebrated Christmas at their home, and if her children felt bad if they didn't get presents. In another example, the students listed attentively to Paul, a Chinese exchange student, talk about art, culture, and history of China. When Paul asked for questions, one freshman asked, "But do you have telephones?" These exchanges served as a vivid reminder that the learners have their own questions and are busy constructing knowledge related to their background knowledge and experiences.

We also learned from the high school students that the negative picture painted by James Loewen in *Lies My Teacher Told Me*[7] was not set in stone. This book was used as a text in the social studies methods class. Loewen asserts that most high school students hate history. In the spring 1996 session, the students at one of the schools rated the micro-teaching classes in social studies as most valuable (compared to classes in the other subjects), specifically mentioning participation in hands-on activities, speakers from other cultures, music, simulations, and the Internet activities.

Some of the criticisms from the high school students were that they were treated like children at the college, that they wanted to receive grades, and that some history preservice teachers, despite guidance from their methods instructor, fell into the role of information givers and were boring.

What We Learned from the Preservice Teachers

Most of the preservice teachers reported that the micro-teaching was the most valuable part of their methods class and that they were better prepared to student teach. The authentic context, "a live audience with real kids," was cited as the most positive aspect of the program by many of the preservice teachers. Many, but not all, of the preservice teachers had the opportunity both to team plan and team teach. Several cited that working with peers was a valuable experience. One person stated,

> The collaborative planning sessions not only helped us to plan each lesson more effectively but gave us a chance to discuss what went well, what didn't work, and what we could do to improve things for the next lesson.

Another preservice teacher commented,

> Working in planning/teaching groups allowed us to focus on teaching; whether or not the . . . students were getting it or learning. We weren't so worried about planning something that would work because we all had good ideas to help . . . and we didn't have to worry about controlling the class so much because we were in groups and could concentrate more on whether or not the kids were learning.

The preservice teachers who worked in groups to plan and teach lessons seemed to profit from the ideas of their peers in the same way that students in cooperative learning groups do, as noted by Slavin,[8] and often perform at higher levels of academic achievement than do the students who are taught primarily using traditional methods. Through our analysis of their comments, the preservice teachers indicated that they were able to focus more on Fuller's second stage, "task concerns" (classroom routines and teaching logistics), and third stage, "impact concerns" (reflection on the influence of teaching on student learning), instead of focusing primarily on first stage, "self concerns" (uncertainty about adequacy in management of the students, time and the material to be taught).[9] One commented, "I think it was terrific to be able to gauge student reactions." Some noted that their confidence increased in their own abilities as a result of their micro-teaching experiences: "I now know that I will make a great teacher. I loved teaching these kids." Another said, "I was able to explore my own methods and develop a style that works for me."

Through the reflections of preservice teachers' journals, we learned that when faced with only a small number of students (four to ten) in a small room, preservice teachers became more aware of the following:

▶ Seeing the glazed-over looks and inattention
▶ Answering their own questions
▶ Recognizing students who dominated and those who did not participate

They also reflected on the challenges of motivating students when no grades were given, the importance of enthusiasm, planning, and background knowledge ("the mountain range in Peru is the Andes, not the Alps"), the importance of not letting personal lives interfere with lessons ("partying all night does not fit with teaching a coherent lesson"), and getting the lesson and available time to fit together.

They experimented with ways to make content more meaningful and to get more student interaction. We observed lessons in which the preservice teachers did the following:

▶ Brought in ethnic food when talking about another culture
▶ Related South American culture to local culture through the use of rodeo
▶ Shared personal travel experiences to Spain and experience in the Gulf War
▶ Made three-dimensional maps to recreate battle scenes
▶ Asked questions that required students to compare and contrast
▶ Played music from Yugoslavia to help students identify with teens who lived there

Many of the methods teachers chuckled over an often-heard reflection from the preservice teachers: "Lessons that involve activities and student interaction take more time. We wish we had more time!" Our response, "So do we!," brought us together as part of a shared experience. Some of the preservice teachers seemed to better understand that making authentic learning experiences fit into given time constraints is a universal issue facing teachers at all levels.

WHAT WE LEARNED ABOUT COLLABORATION

The two most interesting lessons we learned involved the processes of negotiation and the special features of the rural context in which this project took place. Clearly, the collaboration was a process of negotiation between two educational cultures, the school and university. Leming[10] and others describe the interactions between the two cultures of schools and colleges as a conflict between socialization and counter-socialization. According to Leming, the key conflict arises from the schools' assumption that its mission is to transmit knowledge and to socialize students into the existing social order. The college, on the other hand, encourages counter-socialization, independent thinking, and a critical look at the status quo. In our project, a few of the teachers, and especially some of the school board members, were skeptical about new ideas on education coming from university "experts." On the other hand, those of us in teacher education found ourselves voicing concerns about the "folk pedagogy" that informs practice in many schools.[11]

In our methods classes, we actively encourage our students to challenge traditional practices that are not supported by research and sound rationale. We were concerned that some traditional practices and belief systems about teaching that many teachers embrace are sometimes not supported by the research on best practice. We were concerned that our methods students would get advice from teachers who advocated a primary reliance on lecture, for example, and that would be counterproductive in encouraging our preservice teachers to critique all teaching practices, develop multiple approaches to instruction, and include authentic assessments of learning. Early in the project, however, it became clear to the methods instructors that we needed to respect the context in which the teachers' work and the pressures they feel to cover the required curriculum and do well on standardized tests. Respecting each other and putting those issues up front was a key to effective collaboration.

It was very important that the college methods instructors meet with the teachers and administrators and school boards at their respective school sites to discuss differences in policies, politics, logistical problems, accountability, scheduling, and expenses. Since we asked them to bring their students to us, we went to the schools for planning in order to absorb the travel expenses and to meet the teachers and board members on their own turf. We explained that although we, the methods instructors, had ideas about what we wanted for our students, the project needed to have benefits for both college and the school. Having colleges and schools working together in this way is supported by Cochran-Smith.[12] She calls this "collaborative resonance," the assumption that "conjoined efforts to prepare new teachers create learning opportunities that are both different from and richer than the opportunities either the school or the university can provide alone."[13] New ideas about accountability, mutual benefits, and how to prepare future teachers came out of the meetings between the teachers and college faculty.

Neither the college nor the schools in this project offered enough in terms of cultural diversity. Both need to reach beyond their curriculum and setting to provide multicultural perspectives for their students. We consider the short time (six lessons) with the high school students a limitation in making a long-term difference. However, the immediate responses suggest that something powerful is taking place. The seminar with Tanya, the Russian educator, was such an example. Although the high school students were interacting with Tonya for only two hours, the quality of their questions and their rapt attention suggested that students were considering new perspectives.

Our college and schools face severe budget restrictions in a state that ranks in the lower 10 percent in the nation in per capita income. Nevertheless, schools and colleges in rural settings are a good place for discourse and consensus building about how to best prepare teachers. With smaller numbers of people involved who often already know each other ("Cheers" in a rural setting), less bureaucracy, issues that can be more easily defined, and a real sense of place, there is a good chance of effecting change on a small scale with mutual benefits for all.

It is curious that rural communities, which for so long have been marginalized by the dominant culture, have precisely the qualities for which the critics of American schools are now looking. As educators, we need to recognize these strengths, take advantage of them, and build the preparation of rural educators around them.[14]

NOTES

1. Linda Darling-Hammond, *The Right to Learn* (San Francisco: Jossey-Bass, 1997).
2. *Ibid.*, 319.
2. Cynthia S. Brown, *Connecting with the Past* (Portsmouth, N.H.: Heinemann, 1994).
3. Jacqueline G. Brooks and Martin G. Brooks, *The Case for Constructivist Classrooms* (Alexandria, Va.: Association of Supervision and Curriculum Development, 1993).
4. James Welch, *Killing Custer* (New York: Penguin, 1994).

5. Catherine Twomey Fosnot, "Constructivism: A Psychological Theory of Learning," in *Constructivism: Theory, Perspectives and Practice*, ed. C. T. Fosnot (New York: Teachers College Press, 1996): 8-33.
6. Wendell Berry, *What Are People For?* (San Francisco, Calif.: North Point Press, 1990): 168.
7. James W. Loewen, *Lies My Teacher Told Me* (New York: Touchstone, 1995).
8. Robert E. Slavin, *Cooperative Learning: Theory, Research and Practice* (Boston, Mass.: Allyn & Bacon, 1995).
9. Francis F. Fuller, "Concerns of Teachers: A Developmental Conceptualization," *American Educational Research Journal* 6 (1969): 207-226.
10. James S. Leming, "The Two Cultures of Social Studies Education," *Social Education* 53 (1989): 404-408.
11. Jerome S. Bruner, *The Culture of Education* (Cambridge, Mass.: Harvard University Press, 1996).
12. Marilyn Cochran-Smith, "The Power of Teacher Research in Teacher Education," in *Teacher Research and Education Reform: National Society for the Study of Education Yearbook*, eds. Sandra Hollingsworth and Hugh Sockett (Chicago, Ill.: University of Chicago Press, 1994).
13. *Ibid.*, 149.
14. Mary Jean Herzog and Robert B. Pittman, "Home, Family and Community: Ingredients in Rural Education Equation," *Phi Delta Kappan* 77 (1995): 118.

Preserving Oral Historical Resources through a Community, University, and School-Based Collaboration

WILLIAM W. WILEN
LARRY PICICCO

The Scene

"If you could talk to someone who is no longer living, with whom would you like to talk and why?" I (W.W.) asked students this question at our oral history workshop at Theodore Roosevelt High School (TRHS) in Kent, Ohio, each of the past three semesters. The diverse personalities they wanted to converse with still amaze me: Albert Einstein, Princess Diana, Leonardo Da Vinci, Joe DiMaggio, Teddy Roosevelt, Jean Jacques Rousseau, Gregor Mendel, Mother Theresa, Thomas Jefferson, Helen Keller, J. D. Salinger, M. L. King, Babe Ruth, John F. Kennedy. Each semester the list gets longer.

Unfortunately, no student has ever given me the answer I wanted to make my point. Fortunately, I can always count on one of my collaborating teachers. Chris Dreyer, an American history teacher, mentioned her great-grandmother, Anna Herrmann, who emigrated to the United States from the Austro-Hungarian Empire in the early 1900s. Larry Picicco, another American history teacher and chapter co-author, mentioned Vincenzo Picicco, who emigrated from Italy in the early 1900s. I always add my grand-mother, Ida Lindstedt, who emigrated from Finland through Ellis Island in 1909.

I next asked the students what they think might be some of the differences between the people on the long list that they have provided and the short list of three names that my collaborating teachers and I have provided. They realized that their list is made up of well-known people who have been recognized nationally or internationally and are often found in textbooks. In contrast, our list is made up of ordinary people who are never found in textbooks. But history is all around us, and the closer it is to the people in our homes and community, the more potential it has to be personal and exciting. Once my students have gotten the message, I then tell them that this is the purpose of our oral history workshop: to prepare them with the basic knowledge, attitudes, and skills necessary to serve their community. They will become local historians by interviewing senior citizens about their remembrances related to some aspect of Kent's history. Now the workshop is off and running!

Our Conceptualization of Improving Social Studies

ORAL HISTORY

When we think of history, we generally think of written history because our frames of reference are text-books and historical works. But history really begins with the oral tradition reaching back to the early times of the Greek historians. Although the written records, journals, and documents of governments and mostly educated and wealthy individuals became the primary sources for historians over the centuries that followed, the oral tradition was never lost, especially among the common people. After World War II, with the establishment of a major oral history program at Columbia University in New York City, historians rediscovered the oral tradition as an important means of historical research. They realized that recording oral interviews with people from all walks of life offered a historical method that could enhance and complement the traditional written sources. Today, the movement toward investigating social and local community history (home, business, and working life, for example) has heightened the need for oral sources.

Oral history is a method of collecting historical information. It includes tape-recorded interviews, planned in advance, with someone who has firsthand knowledge of an event, person, or way of life that is of some historical interest. The purpose is to preserve the recollections and reminiscences of people living today about their past. The oral history document (audiotape or transcript from the tape) is considered "raw data," and, therefore, is a source for history, typically not history itself. The oral history interview, as raw data, is one source of information; the interpretation and writing of history must include multiple sources.[1]

Oral history is often combined with local history; the subject is community history and the method is interviewing. This provides a convenient opportunity for social studies teachers to involve their students directly in historiography because of the availability of narrators who can serve as primary sources. History comes alive as students "do" history. This complements the more traditional classroom approach of reading about history, listening to the teacher, or viewing a media presentation, to acquire historical information.

Oral history projects can be used to achieve a wide range of social studies goals. Students can use oral histories as a source to prepare histories of community events, institutions, and people. They can be used to explore the impact that national and international events had on a local community. They also can be used to investigate social history topics such as the role of women during war, laborers and the growth of local industry, children and their culture, and changes in various professions in the community.[2] Students can also conduct oral histories for the purpose of investigating social, political, cultural, and economic issues, and they can serve as a data source to solve problems.[3] Oral history projects have the potential to make social studies teaching and learning powerful because they involve students in applying their knowledge about history by doing history. History becomes more meaningful, challenging, integrative, value based, and active.[4]

SERVICE-LEARNING

The broad conceptual base for service-learning in general, and involving students in oral history preservation, specifically, is rooted in the pedagogical framework of constructivism. Developing understanding through the application of new learning to authentic tasks is supported by the best practices that are generalized in research findings.[5] The constructivist/best practice perspective has been adapted by National Council for the Social Studies (NCSS) as a position statement on powerful teaching and learning.[6]

Although the primary purpose of the social studies continues to be civic education, or the development of rational, humane, and active citizens, schools seem to be emphasizing the narrow production of knowledgeable students. One devastating result is that students are disinterested in social studies, uninvolved in their communities, and lacking political competence.[7]

A "strong" or "living" democracy is highly dependent on committed and participating citizens. Students' direct involvement in the community is a way for them to practice and "live" democracy to enhance the public good. This can be accomplished by developing understanding, civic attitudes, and participation skills through social studies. Effective community service-learning (CSL) programs can have a positive impact on students' attitudes and behavior toward their communities, the political process, and even their schools. CSL is a powerful way for teachers to encourage students to achieve the purposes of the social studies.[8]

One of the more recent and comprehensive reviews of research on CSL indicates that, although the research that has been conducted on students' academic and intellectual development in service-learning is limited and inconclusive,[9] some positive findings indicate that students developed problem-solving abilities and open-mindedness, and improved their attendance and grades as a result of participating in service-learning projects.

Wade[10] reported that the best documented outcomes of secondary level CSL projects relate to student gains in personal and social development. Furthermore, evidence of students' increase in self-esteem, self-confidence, and moral development has also been found. The findings on the impact of CSL on political efficacy and participation are mixed with the strongest finding in the area of further community service.[11] A more recent review of research concurred with this important finding that young students who are involved in service-learning "develop an ethic of care and service that fosters civic participation," and this attitude continues into their later school years.[12]

Although there are barriers to implementing service-learning in the schools, they are not insurmountable. The major barriers center on the culture of the school with its high value placed on individual effort and success over collaboration and collective well-being. Traditional conceptions of learning and teaching emphasize the teacher's role in teaching, not the student's role in learning. Collaboration is generally not encouraged among teachers or between the school and the community. Schools that are oriented toward constructivism and "have adopted a more student-centered authentic approach to learning with flexible scheduling and collaborative teaching and learning structures will undoubtedly have an easier time adopting service learning programs."[13]

Our Process of Collaboration and Some Tangible Outcomes (W.W.W.)

The Kent Oral History Project, as it is currently conceived, is a collaboration of three Kent educational and community agencies: the Kent State University Social Studies Education Program, the Kent Historical Society,[14] and the Social Studies Department of Theodore Roosevelt High School. I initiated the project one and a half years ago in my position as a professor of social studies education at Kent State University and as a member of the Board of Trustees of the Kent Historical Society. Five TRHS social studies department teachers, including Larry Picicco, and forty-three of their students have been involved in the project over the past three semesters. Formal written assessments have been completed after each semester, and they clearly indicate that the project has been very successful. Based on this feedback and other more informal assessments conducted by the social studies faculty at TRHS, it is expected that the collaboration will continue well into the future.

The general purpose of the project is to encourage high school social studies students to practice active citizenship by valuing and becoming involved in historical preservation. More specifically, we have the following as goals for the various collaborating groups:

▶ Students will engage in powerful social studies learning by "doing" history, engage in in-depth study of local community topics, participate in cooperative classroom study, learn and practice historical inquiry and the oral history method, apply social studies skills in real-life settings, and demonstrate social and civic responsibility in the community setting.
▶ TRHS social studies teachers will engage students in authentic learning experiences outside the classroom, use a teaching/learning strategy that students have found to be a "peak experience," use an alternative assessment approach to accommodate students' multiple learning styles, and achieve some Ohio Model Competency-Based Program[15] objectives.
▶ Kent State's social studies methods instructor will demonstrate instructional skills to his undergraduate and graduate students and model civic responsibility attitudes and behaviors.
▶ Kent Historical Society will encourage local students to be active and involved citizens in the Kent community, and preserve Kent's history by adding tapes with supporting documentation to its archive of oral histories.

The initial collaboration between Kent State's Social Studies Program and the Kent Historical Society started in 1989. I involved my undergraduate secondary social studies methods students in conducting oral history interviews with Kent senior citizens recommended by the Board of Trustees of the Kent Historical Society. Although I had been conducting oral history interviews for the Board of Trustees since 1983, when I first joined, it was not until I involved my social studies methods students that the number of interviews dramatically increased. This was a symbiotic relationship because, although the Board of Trustees was interested in preserving Kent's past and I could help accomplish this at the same time, I was preparing future teachers to appreciate and learn the skills of historians by actively practicing history.

During this phase of the Kent Oral History Project, more than 120 oral history interviews were conducted by community volunteers, social studies teacher education students, and me. The tapes and their accompanying inventories have been stored in the Kent Historical Society archives. In addition to being available to community members and students, these tapes were consulted for the writing of the recently revised history, titled *Kent, Ohio: The Dynamic Decades*.[16]

Two years ago, I decided to reduce my teacher education students' involvement in the project and to attempt to modify the collaboration by including the social studies teachers at TRHS and their students. Due to changes in the teacher education program at Kent State resulting from the new licensure demands of the Ohio Department of Education, I felt I had less time in my social studies methods classes to train students fully in the method of oral history and less time for students to conduct oral histories and prepare the necessary supporting documentation. Upon approaching the TRHS departmental chair, Bruce Dzeda, who shares some of the oral history materials I would be using in the workshop (described later in this chapter), I found that he and his social studies teachers were very interested in exploring ideas to encourage their students to be more involved in community history and its preservation. Another motivation for the social studies department to be involved, according to Bruce Dzeda, was the demands of Ohio's Model Competency-Based Program, which emphasizes making connections between social studies content taught in schools with students' lives outside school. The oral history method was seen as having the potential to encourage students to become actively involved in "doing" history rather than just reading and discussing it.

After a meeting with social studies teachers interested in participating, at which basic logistical decisions were made, the project began in March 1999. I had made contact and received preliminary approval from narrators for oral history interviews based on recommendations from the Kent Historical Society Board. Four members of the TRHS social studies department identified fifteen "overachieving" volunteer students from their classes, and five teams of three students each were formed. The students had made arrangements with their teachers regarding how they were to receive credit for their participation in the project. With Larry, one of the four participating teachers, serving in the important role as the liaison between the social studies department and the project, I conducted four one-period training sessions in two months on-site at TRHS before the teams of students were given an extended period of time to conduct their interviews and prepare the supporting documentation. A final, fifth session was held for turning in the tapes and supporting materials, and for sharing, reflecting, and evaluating the outcomes of the project.

After the first round was completed, we held a meeting with the social studies chair and teachers to assess the project. We decided to allow participating teachers to select their teams of students by either asking for volunteering students or doing the selection themselves. Everyone agreed that we wanted mature, responsible students who showed a genuine interest in history. We emphasized to the students that they should be willing to devote considerable time outside of school in order to prepare for and conduct the interviews, and complete the related requirements of the project.

Logistical matters were also a concern. We decided to meet three consecutive Wednesdays during first period. After the third session, a two-week break would be provided in order for the students to contact their narrators and send a tentative list of questions. In the sixth week, we would provide more training, but meetings would take place during second period instead of first so that students could stagger their missed class periods. After a four-week interim period to give students time to conduct their interviews and complete all necessary supporting documentation, a final wrap-up session would be held also during second period. A total of five 50-minute class periods were necessary to fulfill workshop objectives.

Workshop sessions were initially conducted in the cafeteria because there were no regular classrooms available. This turned out to be very distracting because study hall students were in the vicinity. Fortunately, Larry discovered an available conference room, which seated approximately twenty students. We conducted the past two oral history workshops in this conference room.

The selection of incentives to encourage students to participate in the project is still an issue. Initially, students worked out contracts for the credit they were to receive from the teachers. This took the form of substituting the project for a major classroom assessment measure, such as a test, semester exam, or in-class project. In some cases, the oral history project was contracted strictly for extra credit. We also added small incentives that might be appreciated by participating students: free membership to the Kent Historical Society (which includes a monthly newsletter), a certificate for participation, and a small juice and dough-nut celebration at the final session. Other possibilities discussed were free movie passes and a pizza party.

The successful collaboration of three educational and community agencies produced many tangible outcomes benefiting the three constituencies. Based on formal written comments from the three cohorts of forty-three TRHS students, the students gained much from interacting with senior citizens and learning from them. The students felt they were performing a worthwhile service for the community by preserving history and adding to the collection of oral history tapes. They also believed that they were helping community seniors by making them feel what they had to say was important. They learned more about community events, people, and issues. And they enjoyed the experience.

The social studies teachers seemed to benefit because they appreciated having the opportunity to involve some of their best students in a challenging project that pushed their capabilities. The departmental chair also appreciated coverage of the goals of the Ohio Model, which call for students to become involved in their local community as active citizens.

My social studies methods students got to experience the successes, issues, and problems of the oral history project because I reported to them on a regular basis. Sometimes they even helped me solve minor problems. As future social studies teachers, they probably have developed some theoretical and practical knowledge of what to do and not to do in implementing service-learning and an oral history project. I also had the experience, and accompanying satisfaction, of serving as a role model of an active social studies methods instructor who "practices what he preaches" by working for the common good as a local commu-nity citizen. My feeling is that in order for future social studies teachers to teach what it is to be rational, humane, and active citizens, they need to be competent citizens themselves.

The Kent Historical Society has the satisfaction of encouraging high school students to get involved in community preservation and has benefited by adding more oral history tapes to its archives. And the TRHS library has started its collection of oral history tapes. A final outcome, judging from the students' com-ments, is that the narrators who talked about their remembrances and reminiscences probably experienced considerable satisfaction in formally contributing an audiotape to the city's archives.

A Teacher Talks to Teachers (L.P.)

Overall, I feel very satisfied about giving some of my students an opportunity to preserve the history of our community. The feedback from the students' perspective provides insight into their appreciation of the opportunity to conduct oral history interviews and the overall effectiveness of the project. Their evaluation, recommendations, and suggestions for future projects are important because we learn how to restructure and adjust the program to serve the needs of the students, program, and school curriculum more effectively.

Initially, when we began the project, the students were not sure of what they were getting into. When we showed them some of the completed oral histories, they expected the project to be very time consuming and involve a great deal of extra work. Once they began to prepare for and conduct the interviews, however, they were relieved to see that the project involved less time and work than they had thought. It was interesting to see how the students compared the oral history project to traditional teacher-driven and textbook-oriented lessons. Most students are not attracted to traditional social studies teaching; that is why they perceived that doing an oral history interview seemed to bring history alive. Teachers can help by encouraging students to see the connection between history and their lives inside and outside the class-room. It is good to hear students explain that they valued becoming involved in someone else's life. I'm also sure that student interest in the life of a narrator does more for that person than we really know.

Oral history is a new approach to learning Kent's history, and we are figuring things out as we move along with the project. Personally, I have come to the conclusion that oral history could be much more effective if the project could be included in the curriculum of my regular U.S. history classes rather than having only three students participate each semester. I found it difficult to coordinate the project.

Participating students had to have permission from the teachers because they were missing classes in order to attend the sessions. Forms had to be made, signed, collected, and recorded, which was not very convenient.

I did not have contact with the other participating teachers' students. I had daily contact with my own team of three and could easily remind them of meeting dates and deadlines, and monitor their progress throughout the project. I could also address concerns they had and provide assistance if needed. I usually had to write notes to teachers reminding them of the workshop sessions and deadlines. They would then have to remind their participating students. It was almost impossible for me to track down the students who were not on my team during the day.

The scheduling and organization of the project is quite hectic. Also, students have to miss three consecutive first-period weekly classes followed by two second-period weekly classes. That is a lot to ask of a student and the teacher. At times, the teachers who gave their students permission to attend the workshop sessions forgot they were involved in the project. Therefore, students were marked as absent. I then had to write excuses or passes to remind those teachers the students were attending the session. I also had to take the time to clear these "absences" at the attendance office.

All of these problems and inconveniences could be eliminated if the workshop were conducted with all students during regular class time. I have suggested that I would volunteer to be the only participating teacher and the project would involve only my U. S. history students in my classroom during my class time. This would allow me to take a more active role in the collaboration because Bill and I would co-teach all the workshop sessions. We are seriously exploring this possibility for the next school year.

An important component of the project has been the collaboration between Bill and myself. When he initially approached our social studies department to discuss the possibility of some of our students' participation, I immediately volunteered. I thought it was an excellent idea, and I could use this as an opportunity to further develop my informal use of oral history interviews in my classes. I offered to be the liaison between the university and the TRHS social studies department. I also saw this as an opportunity to learn more about and incorporate service-learning into our social studies curriculum.

As with all collaborations, commitment, communication, and the desire to make the project work are essential. Bill's role as project director and workshop instructor has been the "meat and potatoes" of the collaboration. My role has been as a facilitator and "middle man" between the students and Bill. Coincidentally, I am working on my master's degree in social studies education and have Bill for a course. This has made it very easy for us to collaborate and communicate. We openly share our ideas with each other in terms of logistical concerns, student and teacher issues, strengths and weaknesses of the project, and how it might be improved. I believe this collaboration has been successful and will continue to improve. We are both trying to achieve the same goal—we want an exciting and effective way for Kent students to learn about the community in which they live and, through the oral history process, become more active citizens.

I asked our social studies departmental chairperson, Bruce Dzeda, to express his views about the importance of oral history and the project. This is what he had to say:

> The past decade or so has seen the rise in the importance of social history as a way of better understanding the past. It has become increasingly clear that oral history has made a distinctive contribution to the discipline of history.

History benefits when eyewitnesses present their viewpoints. Each person who has lived through several decades has a view or vantage point that is unique. No two people see an event or issue in the same way.

Oral history reminds us that ordinary people not only fought the battles of World War II but also worked in defense plants and on labor-short farms. As children, many contributed their pennies to the winning of the war. World War II was not only about generals; it was about the home front. This is also true about the Great Depression, the Cold War, and the events of peace time. The stories of ordinary people deserve to be preserved so that generations to come can learn from these remembrances.

Those who collect oral history accounts are drawn into the stories and experiences of those they interview. There is something magical, even wonderful, about an older, experienced person and a young, inexperienced person talking together about the past. We know that older people want to have their stories told and saved for future generations. Young people also benefit in countless ways from such experiences. Often, long-lasting friendships develop, and both parties feel good about the experience. Thus, young people see their own time and place in history more clearly, with a perspective not available before.

At Theodore Roosevelt High School, we value the chance for our students to talk with friends and citizens of the Portage County community. Everyone benefits—including the future—when the record of the past comes alive.[17]

While the oral history project at Theodore Roosevelt High School is still in its infancy stage, we are going to continue it in the years to come in the hope that it will become an everlasting part of our curriculum and our community. Through the hard work and dedication of Bill, myself, students, narrators, the Kent Historical Society, and community, we will preserve the history of our great city.

A Professor Talks to Professors (W.W.W.)

It is an exciting adventure, professionally and personally, to be the creator and director of a project that is successful. But the real success of the oral history project has been highly dependent on the collaborative efforts of diverse groups of professionals. Without their willingness to contribute a positive attitude, time, flexibility, and resources, the project would not be possible. As Larry mentioned previously, the project has had some problems, but we are working together to resolve them. We anticipate the support of the collaborative groups in order to make significant changes this coming semester.

The following commentary centers on the "nuts and bolts" of planning for and conducting an oral history workshop for students. I thought that it would help you decide if this is something that you want to try. If so, the details will help you plan your adaptation of our oral history project.

In our case, the historical society helps tremendously in identifying potential narrators. I could always count on the Kent Historical Society to come up with two or three times the number of narrators I needed. The alternative is to rely on contact with community groups such as the American Legion, Veterans of Foreign Wars, Lions, Kiwanis, or Masons. Another possibility is to check the local newspapers for stories on people.

An oral history project with the schools requires time. First, you need to contact the principal and social studies chair to arrange a meeting with teachers in order to present the concept and gauge their interest. If you use your methods class or work with one teacher's social studies class, the logistics will be much easier. You will need to budget time to set up a schedule and to carry out the training sessions. It also takes time to contact potential narrators to get enough information to present to the students. I like to make the initial contact with narrators because I can speak on behalf of the historical society, and I think this adds a certain familiarity that helps connect with people who might be a little apprehensive about participating.

My schedule for workshops includes five 50-minute sessions:

▶ First session: I make introductions, hand out the packet of materials, offer a rationale for service-learning and oral history, provide examples of oral histories, and describe the nature of the oral history project.
▶ Second session: Teams are formed, narrators are paired with teams, we review historical sources, teams form initial questions, and teams arrange initial contact with narrators.
▶ Third session: Teams share their impressions from their initial contact, teams hand in a copy of their questions to me for review, we review oral history procedures, students practice procedures with tape recorders by interviewing each other (while I review and return the questions), and teams revise the list of questions and send it to narrators.
▶ Fourth session: Teams share their impressions from further contact with narrators, we review the role of questioning techniques, I conduct a mock oral history interview while students analyze my performance, we discuss interviewing procedures further, I distribute tapes, we review supporting materials to be

turned in with the audiotape at the final session, and teams arrange to conduct interviews and prepare supporting materials.

▶ Fifth session: Teams share their impressions of interview experiences with narrators, I collect tapes, we discuss summaries and inventories as well as grading and follow-up procedures, I conduct the workshop evaluation, and we celebrate accomplishments.

Assuming you received all the tapes and materials at this last session, which was rarely the case in my high school workshop, time is now needed to listen to the tapes; review the summaries, information forms, and tape inventories; and complete the evaluation and feedback forms. The evaluations need to be returned to the teachers for the students to get credit. Because I never received all the tapes and materials in the final session, I was continually phoning, e-mailing, and writing notes to the spokesperson for each of the teams, attempting to get the project completed, and going through Larry to encourage the teachers to push for completion. I am still missing the materials for one team from the fall 1999 group. What happened with the spring 2000 group is another story from which we all learned an important lesson. I should mention that this last round was particularly interesting because my students interviewed narrators who remembered events related to the May 4, 1970, tragedy at Kent State.

A brief elaboration of this spring 2000 oral history effort will clarify the value, benefits, and a major disappointment of the project. Hopes were high when I recruited three narrators through the Kent Historical Society who had direct and indirect connections with the events of May 4, 1970. A group of nine motivated students, recommended by three social studies teachers, formed three interview teams. The three narrators were the former mayor of Kent in May 1970, a businessman who had his pharmacy damaged as part of the disturbances leading to May 4, and a teacher who lived in Kent whose family was deeply affected by the events surrounding May 4.

The training sessions went well with a high level of interest and enthusiasm. The teams devised questions that were sent to, and reviewed by, the narrators, and dates were set for the interviews. The interviews were conducted over a period of two months instead of the one month originally scheduled, but this can be expected because students' and narrators' schedules change. Flexibility and patience are essential. The interviews were conducted, but a major problem developed. Two of the interviews, including one with the mayor of Kent, were conducted on a tape recorder with a faulty microphone. As a result, the tapes were of very poor quality even after I had them analyzed and copied by audio engineers at Kent State. I know we were all disappointed about the faulty tape recorder and resulting incomplete interviews. Our only alternative was to redo the interviews during the upcoming semester, assuming the narrators would cooperate. One consolation was that the Kent Historical Society Board has since suggested that we purchase our own recorders to increase the probability that we won't lose any future taped interviews.

All was not lost, though, because the students participating in this latest workshop reported very favorably on what they learned and the benefits they received from the project. For example, students learned that National Guard troops were quartered in an elementary school in town, that there were tanks on the Kent State University campus, and that one of the narrators had a son in Vietnam at this time. They also learned about the role of police during the rioting, that non-KSU students caused some of the trouble, and that the people of the city of Kent strongly supported the National Guard and were very much against the students. Another interesting story was that the day after May 4, a school levy was approved by the community. One narrator characterized these as both extreme low and high points of this period.

Students, as an outcome of the interviews, wanted to know much more about May 4. In addition to wanting to know more about the incident itself, they wanted to know what the students who were not demonstrating felt about the National Guard being on campus, more about the Weathermen and their radical movement, more about the National Guard's perspective because the focus was so much on the students, and more about the various conspiracy theories surrounding May 4. Judging from their evaluations, the students benefited significantly. They appreciated hearing from people who remembered events of that day. One student said that an interview makes the experience "ten times more intriguing . . . and to have a person tell you exactly how he felt at that moment makes you feel as if you were there." This student realized what this community service project was all about.

Another essential component of the workshop is the packet of materials[18] you will need to provide for students. Listed below are the components of the packet I use:

▶ Introduction about oral history and Kent's Oral History Project
▶ Definition of oral history and its characteristics ("Oral History Is . . .")
▶ Several illustrative commentaries based on oral histories gathered from a variety of sources, including the excellent source *Ordinary Americans* by Linda Monk[19]

The oral histories my students and I have conducted over the years and the tapes are cataloged in the Kent Historical Society archives. An illustrative oral history completed by one of the teams from the previous semester is contained in the packet summary. The general information form, tape inventory, and signed gift agreement are included. Other components of the packet include the following:

▶ Procedures for conducting oral history interviews
▶ Information on using questioning to accomplish oral history goals
▶ Introduction to oral history interview tape
▶ Gift agreement form
▶ Sample certificate of appreciation (sent to narrators)
▶ List of narrators to be interviewed during the current semester, with extended background on each
▶ Schedule for the workshop and assignments for sessions
▶ List of questions for conducting family histories
▶ Debriefing and evaluation forms

Finances have not been a problem because the Kent Historical Society has basically picked up the tab. Major expenses come from copying the approximately forty-page packet for each participating student and teacher; purchase of the audiotapes (three per narrator—one each for the Kent Historical Society and TRHS media center and one for the narrator); and the purchase of some books on Kent's history for students to consult when learning about the investigation topic and creating interview questions. We used the tape recorders for role playing interviews in workshop sessions; they were also checked out when the students did their interviews. Be sure to check the recorders while students are practicing during the workshop sessions. The final cost is the purchase of refreshments for the last session, when a celebration is in order. The Historical Society provided the personalized certificates for the narrators and students.

Care needs to be taken with the products of the project. The tape recordings are stored in the archives of the historical society and the high school media center and are available for community members' and students' use. Each tape is accompanied by the general information form, summary, tape inventory, and permission form. The tapes will be getting further exposure because plans are being made for the historical society's monthly newsletter to feature oral history interviews. The historical society is also transcribing the oral history tapes so that we will have them available for the public in written form. A list of all the oral histories can be found on the Kent Historical Society's web site.[20] The tapes are also cataloged in the TRHS media center[21] and listed on the center's web site with the students' names as the interviewers. This is another reward for the students' efforts.

The problems we have had are being worked out, and we will enter a new, more advanced phase of the project next fall semester. Larry's proposal to implement the oral history project with one or more of his U.S. history classes will be an experiment this fall. One plus, as I see it, is working with a class of students for which the oral history project is a requirement. Another plus is that Larry and I will be working as a team in the workshop sessions. I think this will increase the probability of a powerful teaching experience for the students and the production of high-quality historical artifacts. My only concern about working with a heterogeneous group of students is that some will have only minimal ability and interest in the project, and this may affect the final product. We will have to form teams carefully using Larry's knowledge of the students. I am genuinely looking forward to the next round of the oral history workshop.

In summary, here are what I perceive are the general outcomes and insights gained as a result of our collaborative effort and the oral history workshop:

▶ Community participation and historical preservation are perceived as important goals to be achieved.
▶ Diverse educational and community groups will collaborate when the goal is mutually beneficial to all.
▶ Although a leader is necessary to initiate the collaborative process and coordinate many aspects of the project, the goals of the project will not be accomplished unless leaders within all the collaborating groups are willing to promote the project and do the necessary work.
▶ High school students are very willing to engage in community service projects, capable of applying the oral history method, and relatively dependable in completing the project, and generally produce a quality product.
▶ Community service-learning is a rewarding experience and creates an overall good feeling.

NOTES

1. William Wilen, "Kent's Oral History Project," *Kent Historical Society Newsletter* (September 1997): 1.
2. Social Science Education Consortium, *Teaching the Social Sciences and History in Secondary Schools* (Belmont, Calif.: Wadsworth Publishing, 1994).
3. Samuel Totten, "Using Oral Histories to Address Social Issues in the Social Studies Classroom," *Social Education* 53 (1989): 114-116.
4. National Council for the Social Studies, *Expectations of Excellence: Curriculum Standards for Social Studies* (Washington, D.C.: Author, 1994).
5. Steven Zemelman, Harvey Daniels, and Arthur Hyde, *Best Practice*, 2d ed. (Portsmouth, N.H.: Heinemann, 1997).
6. National Council for the Social Studies, *Expectations of Excellence*, 163-170.
7. Patrick Ferguson, "Impacts on Social and Political Participation," in *Handbook of Research on Social Studies Teaching and Learning*, ed. James Shaver (New York: Macmillan, 1991).
8. Rahima C. Wade, *Community Service Learning* (New York: State University of New York Press, 1997).
9. Rahima C. Wade, "Community Service Learning and the Social Studies Curriculum: Challenges to Effective Practice," *The Social Studies* 88 (1997): 197-202.
10. *Ibid.*, 30-33.
11. *Ibid.*
12. Sheldon Berman, "Integrating Community Service Learning with School Culture," *Constitutional Rights Foundation Network* 7 (1999): 3
13. Wade, "Community Service Learning and the Social Studies Curriculum."
14. Kent Historical Society; Contact James Caccamo, Executive Director, P.O. Box 663, 152 Franklin Avenue, Kent, OH 44240; 330-678-2712.
15. Ohio Department of Education, *Social Studies: Ohio's Model Competency-Based Program* (Columbus: Ohio Department of Education, 1999).
16. Ralph Darrow, ed., *Kent, Ohio: The Dynamic Decades* (Kent, Ohio: Kent Historical Society, 1999).
17. Bruce Dzeda, Communication to Larry Picicco, 2000.
18. William Wilen, *Oral History Project* (packet of training materials and resources) (Kent, Ohio: Kent Historical Society, 1999).
19. Linda Monk, *Ordinary People* (Alexandria, Va.: Close-Up Publishing, 1994), 20.
20. Kent Historical Society web site includes a list of oral histories, www.kenthist.org.
21. Theodore Roosevelt High School Media Center; Contact Jan Wojnaroski, 1400 N. Mantua Street, Kent, OH 44240; 330-673-9595.

Teacher Release to Industry Program as Professional Development of Teachers of Social Studies

Warren Prior
Randal Symons

The Scene

Danica is a teacher of social studies who has been teaching in secondary schools in Australia for about ten years. In 1998, she applied for the Teacher Release to Industry Program (TRIP). Here is a conversation, held early in the program, with her university supervising professor, Warren, at her work place, the Tooling Industry Forum of Australia (TIFA).

Warren: So why did you really apply for the TRIP program?

Danica: Honestly, I have to tell you that I was looking for a break from the classroom after ten years of teaching. Working with challenging teenagers for the last ten years is my achievement, and, now, being part of the TRIP program is my reward! I did know a couple of people who had participated in the TRIP program, and I felt that it might be a good opportunity for me to rethink my teaching and learning in social studies.

Warren: What exactly is TIFA?

Danica: As you know, I was placed here after an initial interview with the manager. It is the peak industry body for toolmakers and looks after training, marketing, and career standards in the tooling industry. I had never heard of TIFA, and as yet still know nothing about toolmaking. But I'm learning fast!

Warren: Tell me about your work program here in the office at TIFA.

Danica: Well, one of the first things I have discovered here is the joy of having a spacious work place! I even have my own phone and can shut the door if I need quiet work time. Little things maybe, but this is a huge cultural shift for me, and I know I can speak for my teacher colleagues. I have had several meetings with my manager. He had done his homework and knew my teaching background in social studies. He wants me to redevelop the entry standards training programs for the industry given the huge cultural shifts to technologies driving the industry.

Warren: But you are a social studies teacher. What can you offer TIFA?

Danica: There is such a difference in how I am perceived and accepted. I believe that I have a lot of relevant skills to this job. As a teacher, I know how to plan teaching and learning programs, set objectives, cohere national benchmarks and evaluate learning. There isn't anyone at TIFA who can do all of this. I have quickly picked up that there is a need for all of these things to be placed in some form of industrial cultural setting. I have been to a couple of meetings where the conversation was really about corporate citizenship, the need to encourage young females into the industry, and the critical need for these young people to have the sort of skills, like problem-solving skills, that I teach in my social studies classes.

Warren: So where to now?

Danica: I feel so revitalized already. I can't wait to get started, and even the other night I was thinking at home about how some of my year 10 social studies students would be amazed to know that some of the things I try to teach them actually are seen to be important in the workplace.

TRIP Created as a Form of Professional Development in Australia

The focus of the university/school collaboration project described here is a professional development program that operates in the State of Victoria, Australia. It is a one-year program in which selected teachers (and principals), including teachers of social studies, from both primary and secondary schools, work in an industry placement for an extended period of time during one school year.

Over the past decade, we have seen a worldwide trend in industry toward restructuring workplace practices. The globalization of economies, the continuing impact of information technologies, and the introduction of competency-based approaches to career entry and progression have all brought about significant changes in the culture and realities of workplace practices.

Teaching, in both schools and universities, has not been immune to these mega-trends. In Australia in the late 1990s, we have witnessed the first attempts by state governments to describe and define what it actually means to be a teacher.[1] At the heart of the issue have been three key questions:

▶ What is a teacher?
▶ What do teachers do?
▶ How can teachers contribute to the *economic* well-being of the nation?

The issues arising from these questions have resulted in shifts in thinking about the goals of education, an examination of the place of schools as agents in facilitating change in workplace practices, and a critical analysis of teachers themselves as suitable models for promoting "outside of school" work practices, that is, in the "real world."

As a result of these trends in Australia, governments forge closer links between the education sector and industry. Most education/industry links programs have been conceived within the social philosophy that takes it for granted that schools and business organizations serve similar social purposes. This argument posits the view that both are instruments of economic growth. In particular, there is the growing perception by governments that schools are agents of economic development and that vocational education is best located in the social studies area. In other words, a socially educated person is one who is skilled for employment and has knowledge and values that will contribute to the economic well-being of the (national) community. Perhaps the most obvious sign of the connection between education and national economic indicators is the recent name change for the government department. No longer called the Department of Education, it is now called the Department of Education, Employment, and Training (DEET).

The emergence of these new relationships between industry and education has highlighted the need to examine and define teachers' work.[2] A common comment heard in the industrial sector is that teachers have no knowledge of the "real world" because they never leave school. These criticisms result in a devaluing of teachers' work.[3] In a recent research project concerning citizenship education, Prior,[4] using a case study of a "typical" high school in metropolitan Melbourne, noted that of sixty-five teachers at the school, only eight had had some form of extensive work experience outside of teaching. None of these eight teachers was a social studies teacher. University professors, too, are not immune to the comments about life in the "ivory tower." In preparing for this chapter, we interviewed ten university professors. Four of these professors were teaching in the social studies curriculum and pedagogy area. Only three of the ten professors had worked outside of the education sector, and none of the four social studies professors had worked outside of teaching in a university/school environment. Critics also point to young people who are about to enter the workforce as not being adequately prepared for changing work cultures and practices.

The curriculum area of social studies is sometimes targeted by industry in Australia as an example of a subject that contributes little to the real world of work. This is a perception that we, as social educators, know is incorrect. At the senior level of secondary school in Victoria, a new social studies subject, called "Industry and Enterprise Studies," has recently been introduced by DEET, probably in response to these criticisms. Here the focus is on the transition from school to work. As part of the requirements of the course, students are required to undertake work experience. Their social studies teacher supervises this experience.

A look at the statement of goals of teaching social studies will confirm that teachers in this key learning area are well aware of their responsibilities toward preparing students to take their place in the community, which includes the world of work.

In the State of Victoria, the Curriculum and Standards Framework, *Studies of Society and Environment* (2000) is an outcomes-based curriculum.[5]

Studies of Society and Environment (SOSE) enables students to participate as confident, responsible and active citizens in a democratic society. . . . Students will gain a broad knowledge, which includes the development of aspects of economics and understandings about the financial systems to enable them to participate as informed, enterprising adults in personal and work situations.

This curriculum framework also identifies six areas of essential knowledge for all students in the teaching and learning of SOSE. One of these further develops the already close links between school and the workplace: Enterprise skills include collaborative decision making, problem solving, exploring issues, and creating work and business opportunities.

In Australia, we have argued that the links being made between school and work are now so strong that it poses a critical issue for us as social educators. What are the key social competencies that we, as social educators, can assist young people to develop, in order for them to become responsible and active citizens in one of the major contexts of their adult lives, namely, the work place?

This is not to say that social studies is, or should be, confined to having only a narrow vocational focus.[6] However, we often define who we are as citizens by the work we do. We take the position that teachers of social studies do have a responsibility to prepare students for life in the work place. This is not a "factory fodder" approach but an approach more in line with the already existing broader goals of social studies. Another key question for us is, How, then, can we, as social educators, enhance our understandings about the "real world" of work?

The conceptual argument is that one of the major goals of the teaching and learning of social studies is citizenship education, and that citizenship controls the access of individuals and groups to scarce (mainly economic, but also cultural) resources in society. Social studies teachers need to be alert to the vagaries of (nonteaching) employment. Although issues of inclusion/exclusion, social injustice, exploitation, the violation of human rights, and inequity remain as features of our industrial societies, the growth of citizenship entitlements fostered by schools has the potential to mitigate the worst features of an unequal world.[7]

In 1990, a salary increase agreement for teachers included in its professional development provisions the introduction of an industry exchange program in which teachers "assist in developing a multi-skilled workforce." Following on from the award agreement, the key stakeholders—Department of Education, Employment, and Training, the Victorian Employers Chamber of Commerce and Industry (VECCI), and the Teachers Federation of Victoria (TFV)—established the Teacher Release to Industry program (TRIP).

Objectives of TRIP

The objectives of the TRIP program are the following:

▶ To give teachers direct experience of industry through extended employment in positions determined by industry, thereby developing their skills to act as change agents in school communities
▶ To provide school students with programs containing up-to-date information about current industry practices as well as industry's expectations of young people entering the work force
▶ To indicate to industry, and to the education community, the various ways in which industry can be a source of information, resources, and support for the educational programs of schools
▶ To encourage education and industry personnel to establish and maintain a diversity of ongoing networks and links between schools and industry

The practicalities of the TRIP program include a negotiated agreement between the industry workplace and the teacher's employer, DEET, to share equally the salary costs of the teacher during the TRIP placement. DEET also replaces the TRIP teacher at his/her school by another teacher.

The third partner in the TRIP program is the university. Participants in the TRIP program undertake a postgraduate qualification during their work placement experience. University staff act as a liaison and support for the teachers while on placement in industry. As the head of the social education area at Deakin University, my role is to coordinate the collaboration among the university, school, and the industry for teachers of social studies who are undertaking work placement. Underpinning the TRIP program with teachers of social studies are principles of professional development[8] conceptually framed to do the following:

▶ Focus on the defined needs of social studies teachers to allow them to validate and extend their existing classroom practices.
▶ Acknowledge their existing understandings and skills and knowledge that they bring to the program so that they are their own researchers and reflective practitioners.

Two key questions, therefore, frame this school/university/work place collaboration:

▶ To what extent do the experiences gained by teacher participants in the TRIP program contribute to the goals of social studies?
▶ Are TRIP teachers any more analytical and reflective about their classroom practices in social studies on their return to the classroom?

How the Collaboration Worked: A "TRIPer's" Perspective (R.S.)

The TRIP experience was a year placement into an area of industry. In my year in 1999, there were fifty-one TRIP teachers. For me, this was my first real experience of work outside of school. I had only been to school, studied to be a teacher, and then finally taught. I have now been teaching for sixteen years, including my participation in a teacher exchange program to Canada in 1996. I have taught at all levels of the primary school, and for one year, I was appointed a specialist computer teacher. My professional development over the years includes further tertiary studies and many short courses. Even so, none has provided me with such a global perspective of the world of work outside of teaching as the TRIP program.

I have always had an interest in social studies as far back as I can remember, even as a student in primary school. As a teacher, it is the key area of the curriculum where social skills, values, and knowledge of the world can be developed, and applied social studies provides a myriad of opportunities for learning about real-life situations.

The placements in industries vary, but to generalize, most positions for teachers of social studies are in the management/human resources and training fields. Industry sometimes recognizes the skills teachers possess in teaching and facilitating, but not often or at least not initially when you start "on the job." Once in the workplace environment, management soon learns that there are other skills that social studies teachers possess—analytical skills, problem-solving skills, cooperative learning skills, corporate citizenship skills (in the sense of understandings about the mutual obligations of organizations to the community), and broad cultural understandings and sensitivities. As a teacher of social studies, I also had a range of social understandings, including a broad global view of a range of societies.

As a TRIP teacher, I brought a kind of "new set of eyes," by being not really an employee. As a result, I was able to analyze workplace practices critically and suggest recommendations for improvement. The TRIP teacher is not a threat to anyone's job. TRIP teachers leave at the end of the placement. Employers mentioned this fact often as I went to meetings before taking up my placement.

I applied for TRIP on two occasions. In 1999, I was successful in gaining a position at the Commonwealth Serum Laboratories Limited (CSL), a large pharmaceutical company based in Melbourne. My position was as a training associate in the human resources area. My role primarily focused on management programs, including the following:

- Computer training for staff
- Workplace training and assessment
- Newsletter production for the middle managers and others on a monthly basis
- Involvement in on-line competency-based recruitment and selection
- Facilitation and updating of the company Induction Booklet
- Development of a Worklife Kit—the balance between work and life

The collaboration process of TRIP required me to form partnerships with three parties. The first was with my school principal. The second was with the university. The third was with the workplace supervisor. There were, of course, links between these.

SCHOOL PLAN

My principal authorized the TRIP application. As a part of the application process, I had to include a school plan that outlined the skills and experiences I believed I would develop throughout the TRIP year. These had to be linked to my school's charter (a three-year document that outlines the goals and priorities of the school in the areas of curriculum, management, resources, and environment). Both the principal and I agreed to the plan. The plan also included a section on how I would share my workplace understandings and skills with my social studies colleagues and how I could maintain contact with the school to assist in the transition phase for when I returned the following year.

UNIVERSITY ROLE

Being on the TRIP program required that I complete the university component, which resulted in my being awarded a Post-Graduate Certificate of Education. In the first week of the program, all teachers complete induction training. During this time, a representative from the university is introduced. Representatives explain their involvement and the expectations of the tertiary component. The week continues with various speakers targeting aspects of industry life as well as the transition into the workplace. Some of the areas included industrial relations, workplace culture, and discrimination. I found this week invaluable. I was able to apply most of the workshop information into my industry placement.

The university tasks included three analytical and reflective synopsis papers written at different phases throughout the year. Also, I collaborated extensively with my university professor to develop a workplace project. Under my agreement with both my principal and my workplace manager, this was to be relevant to both my workplace and school. Most social studies teachers developed resources to assist them directly in their teaching. Others developed management strategies that they planned to use in managing their social studies departments. I developed a *PowerPoint* presentation summarizing the various professional development opportunities that I had experienced at CSL. I chose areas that were relevant to both school and industry. I presented this to my university professor toward the end of the year. At the end of the work placement, many of the participants shared these projects with the other TRIP participants.

My university professor also visited my workplace on several occasions. During these visits, she became increasingly familiar with my work environment, and I could see that she was enjoying being outside of the university. It was also an opportunity for her, myself, and my workplace manager to discuss common issues, usually over a cup of coffee. With e-mail, faxes, and phone calls, the link with the university was never far away. My university professor gave me the confidence that I was on track with my assessment tasks and discussed with me the things that were going well during my placement. She also met with Helen, my workplace supervisor, on two occasions, again making sure that the program was meeting its expectations for all concerned. I suspect that these meetings were also good public relations for the university.

Workplace Supervisor

Each TRIP teacher has a workplace supervisor whose responsibility is to interview the teacher, develop a job description, and then supervise the person's placement for the forty weeks of the program, providing appropriate feedback and support. My workplace supervisor encouraged me in the roles I had, appeared to appreciate the "teacher" understandings, skills, and values I brought to the job, and enabled me to enhance my sense of professionalism, while ensuring I met the company requirements.

Pulling It All Together

The Department of Education, Employment, and Training (DEET) is responsible for bringing these groups together to ensure that the process is a successful one. The Victorian Employers Chamber of Commerce and Industry (VECCI) coordinates the yearlong program and arranges various opportunities for the stakeholders to meet. For example, at the beginning of the year, the principals and employers meet over breakfast. The process of TRIP is explained, as are the responsibilities of those involved.[9]

There were three network days during the year. The first involved a partnership with principals. It was at this time that the "School Plans" were developed. These were collected by the team at VECCI, recorded, and then a copy was sent to my principal. The School Plans helped to make the experience relevant for both parties (teacher and school). The following network days provided an opportunity for teachers to reflect with others on their experiences as well as be exposed to various presenters who targeted areas that were appropriate to that phase of the placement.

Toward the end of the work placement time, a dinner is organized for all the parties in the partnership. This is a time of celebration, and a great deal of networking takes place at the dinner. A two-day retreat was organized toward the end of the placement year to assist in the transition back to school. During this week, workplace visits were organized. This was an opportunity for us to visit other workplaces and gain some insight into the variety of areas in which each teacher was placed. The final network day provided a forum for reflection as well as an opportunity for our workplace projects to be presented.

Once the TRIP year was over, there was a final phase to the program. This occurred in May of the following year. During this professional development day, we discussed the skills, attitudes, and understandings gained from the TRIP experience. Comments like, "I learned the positive connection between my work as a social studies teacher and work outside of school" and "I developed further understandings and skills about working in a multicultural workplace" were common. The coming together of the year's cohort also provided the opportunity to develop network links further.

Links continue through a TRIP Association established in 1996, which circulates a quarterly newsletter to the TRIP "family." The association meets regularly and organizes events to assist in keeping people in touch. It is a chance to reminisce as well as plan activities relevant to previous TRIPers as well as those currently in the program. Also, the association produces a skills directory that lists all of the teachers who have been on the program (more than five hundred at this time), the schools where we are based, and the areas of expertise we possess. The TRIP year creates many partnerships and strong links.

The TRIP Experience for Teachers of Social Studies

To gain a wider understanding of the TRIP experience, a survey of teachers of social studies who have participated in the program was conducted. It should be noted that although the small sample may not meet high levels of statistical reliability, the data collected do provide information that captures a snapshot of the TRIP program for those teachers whose teaching background is in social studies. The survey revealed that very few teachers had work experiences outside of a school environment. The teaching of citizenship education was seen as the major goal of social studies.

The teachers surveyed represent both men and women with at least ten years of teaching experience, prior to entering the TRIP year. They came from both the primary and secondary sector with both city and country represented. Their roles within their schools varied. They all had the common link of working with the SOSE (social studies) curriculum.

Prior to their TRIP year, all teachers spoke of their need and interest in teaching social studies using real-life experiences. A typical comment was:

> Social studies is one subject where I need to have clear understandings about how society operates so I am able to provide my students with the links between theory and practice.

The social studies teachers from secondary schools, particularly those teaching in the middle years, commented on the challenges thrown at them by exuberant students.

> Often my students asked me whether I've actually worked outside of teaching. I have had to say no. It would have given me greater credibility to say yes.

The teachers' reasons for applying to the TRIP program were about both professional development (incorporating career development) and the need to develop understanding of the skills and issues that were relevant in industry which they could then transfer to classroom practice. Common contextual issues included those of social justice, active participation in decision making, and environmental issues. There was also some reference made regarding whether a teacher would be able to "cut it in the real world of work."

The responsibilities of the social studies teachers in the survey in their industry placement were typically in training and development positions. The link between industry and education was further strengthened by the work that some of the teachers did with Vocational Education and Training Program (VET). Human resource management was also an area of involvement.

The collaboration with the university was accomplished through the university's University Liaison Person (ULP). The experience of this collaboration varied. Most teachers mentioned the easy, professional relationship and were positive about the collaboration on the workplace project. There was support for the university connection at the industry placement. In some workplaces, the ULP was able to assist the workplace supervisor in clarifying the role of the TRIP teacher. For some teachers, the tertiary requirements of the program were a distraction from the real task at hand. In many cases, the ULP provided insight into the potential of the TRIP year as many of them had supervised participants on the program from previous years. On one occasion early on in the program, I became really stressed about the staff politics of my workplace. The ULP was able to help me by talking with my supervisor.

The variety of workplace projects is one form of evidence of the success of TRIP. Projects included videos, educational resource kits, CD-ROMs, brochures, articles in educational publications, and web site development. A typical example was of a social studies teacher who was located at a power station. One of her major roles was to act as an education officer/tour leader for the many visitors to the site. During her year, she developed numerous guide sheets about the production of energy that linked to the goals of the social studies curriculum for the many school groups who visited the plant. Finally, she created a video about energy production and environmental awareness, which was funded by the company and distributed to all schools in the state. This form of social studies resource production would not have been possible without both the time release given to the teacher and the cooperation of her workplace.

After the TRIP year, the teachers in the survey highlighted the following understandings in the social studies curriculum that were enhanced. These are taken from the current social studies curriculum. The teachers commented that they were better able to:

▶ Compare different types of work and enterprises in the local community.
▶ Analyze factors that make work at home, at school, and in the community satisfying, safe, and effective.
▶ Explain key factors that influence the Australian economy.
▶ Identify and discuss factors that affect opportunities for current and future work.
▶ Analyze vocational pathways and education and training requirements to develop possible career paths and work opportunities for students.

Teachers in the survey were able to identify some new skills that they felt were developed during the TRIP year. Work-specific computer skills, report writing, and cooperative learning skills were most commonly mentioned. Other skills included the ability to gather information faster and from a wider variety of sources and the ability to analyze the changing nature of work more broadly. In her larger study of TRIP teachers, Perry[10] noted that the concept of professionalism was mentioned many times by the respondents, both in the industry environment where professionalism was expected and on the return to school when the professionalism of some colleagues was questioned. One TRIP teacher commented, "It was not easy to come back as colleagues thought I had been away, having a good time."

Teachers in the survey commented that the TRIP program strongly influenced their classroom practices in social studies by enhancing their ability and willingness to adopt some common workplace practices. For example, they mentioned more student (worker) involvement in classroom decision making, more appreciation of the value of consistent and reliable judgments in measuring student learning (production measurement), and a greater and wider usage of information technologies in classroom projects. In summary, teachers behaved more confidently in articulating the role and value of social studies as a key learning area in the school curriculum.

The TRIP program is in its tenth year and is more successful than ever. As one measure of its success, the number of teachers who now apply far exceeds the number of work placements. So over the years a selection process has had to be developed. Comments from teachers, their principals, and workplace supervisors continue to be very positive. There is something in it for everyone. The growth in membership of the TRIP Association is also evidence of the value placed on networking after the experience.

How the Collaboration Worked: A Professor's Perspective (W.P.)

At Deakin University, the Education Faculty has established a Consultancy and Development Unit (CDU) that creatively seeks opportunities for university and community collaboration. Over the years, the forms of collaboration have diversified and grown as faculty members have come to realize that staff can transfer their understandings and skills from the university to the broader community. This process has been encouraged (some would say forced) on the faculty, by reductions in government funding to universities.

University staff are now expected to think creatively, in an entrepreneurial fashion, in order to create links with possible clients in the community. Over the years, CDU has developed into a multimillion dollar enterprise. The location of the TRIP program at Deakin University is one example of CDU's successfully tendering for a competitive public consultancy. In the case of this program, the client was the Department of Education, Employment, and Training.

This is a fairly hard-nose explanation of the origins and location of the TRIP program at the university, and it would be unfair to suggest that the education faculty works in the program just to generate income for the faculty. Over the ten-year period of the TRIP program at the university, a core of interested and committed staff has worked continuously on the program. Once the industrial matter of convincing the dean of education that working in the TRIP program should not be on top of other activities, like teaching and research, but should be included in the allocation of workloads, university staff now look at the program as a normal part of their working activities.

At the university, there are about ten staff from the education faculty who regularly work in the TRIP program, often contributing to the induction program and then collaborating with a TRIP teacher(s). Members of faculty volunteer to work in the program so they have a high degree of commitment to it. There are four staff from the social studies curriculum area. We see great benefit for us in the TRIP program in terms of our own teaching and research in social education. We teach in the primary and secondary school social studies curriculum area at both the undergraduate and postgraduate levels. All have extensive experience at teaching in schools and universities, but none has had extended work outside of teaching.

In collecting data for this study, I decided to have informal group discussions with my three colleagues from the social studies area arranged. Although an interview schedule was developed, the discussion roamed far and wide, perhaps helped by the offering of wine as an incentive to participate in the discussions. In general, we tried to focus on three aspects of the program. These were the following:

▶ Reasons for participating in the TRIP program as the university partner
▶ Knowledge, understandings, skills, and attitudes explored and developed during the program
▶ Links, if any, made between the TRIP partnership experience and teaching and learning in university-based social studies teaching responsibilities

The initial reasons of all three university professors for participating in the program were very different. Reasons included the opportunity to form liaisons with interesting workplace sites, for example, an Aboriginal Community Centre, and the enhanced ability to connect the goals of social studies with nonschool contexts.

I became involved in the program because of my research interests in collaborative and partnership learning.[11] For some years, I had been working with a number of schools on collaborative projects, mainly in the social studies curriculum area. I had also worked on a number of CDU consultancy projects, but in each of these cases, the context was an education environment. The TRIP program offered me an opportunity to work in a completely new environment.

All three professors commented on the initial difficulty of establishing a sense of collegiality with their TRIP teacher, now not a teacher, but a middle manager. They were initially out of place in a foreign work site. Reflecting on his visits to work sites, one professor shared the view that he now had a better understanding of how his own skills were more generic than he had initially thought. He noted how his focus in his university classes on social education, and in particular on citizenship education, could often be observed in his discussions with his TRIP teachers and the workplace supervisors. Here they talked about corporate citizenship, and on several occasions, he has been invited to talk with workplace staff on aspects of citizenship. Sometimes collaborative professional development practices have unintended outcomes.

The one outcome of the TRIP program that all four of us agree on is the positive impact it has had on our teaching at the university. On a personal level, we believe that it has enhanced our sense of efficacy in that the pedagogy of running a business is sometimes similar to that of running a social studies classroom. In both contexts, there are issues of setting objectives, recognizing the culture of the stakeholders, and measuring outcomes. We believe that although theory has always informed our practice, we can now add that practice, too, informs our theory.

Partnerships and collaborations are now invariably built into consultative work practices with clients of CDU at Deakin University. We have found that some university professors who had hoped to work in the TRIP program have turned out to be unsuited to the job. The establishment of an atmosphere of collegiality among the three key stakeholders requires a degree of humility and a recognition that the focus is on the defined needs of the teacher. These elements take time to develop and regular visits to the workplace. In the workplace, it is the university professor who is sometimes out of his/her depth of understanding.

Conclusion

Over the years, the TRIP program has undergone some significant changes both in its organization and in its conceptual framework. On a practical level, university professors are finding it more difficult to make regular visits to workplaces due to increasing workloads at the university. The effectiveness of the partnership process begins to suffer when one party has to withdraw.

One particularly important challenge facing the Department of Education, Employment, and Training is the trend of some TRIP teachers not to return to their schools but rather to take up offers of positions in their workplaces. (This was more the case in the early years of the program.) It should be noted that often these offers of positions are at far greater salary than teachers would ever earn. In one sense, it is flattering to think that "ordinary" teachers make the transition to greener fields with a set of highly developed generic skills and understandings. On the other hand, this is a great loss to teaching. One outcome of this practice, if only now represented by a small percentage of teachers, has been for DEET to "require" TRIP teachers to return to their schools as part of the initial agreement. We support this approach, and figures over the past two years indicate that once teachers actually return to their schools, they stay. The data from our survey also indicate the high level of enthusiasm of returning teachers keen to apply their "new" skills and understandings back in their classrooms.

Given the nature of the TRIP program as a professional development activity, the nature of social studies teachers' responses on their return to schools is a good indicator of the impact of the program. Several teachers commented on recent developments in vocational education, including the introduction, in Victoria, of several Vocational Education and Training (VET) subjects at the senior end of high school. Other teachers noted how they now incorporate information technologies more easily into their social studies classes. For some teachers, the experience sharpened their ideas about both specific goal setting and long-term planning. In all of these responses, teachers commented on the positive reaction of students to the sharing of TRIP experiences with them. The positioning of skills developed in social studies classes was more readily accepted by students as being generic to the work place. In particular, teachers noted how it was easier to develop ideas about the "good citizen" and the relationship of contributing to the community through work, and not necessarily paid work.

The TRIP program is a significant professional development activity. It has enabled more than five hundred teachers in Victoria to enhance their skills and understandings essential to supporting schools in preparing young people for the world of work. Schools are places where young people should be given opportunities to learn about and practice a range of citizenship skills. Work is one way in which we define our citizenship. Teachers of social education have a critical role to play in this preparation process.

NOTES

1. Terry Seddon, "Who Says Teachers Don't Work," *Education Links* 38 (1990): 4-9.
2. Andy Hargreaves, *Changing Teachers, Changing Times* (New York: Teachers College Press, 1994).
3. Chris Perry and Ian Ball, "What Do Teachers Really Know about Work: Professional Development through Education-Industry Links," *Teacher Development* 2 (1998): 73-86.
4. Warren Prior, "What It Means to Be a Good Citizen in Australia," *Theory & Research in Social Education* 27 (Spring 1999): 215-248.
5. Board of Studies, *Curriculum and Standards Framework: Studies of Society and Environment* (Melbourne, Australia: Author, 2000).
6. W. McLennan, *Australian Standard Classification of Occupations*, 2d ed. (Canberra, Australia: Australian Government Printing Service, 1997).
7. Kerry Kennedy, "Preparing Teachers for the New Civics Education," *Asia-Pacific Journal of Teacher Education* 1 (1998): 24-37.
8. N. Johnson, *Planning Effective Staff Professional Development: Network Implications* (Melbourne University, PD Seminar, 1997).
9. TRIP (Teacher Release to Industry Program), Information Document, 1995.
10. Perry and Ball, "What Do Teachers Really Know about Work?"
11. National Professional Development Project on Informed Citizenship, "Men and Women of Australia" (Report to Department of Education, Employment, Training, and Youth Affairs, Canberra, 1997).

Authors' Biographical Information

(IN ALPHABETICAL ORDER)

Marsha Alibrandi is an assistant professor of social studies education and geography in the College of Education and Psychology at North Carolina State University, Raleigh. A social studies and geography high school teacher for fifteen years on Cape Cod, Alibrandi has collaborated on a number of GIS educational projects and courses.

Tina Allsop teaches seventh and eighth grade English and social studies core classes at Shuksan Middle School in Bellingham, Washington.

Janet Alleman is a professor in the Department of Teacher Education at Michigan State University, East Lansing.

Heather Bakke taught human heritage on the Minneopa Trail at Dakota Meadows Middle School from 1998-2000. She now brings social studies to the special education department at St. Francis High School in St. Francis, Minnesota.

Keith C. Barton is an associate professor in the Division of Teacher Education at the University of Cincinnati, Cincinnati, Ohio, and a former teacher at the elementary and middle school levels in Los Angeles and the San Francisco Bay Area. He conducts research on the teaching and learning of history.

Candy Beal is an assistant professor in middle grades education specializing in social studies and global education at North Carolina State University, Raleigh. She coordinates the Middle Grades Language Arts and Social Studies Undergraduate Teacher Education Program.

Sally R. Beisser is an assistant professor in teaching and learning at Drake University, Des Moines, Iowa. She taught grades 3-6 in Ames and West Des Moines Public Schools for fifteen years.

Jere Brophy is a University Distinguished Professor of Teacher Education at Michigan State University, East Lansing.

Helen Carlson is a professor of education at the University of Minnesota—Duluth, and has been in teacher education at the university level for more than twenty years working in social studies methods, foundations, and field experiences. She taught at the pre-kindergarten, elementary, and middle school levels for nine years.

Mary Christenson has been a teacher since 1974. Most of her experience has been at the elementary level with Columbus City Schools in Columbus, Ohio. She is currently a doctoral candidate in integrated teaching and learning at The Ohio State University, Columbus.

Barbara Cozza is an assistant professor of education at the University of Scranton, Scranton, Pennsylvania, who is presently teaching social studies and mathematics methodology courses for elementary teaching integrating a field-based reflective practitioner component. She is a member of the Board of Directors for The University of Scranton Campus School. In the past, she was director of a multiage elementary program and taught K-6 in the New York City school system for sixteen years.

Portia Downey is a sixth grade teacher at Machesney Elementary School in Machesney Park, Illinois, and district coordinator of the Harlem-NIU Partnership. She has been teaching elementary school for fifteen years.

Laurie Elish-Piper is an associate professor of literacy education at Northern Illinois University, DeKalb, and is the university coordinator of the Harlem-NIU Partnership. Prior to earning her doctorate at the University of Akron, she was an elementary and middle school teacher in Indiana.

David Gerwin is an assistant professor of social studies education at Queens College/City University of New York, Flushing, and has been in teacher education at the university level for five years. He has been an education associate at The Constitution Works and a college history professor. He taught middle/high school history for two years in Maryland.

Lou Guzzi has been teaching in the Scranton Public Schools, Scranton, Pennsylvania, for eleven years. He currently teaches K-8 at The University of Scranton Campus School and has been a Teacher-in-Residence at The University of Scranton.

Rita Hagevik was a middle school teacher in the Wake County Public Schools for ten years and a GIS instructor for four years. She is currently a teacher educator for the North Carolina Department of Public Instruction and a Ph.D. student in Science Education and Forestry (GIS) at North Carolina State University, Raleigh.

Callie Hart teaches eighth grade English and social studies core classes at Fairhaven Middle School in Bellingham, Washington.

Angela M. Harwood is an associate professor of secondary education at Western Washington University, Bellingham.

Lynn Herink is a graduate student of education and interim director of the Center for Service-Learning at Western Washington University, Bellingham.

Gina M. Henig is an early elementary teacher at Winans Elementary School in the Waverly School District, Lansing, Michigan.

Carol Holm has been a teacher in the Duluth Public Schools in Duluth, Minnesota, for eighteen years. She currently teaches social studies and language arts to sixth graders at Woodland School. She also has been an adjunct professor at The University of Minnesota—Duluth for two years.

Jack Hutchison has taught English, history, and physical education at the Lima Public School in Lima, Montana, for thirty-two years. He currently teaches full time, serves as the computer technology contact, and has begun his thirty-third year of coaching varsity athletics.

Michael Intoccia has been teaching K-8 grades in the Scranton Public Schools in Scranton, Pennsylvania, for twenty-four years. He is currently teaching fifth grade at McNichols Plaza in Scranton, Pennsylvania.

Clark Johnson is an associate professor at Minnesota State University, Mankato, where he has coordinated the preparation of secondary social studies teachers for ten years. He teaches the methods seminar in social studies and an introductory class for future social studies teachers. He also coordinates student relations for the College of Social and Behavioral Sciences.

Marilyn Johnston is a professor of social studies education at The Ohio State University, Columbus, and has been in teacher education at the university level for twenty years. She taught K-6 grades in California and Utah for thirteen years.

Mary Lou Kelly has twenty-four years of teaching experience from pre-K to college level. She is currently teaching an intermediate class fourth and fifth grade at the University of Scranton Campus School in Scranton, Pennsylvania.

Barbara L. Knighton is an early elementary teacher at Winans Elementary School in the Waverly School District in Lansing, Michigan.

Leslie A. Kreimer has been an elementary teacher in the Cincinnati Public Schools in Cincinnati, Ohio, for eleven years. Kreimer became a National Board Certified Teacher and credentialed lead teacher in 1998, and currently works as a peer evaluator with the district's performance-based teacher evaluation system.

Joseph Kunkel has been a political science professor at Minnesota State University, Mankato, for twenty-one years. He teaches courses in U.S. politics and political philosophy. This is the fourth year he has taught the citizenship course and directed Mankato Public Achievement.

Betty Godwin Mackie has been a teacher in the Wake County School System in Raleigh, North Carolina, for seventeen years. She currently teaches sixth grade language arts in the Academically Gifted Program at Ligon GT Magnet Middle School.

Nancy Mallory is a teacher at Bexley High School in Bexley, Ohio, who teaches government and economics, and world history. Previously she taught at Bexley Middle School. She has been teaching for nine years.

Vassilios Manolios is a teacher of English at William Cullen Bryant High School in Long Island City, New York.

Tata Mbugua is an assistant professor of education at The University of Scranton, Scranton, Pennsylvania. She has taught elementary grades in both Ohio and Nairobi, Kenya. She is currently teaching social studies and early childhood courses.

Ava L. McCall is a professor and chair of the Department of Curriculum and Instruction at the University of Wisconsin-Oshkosh. For more than eleven years, she has taught social studies methods and supervised clinical students. Her web site, www.socialstudies.esmartweb.com, contains more than 750 annotations of children's books and teacher resources for teaching elementary and middle school social studies.

Merry M. Merryfield is a professor of social studies and global education at The Ohio State University, Columbus, where she works collaboratively in person and on-line with K-12 teachers in African Studies and cross-cultural experiential education. She has taught secondary social studies in Atlanta, Sierra Leone, Nigeria, Kenya, Malawi, and Botswana.

Jason Miller has taught seventh grade English at Dakota Meadows Middle School in North Mankato, Minnesota, for five years. He has worked with Minnesota State University staff and Dakota Meadows staff to coordinate Public Achievement with the Advisor/Advisee curriculum.

Steve L. Miller is an associate professor of social studies and global education at The Ohio State University, Columbus. He has been in teacher education for more than twenty years and specializes in economic education. He is a former high school teacher of government and economics.

Andrew J. Milson is an assistant professor of social studies education at Northern Illinois University, DeKalb. Prior to earning his doctorate at the University of Georgia, he taught middle school social studies in the Dallas, Texas, area.

Patricia Noakes has taught in the Scranton Public Schools for twenty-five years. She is currently teaching third grade at Audubon Elementary School in Scranton, Pennsylvania.

James Nordstrom is the principal at Machesney Elementary School in Machesney Park, Illinois. He has been with the Harlem School District for twenty-four years and has served as principal at Machesney for nine years.

Jim Norris has been a high school social studies teacher in the Columbus Public Schools for twenty-eight years. He currently teaches U.S. history and government at Whetstone High School and is a field professor in the Social Studies and Global Education Professional Development School at The Ohio State University, Columbus.

Sandra Brenneman Oldendorf is a professor of social studies education and educational psychology at Western Montana College of the University of Montana, Dillon, and is co-coordinator of the Indian teacher education program with Salish-Kootenai Tribal College. Prior to her twenty years of college teaching, she taught English and social studies in grades 5-12 for nine years in Illinois.

Virginia Owens has taught science at Ligon GT Magnet Middle School in Raleigh, North Carolina, since 1995. Her interest and involvement with the Ligon History Project began when she and Mrs. Mackie witnessed Ligon's trees being felled. Since then, her investigations with students have led to dendrochronology projects, exhibit design, and applications of GIS.

Larry Picicco has been a U.S. history and sociology teacher for the Kent City Schools for the past seven years. This past summer he completed his master's degree in social studies education at Kent State University in Kent, Ohio.

Warren Prior is a senior lecturer in social education at Deakin University, Melbourne, Australia. He was formerly a senior high school teacher of history for ten years.

M. Reisz Riney is an assistant professor of teaching foundations and educational psychology and co-director of a Professional Development School at Western State College in Gunnison, Colorado. He taught English, language arts, and history in grades 7-12 for fourteen years and has taught for four years at the college level.

Thelma Ristow teaches at Webster Stanley Elementary School in Oshkosh, Wisconsin. She has been teaching for more than twenty-five years. Recently, she was chosen to mentor new teachers in a special school district program.

Diana Schmidt has been an elementary teacher in the Ames Community Schools in Ames, Iowa, for twenty-five years and was previously with the Des Moines Public Schools. She received the 1999 Presidential Award for Excellence in Mathematics and Science Teaching.

Steve Shapiro has been a social studies teacher at Reynoldsburg High School in Columbus, Ohio, since 1990. He is also a field professor at The Ohio State University, Columbus, and a consultant to educators in the United States, Poland, and Ukraine.

Neville Sinclair has taught social studies at Ligon GT Magnet Middle School in Raleigh, North Carolina, since 1992, where she offered an architectural history elective as part of the Ligon History Project. She has held several social studies and schoolwide leadership positions during her tenure.

Randal Symons has been a primary school teacher for seventeen years. He is currently on secondment to the Consultancy and Development Unit at Deakin University, Melbourne, Australia, where he manages a range of consultancy projects.

Ann Thompson has taught a variety of middle school courses for nineteen years, including language arts, social studies, ESOL, and technology electives. She is currently an Educator on Loan at the North Carolina Department of Public Instruction and a technology consultant with Centennial Campus Middle School in Raleigh, North Carolina.

William W. Wilen is a professor of social studies education at Kent State University, Kent, Ohio, and has been involved in teacher education for more than thirty years. He has taught at the high school level in Maryland and at colleges and universities as a visiting professor in six states and on four continents.

Anna V. Wilson is an assistant professor of curriculum theory at North Carolina State University's College of Education and Psychology, Raleigh. From among her graduate and undergraduate courses in curriculum theory and research methods, her historiographic methods of school inquiry students participated in this project.

Index

A

B

F

G

H

K

L

M

N

O

P

Q

R

S

T

U

V

W

X

Y